# QUALITATIVE RESEAI
# VULNERABILITY

CW00741798

*Qualitative Researcher Vulnerability* provides conceptual, experiential, and practical insights into the vulnerability of the qualitative researcher. Compared to participants' vulnerability, researcher vulnerability has seen limited attention in the qualitative research process, but yet it is an important consideration.

Drawing on an interdisciplinary group of authors—across criminology, education, feminisms, geography, health, kinesiology, nursing, management and organisation, policy, political science, psychology, sociology, and qualitative inquiry writ broad—the book explores the ways in which we might understand and work with researcher vulnerability, most notably in relation to ethics, risk, empathy, emotion, and power. Ultimately, the authors suggest researcher vulnerability is a vital component of our research practices throughout the research process, for emerging as well as experienced researchers. Whilst researcher vulnerability can be something to protect against, it is also something to be aware of, explore, learn from, work with, and at times (and with care and consideration) embrace.

This book is suitable for undergraduate, postgraduate students, and emerging and established researchers who are utilising qualitative research. It will be especially useful for researchers examining (potentially) sensitive topics, or for those who wish to develop more responsive, responsible, ethical, or reciprocal approaches to qualitative practices.

**Bryan C. Clift** is Senior Lecturer (Associate Professor) and Director of the Centre for Qualitative Research (CQR) in the Faculty of Humanities and Social Sciences and Department for Health at the University of Bath, UK.

**Ioannis Costas Batlle** is Lecturer (Assistant Professor) in the Department of Education at the University of Bath, UK, and a Co-Director of the Centre for Qualitative Research.

**Sheree Bekker** is Senior Lecturer (Associate Professor) in the Department for Health at the University of Bath, UK. She is a member of the Centre for Qualitative Research, Centre for Health and Injury and Illness Prevention in Sport (CHI2PS), and UK Collaborating Centre on Injury and Illness Prevention in Sport (UKCCIIS).

**Katharina Chudzikowsi** is Senior Lecturer (Associate Professor) in Organisation Studies at the School of Management, University of Bath, UK.

# QUALITATIVE RESEARCHER VULNERABILITY

## Negotiating, Experiencing and Embracing

*Edited by Bryan C. Clift, Ioannis Costas Batlle, Sheree Bekker and Katharina Chudzikowski*

Routledge
Taylor & Francis Group

LONDON AND NEW YORK

Designed cover image: Photo by marianna armata / Getty Images

First published 2023
by Routledge
4 Park Square, Milton Park, Abingdon, Oxon OX14 4RN

and by Routledge
605 Third Avenue, New York, NY 10158

*Routledge is an imprint of the Taylor & Francis Group, an informa business*

*British Library Cataloguing-in-Publication Data*
A catalogue record for this book is available from the British Library

*Library of Congress Cataloging-in-Publication Data*
Names: Clift, Bryan C, editor. | Costas Batlle, Ioannis, editor. | Bekker, Sheree, editor. | Chudzikowski, Katharina, editor.
Title: Qualitative researcher vulnerability : negotiating, experiencing and embracing / edited by Bryan C. Clift, Ioannis Costas Batlle, Sheree Bekker, and Katharina Chudzikowski.
Description: Abingdon, Oxon ; New York, NY : Routledge, 2023. | Includes bibliographical references and index.
Identifiers: LCCN 2023010066 (print) | LCCN 2023010067 (ebook) | ISBN 9781032393292 (hardback) | ISBN 9781032393339 (paperback) | ISBN 9781003349266 (ebook)
Subjects: LCSH: Qualitative research. | Social sciences--Research.
Classification: LCC H62 .Q3566 2023 (print) | LCC H62 (ebook) | DDC 001.4/2--dc23/eng/20230316
LC record available at https://lccn.loc.gov/2023010066
LC ebook record available at https://lccn.loc.gov/2023010067

ISBN: 978-1-032-39329-2 (hbk)
ISBN: 978-1-032-39333-9 (pbk)
ISBN: 978-1-003-34926-6 (ebk)

DOI: 10.4324/9781003349266

Typeset in Bembo
by SPi Technologies India Pvt Ltd (Straive)

The Open Access version of Chapter 11 was funded by Swansea University.

# CONTENTS

# ILLUSTRATIONS

## Figures

## Table

# CONTRIBUTORS

**Kia Banks** is a Research Assistant at the Centre for Qualitative Research and a student on the BA (Hons) Education with Psychology course at the University of Bath. Her current primary interests lie in epistemic injustices, climate justice, and curricula analysis each understood through an educational and sociocultural anthropological lens. Kia hopes to contribute to research and policy analysis in education post university.

**Mark Batterham** is a Registered Nurse and currently works in a specialist community mental health service in the south of England. He has a background of working with young people with complex needs, as well as their families and carers. Mark has studied Housing Policy and Urban Planning at the master's level and volunteers for a neighbourhood planning group. He is also a keen amateur housing historian and leads local group walks focusing on this topic. Mark is interested in how mental health services can broaden and enhance their understanding and treatment provision by utilising and adapting knowledge and methods from other disciplines, specifically human geography and urban studies.

**Sheree Bekker** is Senior Lecturer (Associate Professor) in the Department for Health at the University of Bath. She is a member of the Centre for Qualitative Research, Centre for Health and Injury and Illness Prevention in Sport (CHI2PS), and UK Collaborating Centre on Injury and Illness Prevention in Sport (UKCCIIS). Her transdisciplinary research focuses on (feminist) Sport and Exercise Medicine, with specialisation in sports injury prevention. Her current research is comprised of two key strands: 1) understanding the influence of gendered environments on sports injury and 2) conceptualising gender inclusive sport. She takes a translational approach to this research, with the aim of providing innovative considerations that are useful in policy and practice. Sheree is an Associate Editor of the British Journal of Sports Medicine, and a Qualitative Research Editor of BMJ Open Sport and Exercise Medicine. She completed a Prize Research Fellowship in Injury Prevention at the University of Bath from 2018 to 2020, and received the 2019 British Journal of Sports Medicine Editors' Choice Academy Award for her PhD research.

**Nicole Brown** is a writer, social researcher, and Associate Professor working on the cusp of research/practice/teaching. She is Director of Social Research & Practice and Education Ltd and Associate Professor at University College London. Nicole's creative and research work relate to physical and material representations of experiences, the generation of knowledge, the use of metaphors, and more generally, research methods and approaches to explore identity and body work. Her books include *Lived Experiences of Ableism in Academia: Strategies for Inclusion in Higher Education, Ableism in Academia: Theorising Experiences of Disabilities and Chronic Illnesses in Higher Education, Embodied Inquiry: Research Methods,* and *Making the Most of Your Research Journal.* Her next books are *Creativity in Education: International Perspectives* and *Photovoice, Reimagined.* Nicole's creative nonfiction has been published in the *Journal of Participatory Research Methods, So Fi Zine* and *The AutoEthnographer.* Nicole shares her work at https://www.nicole-brown.co.uk and she tweets as @ncjbrown and @AbleismAcademia.

**Olivia Brown** is Assistant Professor in Organizational Behaviour at the University of Bath, School of Management. She is a social psychologist, interested in how intra- and inter-group processes influence individual and group behaviour. Her award-winning research has two core strands—identifying what supports effective teamwork and decision-making in uncertain and stressful environments and examining how online interactions can influence offline behaviour. Olivia serves on the Editorial Board of the *Journal of Occupational and Organizational Psychology* and is a member of the Bath Beacon, *The Value of Data,* that considers how the cultural, economic, and psychological value of digital traces can deliver positive societal impacts.

**Hugo Ceron-Anaya** is Associate Professor of Sociology at Lehigh University, USA. His work focuses on social inequalities and privilege, examining how notion of whiteness (within a Latin American context), perceptions of masculinity, and class dynamics impact the behaviour of affluent people. He is particularly interested in the wide array of ordinary and everyday practices that reproduce privilege. He is the author of *Privilege at Play: Class, Race, Gender, and Golf in Mexico* (Oxford University Press, 2019), which received the 2020 Outstanding Book Award from the North American Society for the Sociology of Sport. His work has also been published in the *Journal of Sport and Social Issues, Journal of Contemporary Ethnography, Latin American and Caribbean Ethnic Studies,* and *Esporte e Sociedade.*

**Katharina Chudzikowski** is Senior Lecturer (Associate Professor) in Organisation Studies at the University of Bath, School of Management. Her research explores careers in a variety of contexts, including professionals in the area of consultancy and academia as well as former apprentices in the respective professional context.

**Bryan C. Clift** is Senior Lecturer (Associate Professor) and Director of the Centre for Qualitative Research (CQR) in the Faculty of Humanities and Social Sciences and Department for Health at the University of Bath, UK. His research is oriented around sport and physical activity in relation to the cultural economy and qualitative inquiry. He recently co-edited with Alan Tomlinson *Populism in Sport, Leisure, and Popular Culture* (Routledge, 2021), and with colleagues in the CQR *Temporality in Qualitative Inquiry* (Routledge, 2021).

**Ioannis Costas Batlle** is Lecturer (Assistant Professor) in the Department of Education at the University of Bath, and a Co-Director of the Centre for Qualitative Research. His research qualitatively explores the role of non-formal and informal education in young people's lives, particularly looking at both structured learning opportunities and unplanned, spontaneous opportunities outside school environments. Ioannis' experience researching young people's lives focuses primarily on charities, youth groups, youth sport, and young people not in education, employment, or training.

**Michael Dao** is Assistant Professor and Associate Chair in the Department of Kinesiology at San José State University, USA. His research interests are rooted in sport as tool for development internationally, and sport studies in Vietnam and the Vietnamese diaspora. He is an advocate for equitable and diverse practices in sport and physical activity, and aims to build bridges between the Department of Kinesiology and communities around San José to address social barriers that may prohibit marginalized from participating in sporting spaces. His work has been published in a variety of journals, including *Qualitative Research in Sport, Exercise, & Health, Journal of Sport Development, Journal of Global Sport Management*, and *Third World Thematics*.

**Natalie Edelman** is an Independent Consultant in Trauma-informed Research, Service Support & Training and Principal Research Fellow at the University of Brighton. Natalie's training is primarily epidemiological and as a mixed methods researcher she has explored the application of criticality to quantitative methods, and augmentations to research ethics conventions that aim to improve inclusivity and participant experience. During her career, she has researched community-based syphilis and HIV testing, the sexual health needs of women with problematic drug use and care experienced young people, integration of hepatitis care within drug treatment services, and psychosocial predictors of sexual and reproductive health. Her current interests and expertise focus on clinical prediction modelling, the interface between the population and the individual and the application of trauma and resilience informed approaches to sexual health research and care.

**Michael D. Giardina** is Professor of Physical Culture and Qualitative Inquiry in the Department of Sport Management at Florida State University, USA. He is the author or editor of 24 books, including *The SAGE Handbook of Qualitative Research* (6th ed.; with Norman K. Denzin, Yvonna S. Lincoln, and Gaile S. Cannella, 2023),

*Qualitative Inquiry—Past, Present, & Future* (with Norman K. Denzin; Routledge, 2015), and the award-winning *Sport, Spectacle, and NASCAR Nation: Consumption and the Cultural Politics of Neoliberalism* (with Joshua Newman; Palgrave Macmillan, 2011). He is a two-time recipient of the North American Society for the Sociology of Sport (NASSS) 'Outstanding Book Award' (2006, 2012), and a 2017 inductee as a NASSS Research Fellow. He is the co-editor of three SAGE journals—*Qualitative Inquiry, Cultural Studies ↔ Critical Methodologies*, and *International Review of Qualitative Research*—past-editor of the *Sociology of Sport Journal*, co-editor of three book series on qualitative inquiry for Routledge, and Director of the International Congress of Qualitative Inquiry (ICQI).

**Julie Gore** is Professor of Organizational Psychology in the Department of Organizational Psychology, Birkbeck, University of London. Previously, she was Director of the Centre for Qualitative Research (CRR), University of Bath, UK, and now an external affiliate. A Chartered Psychologist and Fellow of the British Psychological Society, her research focus is on the psychology of expertise and naturalistic decision-making (NDM) across a range of professions working under uncertainty. An expert in cognitive task analysis, Prof. Gore is Editor for *Journal of Occupational and Organizational Psychology*, Associate Editor of the *Journal of Cognitive Engineering and Decision Making*, and serves on the board of the *British Journal of Management*. Prof. Gore holds a PhD in applied cognitive psychology (one of the world's first in the field of NDM) from Oxford Brookes University, UK. For her most influential work see—*The Oxford Handbook of Expertise*.

**Alexandra C. Hartman** is Associate Professor in the Department of Political Science at UCL in London. She completed her PhD in Political Science at Yale University in 2015, and her research and writing explore local property rights, the causes and consequences of forced displacement, and methodology.

**Rhea Ashley Hoskin** is an *AMTD Global Talent Postdoctoral Fellow* at the University of Waterloo and St. Jerome's, where she is cross-appointed to the departments of Sociology & Legal Studies, and Sexuality, Marriage, & Family Studies. Hoskin's work focuses on Critical Femininities, Femme Theory, and femmephobia. More specifically, her work examines perceptions of femininity and sources of prejudice rooted in the devaluation or regulation of femininity, as well as strategies for revaluing and rethinking femininity. Hoskin completed her MA in Gender Studies and her PhD in Sociology from Queen's University. In 2019, she was awarded the Governor General's Academic Gold Medal at Queen's University for her work on Femme Theory. Dr. Hoskin is an associate editor of *Psychology & Sexuality*, and co-founder of LGBTQ Psychology Canada.

**Zoe John** is Lecturer in Criminology at Swansea University, with a particular interest in ethnography, gender, and sporting violence. Her previous research focussed on gender, violence, and embodiment in mixed martial arts (MMA), including a flexible research role in which she participated in MMA. These outlined areas of interest were central not just to the sport of MMA but to bodies in everyday life, including sexual harassment, boundaries of humour, and the liminality of violence in interaction. Zoe continues to research and teach in these areas.

**Adam Joinson** is Professor of Management at the University of Bath. His work focuses on the interaction between human behaviour and technology, with specific foci on issues of how the design of systems influences behaviour ranging across privacy and self-disclosure, cyber-security, social relations, and patterns of influence.

**Milli Lake** is a feminist, a researcher, and Associate Professor at the London School of Economics' Department of International Relations. She completed her PhD in Political Science at the University of Washington in 2014, and her research and writing focuses on political violence, institutions, and methodology.

**Cassie Lowe** is Senior Teaching Associate at the University of Cambridge in the Cambridge Centre for Teaching and Learning. Prior to Cambridge, Cassie was a Senior Researcher in Learning and Teaching at the University of Winchester, where she taught on the MA Learning and Teaching in Higher Education and was the lead Editor for the student research journal *Alfred*. In the scholarship of Learning and Teaching, Cassie's research interests are student engagement, students as partners, and curriculum development. Cassie's doctorate research brought together Julia Kristeva and Sigmund Freud's psychoanalytic theories to advance the theory of abjection through exploring repetition compulsion and life writing.

**Dawn Mannay** is Reader in Social Sciences (Psychology) at Cardiff University, Wales, UK. Her research interests include class, gender, education, and inequality, and she employs creative participatory methods in her work with communities. Dawn's publications include *Visual, Narrative and Creative Research Methods: Application, Reflection and Ethics* (2016), *Our Changing Land: Revisiting Gender, Class and Identity in Contemporary Wales* (2016); *Emotion and the Researcher: Sites, Subjectivities, and Relationships* (with Tracey Loughran, 2018), *Children and Young People 'Looked After'? Education, Intervention and the Everyday Culture of Care in Wales* (with Alyson Rees and Louise Roberts, 2019); *The SAGE Handbook of Visual Research Methods* (with Luc Pauwels, 2019); and *Creative Research Methods in Education: Principles and Practices* (with Helen Kara, Narelle Lemon and Megan McPherson, 2020). Dawn is committed to moving beyond academic publications to generate policy and practice impacts and draws on film, artwork, and music to engage with diverse audiences.

**Julie Riddell** originally started as a research assistant within Education Services at Glasgow City Council. She has been a research assistant within the MRC/CSO Social and Public Health Sciences Unit since 2013 and currently works within the Social Relationships and Health Improvement Programme. Julie has worked on a variety of projects within the unit and is particularly interested in menstruation and its impact across the lifecourse. Julie also has an interest in the use of creativity in research, both in the research process and dissemination. Alongside Susie Smillie, she coordinates the Emotionally Demanding Research Network in Scotland.

**Josie Rodohan** is a Research Assistant at the Centre of Qualitative Research and also studying BSc (Hons) in Sociology and Social Policy at the University of Bath. Her research interests include the sociology of work, power relationships, and pension policy. She aims to pursue a career within policymaking related to work and pensions.

**Aled Singleton** is a Research Officer in the Geography Department at Swansea University. He has a background in managing place-based projects, including community and urban renewal schemes for local government and arts-led regeneration in the third sector. His PhD (2021) focuses on the attachments to place that individuals make as they grow up, through early adulthood and how people negotiate moving home in older age. Aled is committed to developing and teaching techniques in spatially led conversations and outdoor walking interviews, helping researchers and individuals to connect with deeply held emotions and memories. Such approaches were deployed in the case explored within this book, revealing rich details of everyday organisational practice that may otherwise be hard to explore. In his wider work, Aled uses creative writing and collaborations with artists to stage public events and make films. Aled has an ongoing relationship with Mark and colleagues working in mental health.

**Susie Smillie** studied medicine, then psychology, going on to work in counselling and therapeutic settings in the NHS and third sector before joining the MRC/CSO Social and Public Health Sciences at University of Glasgow in 2010. As a qualitative research assistant there she worked on evaluations of a range of interventions including those focussed on reducing suicidal behaviour, and on improving social and emotional wellbeing in primary school pupils. She is now a PhD student in sociology at University of Glasgow researching young people's wellbeing and creativity during school holidays. Alongside Julie Riddell, she coordinates the Emotionally Demanding Research Network in Scotland.

**Devra Waldman** is Assistant Professor in the Department of Sport Management at Florida State University, USA. She has conducted ethnographic research in India, Italy, and the UK on questions of sport and urban geographies. Her work has been published in academic journals such as *International Review for the Sociology of Sport*, *International Journal of Urban and Regional Research* and *Geoforum*, as well as in books such as *The Palgrave Handbook of Feminisms in Sport, Leisure, and Physical Activity*, *The Routledge Handbook of Physical Cultural Studies*, and *The Routledge Handbook of Sport and Politics*.

**Lilith A. Whiley** is Senior Lecturer and interdisciplinary researcher in Occupational and Organisational Psychology (Management) at the University of Sussex Business School. Her work brings together Occupational Psychology, HRM, and Social Psychology to explore inequalities at work and improve inclusion in the work-place—and beyond. Lilith is especially interested in 'otherness', vulnerabilities, and the intersection of stigmatising identities.

**Kate Woodthorpe** is Reader in Sociology in the Department of Social and Policy Sciences at the University of Bath, where she is Director of the Centre for Death and Society, the UK's leading interdisciplinary research centre devoted to under-standing the social contexts of death, dying, and bereavement. She has undertaken research and published on funeral practice, costs, and family at the end of life, and has advised the UK and Scottish governments on funeral policy.

# ACKNOWLEDGEMENTS

Over the last several years, students, research assistants, and professional and academic staff have come together to create and develop the *Centre for Qualitative Research* (CQR) at the University of Bath. The Centre engages in several activities within the University and outside of its walls, all of which coalesce around education and training, industry collaboration, and research. One of our primary activities is hosting the *Qualitative Research Symposium* (QRS), an annual Symposium that is organised around one common theme. The Symposium is intended to be a space for qualitative researchers across all disciplines to come together to discuss, debate, explore, transfer, and translate their knowledge and understanding of qualitative research across our respective disciplines, institutions, organisations, and contexts. To date, the Symposium has hosted more than 900 participants across the spectrum of career stages, and we hope will continue to attract the research voices of multiple, diverse individuals and groups.

The impetus for this book grows out of the eighth annual QRS hosted at the University of Bath in February 2022. The theme for the 2022 Symposium was *Researcher Vulnerability*. Leading up to, throughout, and after the Symposium, we reviewed several resources on the topic (many of which are incorporated here). In reading the diversity of scholarship on vulnerability across disciplines, and in seeing the limited exploration of vulnerability in relation to the qualitative researcher (although this is changing…), this book became a way to focus on how researcher vulnerability is framed, negotiated, experienced, managed, or embraced. We feel it is a useful contribution to how qualitative researchers think about themselves in relation to their work and participants.

We hope that this book becomes a supplementary text for undergraduate, postgraduate students, and researchers who are utilising qualitative research in their teaching and research. It will be especially useful for researchers examining (potentially) sensitive topics, or for those who wish to develop more responsive, responsible, ethical, or reciprocal approaches to qualitative research practices.

As with all Symposia, there is a tremendous amount of support and work that goes into a successful event. That collective effort in turn creates the possibility for this book. At the University of Bath, several people have provided support for the 2022 QRS. Institutional support from David Galbreath, former Dean of the Faculty of Humanity and Social Sciences, and Neil Bannister and Ana Bullock in the Doctoral College make the event feasible within the institution. In the Department for Health, Fiona Gillison, former Head of Department, has consistently supported the Symposium in a variety of ways, all of which enabled us to work on this collective project. Administratively, Michelle Hicks, Stephen Coles, Krisztina Perecsenyi, and Harriet Fender provide indispensable guidance and assistance in several forms. For the 2022 QRS, a postgraduate team helps organise and facilitate the event, including: Amber Van Den Akker, Hala Alaouie, Sarra Boukhari, Katharina Hug, Imene Taibi, and Emrah Yildirim. Each attendee and presenter created the atmosphere wherein sharing, discussing, and exploring qualitative research takes shape. Notable at the event this year was Milli Lake, whose keynote talk prompted thought-provoking considerations of power within qualitative research in relation to vulnerability, and Nicole Brown, whose plenary session offered insight into how we all might utilise researcher journaling to monitor, inspect, and negotiate vulnerability.

To all authors in this text: We are grateful to each of you for working with us on this interdisciplinary project. The lingering effects of COVID-19 continued around us all in various ways while working on this book. Your care, insight, and effort to bring this collaborative project to fruition were both supportive and inspiring.

At Routledge/Taylor & Francis, we continue to enjoy and appreciate the sublime Hannah Shakespeare and Matt Bickerton for their help in numerous ways, and to Lucy Kennedy for helping us finish this project.

We would also like to particularly recognise two indispensable, wonderful, and now-missed research assistants with the CQR during the 2021–2022 academic year, Kia Banks and Josie Rodohan. Additionally, we appreciate the constructive feedback from Jessica Francombe-Webb on earlier drafts of the introduction.

As another product of the CQR, we are continually inspired by the collective and conscientious ethos of everyone involved. You can find the CQR on Twitter @CQRBath or the University of Bath website.

Bryan C. Clift, Ioannis Costas Batlle, Sheree Bekker,
and Katharina Chudzikowski (Editors)
November 2022

# INTRODUCTION

## The relevance and importance of researcher vulnerability in qualitative research

*Bryan C. Clift, Ioannis Costas Batlle, Kia Banks,
Josie Rodohan, Sheree Bekker, and
Katharina Chudzikowski*

### Researchers as vulnerable?

Thinking of researchers as vulnerable has received limited attention in the qualitative research process. From the early stages of planning through to the reporting and lasting presence, qualitative projects more frequently bring considerations of ethics and risk to the fore more so than vulnerability. Relatedly, risk and vulnerability are often conflated. Whilst the risk and vulnerability of participants are considered in some projects, consideration of the vulnerability of the *researcher* as related to but distinctive from risk in the process is rarely discussed. Still fewer consider how vulnerability can or might be thought of as something more than that which to protect or guard against, but also as an aspect to embrace, think with, or work with.

Here, we foreground the vulnerability of the qualitative researcher. In doing so, we suggest that vulnerability is more than a state or condition. Rather, like ethics, risk, or empathy, vulnerability and specifically *researcher vulnerability* is another means through which to think about our research, ourselves within it, and where human participants are involved our relationship with them.

To begin this exploration of vulnerability, we set out to respond to several questions:

- What is meant by vulnerability and researcher vulnerability?
- What is the difference between risk and vulnerability?
- How is vulnerability related to ethics and risk?
- How do our emotions intertwine with vulnerability?
- Should researchers be vulnerable? How do we plan or prepare for this?
- What do we make of our own vulnerability?
- If we ask participants to be vulnerable in some respects, should we also ask this of ourselves? Can or should we embrace vulnerability?

DOI: 10.4324/9781003349266-1

- How is a researcher's vulnerability related to the research process?
- How can vulnerability inform understandings of positionality and reflexivity?

In thinking through these questions with one another, colleagues, participants of the 2022 Qualitative Research Symposium hosted at the University of Bath,[1] peers in the Postgraduate Qualitative Support Group at Bath, and the authors in this text, the aim of this book is to provide practical, experiential, and conceptual illustrations through which we explore the vulnerability of the qualitative researcher. As an introduction to this exploration, we proceed in the following ways: a) putting forward a diverse and interdisciplinary exposition on the idea of researcher vulnerability; b) discussing relationships and distinctions amongst ethics, risk, empathy, emotion, and vulnerability; c) placing researcher vulnerability in dialogue with positionality and reflexivity; and d) outlining the chapters within this book with thoughts and questions for readers to consider in their work.

As a whole, the text explores conceptualisations of researcher vulnerability, researcher experiences with it, and approaches to working with it. Ultimately, we suggest researcher vulnerability as a vital component of our research practices at several stages in the research process, one to be aware of, explore, learn from, work with, and at times (and with care and consideration) embrace.

## Vulnerability, empathy, and emotional demands

Vulnerability does not carry a ubiquitous understanding and its meaning should not be taken for granted. As a multifaceted and interdisciplinary idea, it has been conceptualised within a broad range of domains within scholarly inquiry. These include, for example, public health, legal scholarship, feminisms, critical social and cultural studies, psychology, computer science, geography, political science, development studies, and bioethics, wherein vulnerability is considered in relation to social, cultural, physical, psychological, financial, ethical, political, technological, or legal dynamics. In science and technology studies, for example, risk recognises the potential for loss or damage, and vulnerability refers to a weakness in software or hardware that exposes threats. Across economics, political science, ecology, or engineering, Wisner (2016) articulated how the word operates as a metaphor for an entire system's stability in response to shocks or unanticipated changes. Internationally, the United Nations (UN) uses the Environmental Vulnerability Index (EVI) to assess the severity of issues likely to occur amongst nation states across the world; it also uses an economic vulnerability index to assist in the classification of national developmental stages and status. In human health, biomedical models of research rely on a range of indicators, metrics, and measurements of risk where the status of individual or collective vulnerability increases the chances of negative health outcomes. In social sciences, vulnerability can assist in recognising individual or group susceptibility to harm. As several have previously illustrated (e.g., Davison, 2004; Gilson, 2016; Luna, 2009; Wisner, 2016), the elasticity of 'vulnerability' makes it a common feature across disciplines, but it is also a challenging one to pin down.

Amidst this diversity and complexity of vulnerability, a common theme underpins the previous examples: vulnerability is generally positioned to be viewed and understood problematically if not negatively, as a formation of weakness that can be troublesome, unwanted, or even exploited. Writing in response to the discourses framing sexual violence against women in relation to vulnerability, Gilson (2016) wrote:

> … a particular understanding of vulnerability dominates the sociocultural imaginary of the industrialized, capitalist Western parts of the world, especially the United States, and wields a detrimental power over our ability to respond well to vulnerability when we experience it ourselves and when we encounter it in others. This common view of vulnerability is what I term a reductively negative understanding.
>
> *(p. 74)*

Gilson highlighted the negativity of this understanding in two ways: first as a condition liable in which to be harmed; and second as a character trait, property, or state imbued with negative value and thus to be avoided. She then points out several ways in which this understanding of vulnerability is reductionist: a) its meaning has become a homogenous property because to carry a consistent meaning for numerous people and disciplines necessitates narrowing connotations of the term; b) it becomes relatively fixed and difficult to change, and as a result separates groups of people into different categories; and c) it affixes a hierarchy of value that enables agency or other preferable traits in attribution to some but not others. In troubling the idea of vulnerability and reworking it conceptually, Gilson and other feminist and bioethics scholars provide a way forward for thinking about vulnerability *productively* in the research process not just for participants but also for researchers.

In their critical examination of vulnerability within bioethics, Rogers, Mackenzie, and Dodds (2012) pushed back on the dominant negative attributions of vulnerability. They concluded that vulnerability is not exclusively "a property of only those people who fall into the category 'vulnerable groups' or 'vulnerable populations'" but rather that "all human life is characterized by vulnerability" (p. 31). Whilst the term can be used to highlight greater conditions of exposure to risk, in doing so we cannot let go of vulnerability as conditioned by the embodied, finite, and socially contingent character of human (and non-human) life. In this way, vulnerability is not restricted to protecting against harm, nor is it detrimental, but is "an ontological condition of humanity" (p. 12). In place of a reductively negative position on vulnerability, approaching vulnerability as a shared ontological condition opens the possibility of considering how we as researchers can (and perhaps should) be open to affecting and being affected in research, be it by our fellow researchers, participants, or content. Indeed, Glass and Davis (2004) understood vulnerability as it relates to a capacity for growth or emotional resilience:

> Vulnerability named within a safe environment can be reconceptualized as a movement between negativity and positivity as it brings about a conscious realization of the need for nurturing by self and/or others. It is this movement that results in healing, strengthening, and fulfilling personal and professional growth and integration.
>
> *(p. 91)*

Vulnerability, thus, can be a fundamental and shared means through which we relate to and understand research participants, ourselves, and our projects. In this way, vulnerability brings researchers and participants into a shared space that is less hierarchically organised. Rogers, Mackenzie, and Dodds (2012) say as much—and in concert with more sensitive, diverse, ethically attuned, politically driven, and reflexive orientations to qualitative research—in suggesting that the research process itself might be thought of as space in which to foster resilience, agency, and autonomy amongst *all* involved.

Though vulnerability can aid how we relate to research participants, we suggest it does so whilst overlapping with (but remaining distinct from) empathy. Empathy can be broadly understood as the ability and practice of understanding or sharing in the feelings of another, or to perceive situations or phenomena from the perspective of another. Brené Brown (2006)[2] articulates empathy as means of fostering connection, power, and freedom. In the use of qualitative methods where human interaction with others is central (e.g., interviews, focus groups, participant observation, community-based work, etc.), empathy has played an important role because of its recognition as a way to think through relating to participants, demonstrating positive and ethical means of interaction, and building rapport. Consequently, for many qualitative researchers, empathy has become a useful technique for ethical conduct and the relationship between researcher and participant. Furthermore, in terms of data quality, it is also recognised as enabling access to better, or at least different or more trustworthy, data (Watson, 2009). Whilst empathy is undoubtedly helpful and appropriate in many respects, we suggest that it alone falls short of the shared ontological condition intimated by vulnerability.

Invoking empathy can be slippery in multiple ways. Watson (2009) suggested that when employed insincerely or simplistically, assumptions about empathy can stifle research and give rise to unethical practices. Stout (2019), too, noted that our feelings within empathy are different from the feelings of the person you might be empathising with:

> Feeling like expressing outrage on someone else's behalf is not quite the same as feeling like simply expressing outrage. Feeling like expressing how frightening this situation is from the other person's perspective is not the same as feeling like simply expressing how frightening this situation is. Feeling for someone or 'into' someone are their own kinds of feelings, related to but not identical to the feelings of the person you are empathizing with. We would describe you as being moved in the empathic encounter, but we might have no standard emotional term for precisely what you were moved to feel.
>
> *(pp. 351–352)*

This difference is important: it generates two different perspectives (yours and the other person's); someone else's perspective may be threatening to you; and spaces between you and the other person could be sensitive or problematic. To truly adopt the perspective of someone else, Stout noted, you must *feel* like them in expressing their perspective. To bridge the space between perspective and achieve empathy involves a degree of vulnerability.

Like Watson and Stout, Lather (2000) problematised empathy. Pushing against scientistic thought towards different ways of thinking and producing knowledge, she suggested that empathy and voice as indicators of quality or authenticity bring challenges to ethical research practice. Where research is framed as a space for the practicing of empathy, she contended that the researcher takes on a role as a facilitator for voice and authenticity, which may well deny the visibility of the researcher in the process, risking naturalising categories, relying on clean and tidy narratives, enforcing epistemic cultural convention, and ethically assuming a right to know. Empathy, she suggests, can enable the appropriation of others and potentially make it easier for researchers to tell tales that are all-too-familiar to the categories and experiences commonly understood. Representationally, she suggested that strategies like shifting counter voices and subtextual under-writing can force an open-ness and variability towards reading that de-authorises researchers as "the ones who know" (p. 22) against participants and others who do not. Keen (2006) submitted that empathy has been used immorally, even becoming "pornographic" in its "indulgence of sensation acquired at the expense of suffering others" (p. 223). Consequently, whilst we encourage qualitative researchers to draw on empathy, we agree with Watson's (2009) suggestions that our own empathy should be subject to scrutiny; that it is something of which to be suspicious, to examine, and from which to learn about ourselves, research relationships, and the topic. Our own vulnerability carries the potential to scrutinise ourselves in this way by challenging the distance that empathy can create in our relationship with participants and the research. Ontologically, it brings us into the work that shares in the constitution of our lives with participants'.

Closely related to empathy and vulnerability is emotion and emotionally demanding research. Arditti (2015) argues that involvement in almost any project creates opportunities to experience emotions within the work. Gilbert (2001) likewise illustrated how entering the subjective world of other peoples' lives brings forward emotions in the researcher. For those areas of inquiry around sensitive topics or emotionally demanding research (e.g., illness, bereavement, death, difference, inequities, bullying, trauma, forms of abuse, violence, etc.), we know well that researchers are often affected (Batty, 2020; Bloor, Fincham, & Sampson, 2007; Borgstrom & Ellis, 2021; Campbell, 2002; Davison, 2004; Dickson-Swift, James, Kippen, & Liamputtong, 2007, 2008; Johnson & Clarke, 2003; Kumar and Cavallaro, 2018; Lee & Renzetti, 1990; Rager, 2005; Sherry, 2013; Silverio et al., 2022; Woodby, Williams, Wittich, & Burgio, 2011). Kumar and Cavallaro (2018) understand that emotionally demanding research "demands a tremendous amount of mental, emotional, or physical energy and potentially affects or depletes the researcher's health or wellbeing" (p. 648). Pushing on this further, a range of research practices can affect us emotionally, not just the topics considered sensitive. For instance, where researchers invest their personal selves to significant degrees into the work (e.g., fieldwork, participatory action or community-driven projects, autoethnography, etc.), emotional demands on the researcher are important considerations. In all instances, and especially those researching sensitive topics, our emotions, and participants', require attention and care. Attending to these demands, and vulnerabilities amongst participants and researchers, can bring different understandings and foster meaning-making.

Arditti (2015) contends that becoming aware of our emotions implies we have encountered another's (or our own, we would add) suffering. Instead of pushing these emotions away, she encourages us, as do Glass and Davis (2004), to develop and use emotional literacy as a means of insight into what is going on. Emotion in this sense, like vulnerability, can be a catalyst to be more responsive to participants and ourselves. Hubbard, Backett-Milburn, and Kemmer (2001) forward that improvement, development, or betterment implies researchers learning how to 'manage' their emotions:

> The purpose of this emotion management is not to learn how to avoid emotional experiences but to learn how to acknowledge and utilize them effectively throughout the duration of the project. One result of sharing experiences of emotion throughout the research process may be to facilitate a collaborative learning culture whereby researchers learn from each other how to manage emotional risk in specific contexts and this may make a significant contribution to professional development. But this involves the development of trust and willingness to accept emotion as a valuable and inevitable part of the research experience.
>
> *(p. 134)*

Therefore, being attentive to our emotions is a core aspect of vulnerability. Indeed, Stout (2019) contends that being open to a perspective not one's own involves being vulnerable to that person and perspective. Despite the individuality of each person's 'emotional make-up', we take and extend Hubbard, Backett-Milburn and Kemmer's (2001) approach that 'emotion management' and researcher vulnerability should be both individual and, importantly where appropriate, *collective* processes.

Unfortunately, one of the central barriers to creating a collective space for 'emotion management' is the time and care to do so. Too frequently, the individualistic ethos of the neoliberal academy entails "being asked to be productive in ways that create a sense of having to do more and do it faster [...] often even before we have completed our tasks at hand" (Adams, Burke, & Whitmarsh, 2014). Educational institutions are rooted in a biomedical model that privileges research efficiencies, and its associated and institutionalised ethics processes, often expelling emotion as extraneous, unwanted, tangential, or irrelevant. The stranglehold on what constitutes 'good' use of time within the neoliberal academy emphasises tangible outputs, like grants and publications (Martell, 2014; Shahjahan, 2015), whilst suggesting that time used to reflect on our emotions and their ensuing impact on researcher vulnerability is 'wasteful'. We challenge this logic and suggest that the emotion management aspect of researcher vulnerability is worthwhile, important for individual and collective wellbeing, and a much-needed use of time.

In bringing together vulnerability, empathy, and emotional demands, we suggest that our own vulnerability, distinct from but in relation to empathy and emotion, can assist in scrutinising empathy, ourselves, research practices, and what our work might achieve. Empathy independent of vulnerability falls short of the ontological character that seems a prerequisite for ethically attuned, politically driven, diverse, and reflexive approaches to qualitative research. The attentiveness to our and others' emotional needs cannot be achieved without vulnerability. At the intersection of vulnerability, empathy, and emotion is, as Stout (2019) wrote, being open to someone else's perspective. This, he posits, usually involves something akin to vulnerability precisely because it places your own perspective under challenge. Whilst at times vulnerability may be something we need to protect against; at others, it is something we could embrace and work with. There is no one-size-fits all approach when it comes to determining whether vulnerability—particularly, researcher vulnerability—should be guarded against or welcomed. This is why vulnerability, as a productive aspect of research, tinting empathy and emotional needs, should be intimately woven into the fabric of our work. As such, we suggest that vulnerability offers an additional practical-conceptual tool for thinking about how we relate to the multiple dynamics of qualitative research that is not often present in or incorporated into current conceptualisations of empathy, nor (as we outline in the following section) ethics and risk.

## Ethics and risk

Pick up any qualitative research design book, and ethics and risk are likely to be central aspects covered. At a fundamental level, we take Hammersley and Traianou's (2012) twinned-meaning of ethics.[3] In the first instance, ethics is a field of study "concerned with investigating what is good or right and how we should determine this" (p. 16). In the second, ethics refers to "a set of principles that embody or exemplify what is good or right, or allow us to identify what is bad or wrong." In research, ethics involve a judgement or evaluation about what is and is not ethical. Choices, decisions, behaviours, or actions in qualitative research vary in several ways, but can be abstracted into two basic arguments: judgement, in terms of the extent to which our actions adhere to relevant rules and expectations in a given scenario; and assessing actions according to the extent to which behaviours intended, likely, or actual *outcomes* are good (p. 20). These encapsulate *doing* the things we say we are going to do in our work, carrying good intentions and desired outcomes, but also pushing beyond this to consider how consequences and taking precautions mitigate or avoid negative results or impacts.

Yet, more often than not, the ways we learn about ethical processes in research writ broad are rooted in positivistic approaches. As students and young scholars, we learn about the ethical obligations that researchers carry, the rationale for ethics, ethical processes of an institution, and historical examples demonstrating the checks needing to be placed on researchers. Historical and contemporary examples are often drawn from *scientific* atrocities (e.g., Nazi experimentation on human subjects during the holocaust; the Milgram obedience experiments; the Tuskegee syphilis experiments; or the enslavement of African-American women in the pursuit of gynaecological advancement by James Marion Sims and colleagues). As a result, Gunsalus (2002) suggested that approaches to ethics are derived from scandal. Ethical practices in higher educational institutions during the 1980s and 1990s in North America were infused with the development of ethical codes by professional bodies (e.g., universities, research councils, funders, foundations, etc.) in response to appalling research practices and resulted in installing review processes by institutional boards or committees. *Protectionist* approaches were rightly warranted in many cases, especially in consideration of the extreme extent of historical ethical and moral violations. However, the largely biomedical model that emerged in this response (Denzin, 2003) does not always fit well with qualitative research.

In its institutional form—that is, in the way that risk is shaped by institutional ethical review processes anchored to biomedical models and thus often the primary way in which researchers come to think of it—risk and vulnerability are things to be managed and guarded against (see, e.g., Cross, Pickering, & Hickey, 2015; Flicker, Travers, Guta, McDonald, & Meagher, 2007). Understood as a situation in which exposure or danger exists with a possibility that something unpleasant or unwelcome may transpire for either researchers or participants, risk comes in numerous forms (e.g., physical, psychological, social, financial, emotional, reputational, or institutional). The protectionist orientation is arguably *the* dominant mode of thinking about and managing risk to researchers and participants in research inquiries. It is characterised by focusing on issues of harm, wrongs, illness, violence, threats, abuse, or violence participants may face. For example, when conducting research with disadvantaged, marginalised, or Othered groups, the stated risks of participation should be appropriately and thoroughly considered both prior to and throughout a project. So too with vulnerability when associated with its predominantly negative connotations.

Although no singular ethical protocol exists to cover every single project, possible risk, or vulnerable aspect, Bryman (2012) noted several foundational principles common enough to most qualitative researchers that serve as a useful starting place: research should be worthwhile and not make unreasonable demands; participation should be voluntary, based on informed consent, and free from coercion; adverse consequences should be avoided and risks of harm transparent; and that confidentiality and anonymity should be respected. Especially where research participants are involved, preparing and submitting a research ethics application is often seen as the first step in working through the (potential) ethical aspects of the project. Even beyond the formal process through which we seek ethical approval from the review panel or board, we are expected also to anticipate what dilemmas or ethical issues may arise through the course of research (Berg, 2001; Creswell, 2009; Punch, 2005;

Silverman, 2010). Within these general protectionist practices, however: there is little unique to qualitative research; a utilitarian risk-reward structure shapes communication (Denzin, 2003); and the neutral, value-free, or objective human subject (participants and researchers) remains intact. Correspondingly, there exists an extensive literature on the risks of harm for participants, but a comparably less robust and familiar debate and discussion focusing upon the harm, distress, or risk for researchers (Davison, 2004). Lather (2012) noted that not only is the real value of subjectivity precluded in the ethics processes and the research process, but also that the human status of the researcher is not acknowledged, fully considered, or incorporated. Even less exists on the vulnerability of the researcher as related to but distinct from risk.

The foci of ethical practices and risks to participation are overwhelmingly oriented towards participants rather than researchers, although risk to researchers is often given basic acknowledgement (e.g., physical safety). In the relative position of power in the researcher-participant relationship, it is the responsibility of the researcher(s) to delineate and tend to ethical obligations. There are of course instances where this is not true (e.g., researching people in powerful positions, some of whom may hold a form of power over a researcher), but the predominant relationship is an asymmetrical one in favour of the researcher (Brinkman, 2007; Kvale, 2006). As such, ethics in the first instance is focused upon participant(s).[4]

For qualitative researchers and their relationship to participants, a project, and the research process, the protectionist approach to risk is, on the one hand, undoubtedly important and much needed. On the other hand, that sense of protectionism can sometimes feel an inadequate (even blinkered) response to the diversity of ways in which risks, relationships, vulnerabilities, or ethics manifest during research practice. In a protectionist understanding, any part of the research process that could be perceived as heightening risk or exposing vulnerability would raise red flags and potentially be excluded from a project, either prior to or during the work. To reiterate, in some work this is much needed. Topics around violence, sexual assault, or death may be dangerous for both researchers and participants. However, in some instances and topics, avoiding risk or vulnerability may inadvertently or even intentionally preclude understanding, insight, or knowledge. For instance, works exploring issues of exploitation, denigration, oppression, or harm are likely to be infused with an aversion to risk that may predetermine what is and is not on the table of research. Further, 'at risk' or 'vulnerable' labels threaten reconstituting the very institutional power structures that contribute to the creation of the conditions through which people live/experience such labels. Overly-reductivist or simplistic orientations to risk and negative understandings of vulnerability rely on the presumption that we know relatively assuredly the sensitive and distressful areas in advance of doing the work, which is not always possible as risk is not always easy to predict (Davison, 2004). Moreover, if we are to place ethics at the very heart of qualitative research (Ritchie, Lewis, Nicholls, & Ormston, 2014), then we need ideas, concepts, and tools that depart from the protectionist, biomedical model. Vulnerability as a productive and shared ontological condition can assist with this task.

For more than 40 years, qualitative researchers have encouraged better ways of attending to research that is not neutral, value-free, or objective. A primary advancement in such qualitative research has been to develop research that is diverse (in terms of content, *who* does the research, and how it is carried out), ethically attuned, politically driven, and sensitive to issues of power (notably but not exclusively in relation to identity/subjectivity, and structural and institutional systems and processes)—products of interpretivism, feminisms, multiculturalism, post-orientations, and the cultural and relational turns. A protectionist orientation wherein objectivity and researcher neutrality are central does not line up well with research that focuses upon, for example, participatory projects, emancipatory agendas, and empowerment of people and communities facilitated by research itself. As Davison (2004) aptly phrased it:

> When a researcher is no longer judged to be an objective medium through which knowledge is merely 'discovered' he or she is acknowledged—and judged—as being a critical 'constructor' and 'interpreter' of such knowledge.
>
> *(p. 380)*

In brief, the researcher matters. A researcher's personal experience, ethics, morals, and knowledge shape the entire process of research, from first idea, through planning, to writing the final products (Coffee, 1999; Denzin, 1997; Ellis, 2004; England, 1994; Hammersly & Atkinson, 2007; Lather, 1986; Wolcott, 2008). As the primary interpretive instrument within the qualitative research process, a researcher can purposefully (or inadvertently) deny participant perspectives, interpretations, voices, or identities. Consequently, regardless of whether research topics may be more or less sensitive, ethically or morally challenging, taboo, or transgressing disciplinary or institutional boundaries, we contend—as others have before us—that a reorientation of 'risk' is *necessary*. This shift—a gesture towards a re-conceptualisation and consideration of 'researcher vulnerability'—requires consideration of and appraising how we as researchers relate to the people and processes involved in the research process, and indeed ourselves. Researcher vulnerability can be a useful means by which we acknowledge and work our relationship to research foci and participants (positionality) and the ways in which we consider and act upon our position throughout the course of research (reflexivity).

## Vulnerability in positionality and reflexivity

Finlay (2002a, 2002b) commented that reflexivity in qualitative research involves explicit self-awareness of how researchers understand, inform, impinge, or even transform research. A researcher's position—their perspectives, values, identities/subjectivities, social location, presence in the work, and so forth—shape all aspects of the qualitative research process. Underpinning reflexivity and positionality, Berger (2015) noted, is the need for qualitative researchers to:

... increasingly focus on self-knowledge and sensitivity; better understand the role of the self in the creation of knowledge; carefully self monitor the impact of their biases, beliefs and personal experiences on their research; and maintain the balance between the personal and universal.

*(p. 220)*

Yet, Finlay also noted that reflexivity does not mean one thing. Rather, it can carry a multitude of meanings and serve multiple purposes within a specific project:

The functions of reflexivity shift from employing it to offer an account of the research to situating the researcher and voicing difference; from using reflexivity to interpret and understand in terms of data analysis to attending to broader political dimensions when presenting material.[5]

*(p. 224)*

Across different paradigmatic shifts within qualitative research, reflexivity shifts, too. Amidst the growth of qualitative research and proliferation of research paradigms (Lather, 2006, 2012), reflexivity has grown to be considered more than just a researcher's introspection into their position and role in research. Instead, it embraces and works with researcher positions and subjectivities, particularly so in more critical self-reflexive methodologies wherein reflexivity is inseparable from the work (Finlay 2002a, 2002b). Post-positivist paradigms would consider reflexivity anathema to rigorous objective, scientific research (Lincoln & Guba, 2000), preferring a separation and management of biases or preconceptions. Constructivist orientations, as Bowden and Marton (1998) detailed, accept and invite reflexivity within research as a cognitive process in the shaping of knowledge. In locating ourselves as human researchers within research, England (1994) likewise outlined that we are tasked with considering how our position and presence shape a project from the very beginning; from thoughts on a project, the questions we ask, and how we conduct and change our practice, through to how and where we represent it. Further, in deeply immersive research using a variety of methods, more participatory forms of research, or more recent writing-as-research research practices (see Richardson, 1994, 2000), reflexivity is pushed still further as researchers are also subjects of and within research. In working with our position within the research process and engaging in the reflexive process, vulnerability can be a useful resource across these various paradigms and methods.

Ethnography, as emanating from its roots in Anthropology but taken in different ways in numerous disciplines (Atkinson, Coffey, & Delamont, 1999; Atkinson, Coffey, Delamont, Lofland, & Lofland, 2001), has been one of the central methodologies through which positionality and reflexivity were developed. Over time they became an expected part of the research process. Part of the reason for this is owed to acknowledging and responding to the methodology's historical and considerable colonialist roots (Denzin, 1997) and the ways that the researcher correspondingly shapes the research process—from objectivism to constructivism to subjectivism.

Yet, researcher vulnerability does not come through ethnography or ethnographic texts with the same level of attention as risk, ethics, emotions, or empathy. It is present in several texts, and indeed it can be read into the push for ethnographic texts wherein the author's positionality and reflexivity are part of the work. As a methodology, ethnographers incorporate forms of participant observation and interaction in ways that often render researchers vulnerable in and to the contexts in which they find themselves and the people therein. More contemporary ethnographic accounts, in acknowledging the researcher's interpretive and subjective position, often implicitly or explicitly, draw on vulnerability.

For example, Ruth Behar in *The Vulnerable Observer* (1996), which is based on her anthropological fieldwork in Spain, Cuba, and the US, takes up the debate about how researchers are present in their texts. The vulnerability of the researcher and more specifically her emotions are vital for navigating the enduring dilemma around a researcher's *presence*. In doing so she reiterates Devereux's (1967) assertion that "that observers in the social sciences had not yet learned how to make the most of their own emotional involvement with their material" (p. 6). Balancing between author-saturated and author-evacuated texts, she encouraged far more towards the former while recognising vulnerability both in terms of the relationship between researchers and participants, but also representationally. Physical vulnerability has also been featured in ethnographic texts, but like the emotional or representational vulnerability in Behar, it has yet to be specifically drawn out conceptually.

Drawing on Wacquant and Behar, amongst many others, Courpasson (2020) says as much about vulnerability in observational and ethnographic practices from being in the field to writing up our work:

> [...] we social scientists can and probably should work, while [in] the field, to become 'vulnerable observers' in our practice of investigation; the same goes with our practice of writing because ethnographers can decide to depart from the supposed truthful scientific interpretation that induces a posture of overhanging neutrality, and instead 'write vulnerably' by injecting large doses of "subjectivity into ethnography, as proposed by Ruth Behar [...]"
>
> *(p. 103)*

Notable in Courpasson's words, and indeed ethnographers who have taken a more visceral or corporeal turn (e.g., Conquergood, 1991; Giardina & Newman, 2011a, 2011b; Madison, 2009, 2011; Wacquant, 2015),[6,7,8,9] or relational turn (Desmond, 2014), is the relationship with paradigmatic changes in research practices and the role and presence of vulnerability. While not necessarily explicit in their unpacking of vulnerability, such works strive to embrace the idea that research is a shared experience with participants wherein vulnerability carries an ontological presence. Ethnography is not alone in this, and it has contributed to developing other forms of research that push vulnerability still further. Amongst those are participatory research practices and what Denzin (2013) refers to as "new life story forms."

Participatory research[10]which includes all processes where research projects are developed, data collected, or data analysed in a participatory way (Ospina, Burns, & Howard, 2021) further pushes reflexivity and positionality in qualitative research that ethnography advanced. The nature of participatory research— involving community members or participants in the research process to tackle an issue or problem that affects them—necessitates a deeper capacity for reflexivity. It is no longer just the 'academic' researcher whose positionality shapes a project beyond participants as a source of data; it is also those of the 'community' researchers. Whilst researcher vulnerability is well situated to engage with these layers of complexity, recent reviews (Bradbury-Jones, Isham, & Taylor, 2018; Lenette et al., 2019; Wilson, Kenny, & Dickson-Swift, 2018) suggest issues of reflexivity and positionality have rarely been conceptualised with a researcher's explicit vulnerability. Instead, they are often categorised as ethical conundrums (navigating the 'grey area' between academic and community spaces means there are no 'right' answers), reflections on positionality (the role gender, history, and social background play in how researchers are perceived), awareness of power differentials (power dynamics across a community, including children), or accounts about the complexities of conducting participatory research (e.g., contexts where communities carry a strongly hierarchical or undemocratic social structure despite the democratic heart of participatory research).

Within the complexities of participatory research, researcher vulnerability brings a capacity to re-evaluate many of the above in relation to reflexivity and positionality. Whilst these works are undoubtedly useful, we contend there is space to re-evaluate many of the above reflexivity and positionality issues by drawing on researcher vulnerability. Doing so would enable a deeper recognition of the role emotional needs can play in research, as well as a more (we argue) suitable approach to ethics that departs from a protectionist default starting point. This re-formulation matters because, as Chataway (1997, pp. 760–761) posits, "participation leads to both perceived and real identification with a group product. However, identification means leaving one's values open to critique". To cope with having one's values open to critique, Guishard (2009, p. 88) emphatically states that participatory research "requires researchers to be *more* reflective and *more* transparent about our respective standpoints, vulnerabilities, and the limits of our theories and analytical strategies" (italics in original). In doing so—embracing vulnerability—researchers can leverage the strengths of participatory research: developing trusting relationships with community members to collectively address social problems. Fields (2016) provides a thought-provoking reflection on researcher vulnerability through her queer feminist participatory action research as she examined the place of racialised, gendered, and sexualised erotics:

> Perhaps I should have extricated myself from these moments with Bianca, Jaye, and Caia once I noticed their erotic character. Readers might worry that allowing for the erotic compromises researchers' ethics, invites coercion, and undermines absolutely the possibility of democratic knowledge production.

[…] [However] the erotic laid the grounds for connection, empathy, recognition, and betrayal in institutions and interactions marked by persistent yearnings, vulnerability, and victimisations.

*(p. 45)*

Consequently, whilst we celebrate the extant reflections linked to reflexivity and positionality in participatory research, we encourage future works to unpack them in relation to researcher vulnerability. We posit this is a further avenue to continue fostering the humanity of participatory research; a humanity akin to that of a Native scholar in Muhammad et al.'s, 2015, p. 1052) work: "You know I've always said CBPR [Community Based Practice Research] allowed me to be who I am […] I haven't had to be someone else in the research process."

Whilst ethnography initially sparked changes in qualitative research regarding reflexivity and positionality, in turn, and in part enabling participatory research to advance the boundaries of those changes, new life story forms push reflexivity and positionality further still. Integrating the research more substantively, and researchers' accompanying positionalities, subjectivities, and experiences, has been a central feature of new life story forms (Denzin, 2013), like narrative ethnography, autoethnography, performance ethnography, collaborative ethnography, ethnodrama, or sociopoetics to name a few. These are innovative attempts to make sense of our individual and collective lives that push positionality and reflexivity into the very impetus of the work. Moreover, several forms of reflexivity can be put to use in these texts.[11] The poetic or narrative text, Denzin (1997) wrote,

… is reflexive, not only in its use of language but also in how it positions the writer in the text and uses the writer's experiences as both the topic of inquiry and a resource for uncovering problematic experience.

*(p. 217)*

Such approaches are illustrative of the ways in which a researcher's vulnerabilities are made productive in the course of the research. Often situated initially at turning points in an author's life, such texts then work outward towards culture, discourse, history, and ideology. Turning points can be and often are emotional, traumatic, violent, or difficult (e.g., Ronai, 1995, recounting her experiences of being sexually abused as a child); or indeed occurring within the seemingly mundane or trivial, amidst the push and pull of the forces, structures, and processes that govern them (e.g., Jago's (2011) reflecting on cohabiting with her partner and her partner's children, focusing on the difficult relationship with one of them). Authors of these new life story forms present, represent, and make use of their vulnerability in myriad ways, often by deliberately placing themselves in the research and disclosing and working with their own histories, doing so at times as they work with participants.[12]

Where field-based methods or creative analytical practices (e.g., ethnography, participatory research, new life story forms) are useful for illustrating the role vulnerability can play in relation to positionality and reflexivity, the conversation between these concepts is also evident in more common and widely used methods, like interviews. Though we earlier forwarded that ethnography may have served as a foundational cornerstone in changing how reflexivity and positionality are addressed in qualitative research, interviews have been arguably a primary method in which emotional sensitivity and vulnerability have been explored to date—perhaps owed to their travel across use in numerous disciplines. For instance, health researchers in particular have explored sensitive topics (Bashir, 2020), and there is a substantive body of literature that reflects the extent to which "the emotional dynamics of interviews can be intensely personal" (Edwards & Holland, 2013, p. 86). These emotional dynamics, as both Dickson-Swift, James, Kippen, and Liamputtong (2007) and Ellis and Berger (2001) articulate, often encompass developing rapport with participants, researchers self-disclosing, demonstrating emotionality when listening to participants' stories, and, at times, feelings of guilt. Depending on the research topic and the researcher's own social, cultural, and historical life trajectory, any (or all) of the listed dynamics can have a profound impact on them.

Such blurring of boundaries (Dickson-Swift, James, Kippen, & Liamputtong, 2006) between participant and researcher, regardless of whether or not a topic is highly sensitive, leads to researchers wrestling with reflexivity and positionality and the extent to which they should separate the researcher in them from the empathetic human. Whilst developing closeness with participants is a core aspect of gathering rich, in-depth data, the confusion of roles can lead to "compassion stress" (Råheim et al., 2016) or "vicarious traumatisation" (Elmir, Schmied, Jackson, & Wilkes, 2011). Furthermore, these blurred boundaries may force the researcher into considering what they self-disclose and how. Whilst a degree of self-disclosure (revealing information about one-self to interviewees) may be necessary to develop trusting relationships, too much—or what a participant may perceive as an inappropriate or jarring self-disclosure—could result in "researcher vulnerability and scrutiny" (Elmir, Schmied, Jackson, & Wilkes, 2011, p. 14).

To navigate these murky reflexivity and positionality waters, McClelland (2017) advocates focusing on an aspect that is at the heart of interviews: listening. Despite being perceived as a relatively easy skill, she argues it is rife with possibilities and challenges. Consequently, she advocates for 'vulnerable listening' to gather data whilst being attentive to both the researchers' and participants' vulnerabilities:

> My aim in detailing qualities of vulnerability is not to argue that being more vulnerable leads to "better" or "worse" research. Nor do I mean that researchers must protect themselves from vulnerability. Instead, I propose that we must continue to be vulnerable in research and we must care for this vulnerability. This focuses attention on the emotional aspects of data collection that require metabolization, debriefing, and collegial support, rather than warnings about potential trauma, requiring safety precautions, or avoiding danger.
>
> *(pp. 1–2)*

Therefore, regardless of the research topic, undertaking qualitative interviews can trigger issues of reflexivity and positionality that researcher vulnerability is better prepared to navigate. Vulnerability is worth embracing. Instead of attempting to minimise or reduce risk, acknowledging vulnerabilities when conducting interviews can help us, like it helped Ashton (2014), address the "unrealistic expectation of my ability to cope with my feelings" (p. 31).

Vulnerability, we attest, can make a significant contribution to how researchers engage with the constant changes of and within qualitative methods, expectations, and norms. Given its capacity to further emphasise and deepen considerations associated to reflexivity and positionality, researcher vulnerability can be a useful means for situating and making use of ourselves in the work throughout the research process. This is made possible because 'researcher vulnerability' is a concept capable of a) helping researchers scrutinise empathy and emotional management, and b) problematising ethics and risk in a manner more attuned to the (less 'scientific') nature of qualitative research. Doing so can contribute to animating several possibilities in the process, such as disrupting the traditional hierarchy between researchers and participants; forming a basis for fostering trust; developing knowledge that is collectively derived rather than simply extracted; constructing a more ethical or relational mode of knowledge production; seeking dialogue and a dialogical relationship with participants; scrutinising empathy and emotion; deepening and problematising ethics and risk more consistently with the needs of qualitative research; or facilitating praxis amongst a group. Consequently, we posit the vulnerable researcher is a consistent feature of much qualitative research that deserves more substantive exploration.

## This book

Building upon some of the few that have directly explored researcher vulnerability in different disciplines—for example, social work (Davison, 2004), psychology and marketing (Downey, Hamilton, & Catterall, 2007), feminisms (Gilson, 2016), feminist bioethics (Luna, 2009; Rogers, Mackenzie, and Dodds 2012), or education (Aberasturi-Apraiz, Gorospe, & Martínez-Arbelaiz, 2020; Howard & Hammond, 2019; Huckaby, 2011; Keet, Zinn, & Porteus, 2009)—this book creates space for discussion and inter- and multidisciplinary understanding and deployment of how vulnerability is constructed, and what vulnerability looks and feels like for researchers, our research projects, and the methods we use. We recognise the care so often *care-fully* taken for our research participants, particularly those who are marginalised, Othered, or experiencing precarity, and ask whether and how qualitative researchers might also learn from recognising and tending to our own vulnerabilities. Of incorporating vulnerability into research, Behar (1996) wrote:

> Vulnerability doesn't mean that anything personal goes. The exposure of the self who is also a spectator has to take us somewhere we couldn't otherwise get to. It has to be essential to the argument, not a decorative flourish, not

exposure for its own sake. It has to move us beyond that eclipse into inertia, […] in which we find ourselves identifying so intensely with those whom we are observing that all possibility of reporting is arrested, made inconceivable. It has to persuade us of the wisdom of not leaving the writing pad blank.

*(p. 14)*

In addition to making use of our own vulnerability and weaving it into our work, there are also important considerations for negotiating such experiences. The broad range of these considerations—and the complexity within them—became apparent to us during the conference presentations and discussions that sparked the idea of this book. Negotiating vulnerability may entail, for example, developing a robust group of people with whom we are confident and disclose the challenges of being openly vulnerable, temporarily stepping away from projects, or identifying small points of progress and achievement that keep us moving forward in research and working with our vulnerabilities. Additional approaches could involve using a research diary to record, write, and reflect; remembering why we care about and our work in the first place; having faith or belief in the quality of work even when we cannot see the immediate value; or managing our own expectations of achievement. Lastly (for this non-exhaustive list), further techniques could include making the time and space it takes to reflexively engage our vulnerabilities (despite competing life and work pressures); coming to accept the human condition and its associated and multiple vulnerabilities; or recognising that data are not inherently good/bad or better/worse based on our decisions, it is simply different. Underscoring all these issues is the fact that engaging with and practicing identifying and working with our own vulnerabilities is deeply personal and challenging. Correspondingly, the upside of doing so can also be powerfully rewarding for ourselves, our work, and our participants if working with others.

This book, therefore, hosts a selection of multidisciplinary authors to reflect on their experiences of researcher vulnerability, to raise awareness of its potential, and to explore reimagining and embracing researcher vulnerability. In recognising researcher vulnerability as a productive space, we understand that our own vulnerability tells us something about ourselves, our participants and our relationship to them, the ways research is organised within certain contexts and power relations, and the nature of our work. It is a sign that *something* is going on. In this way, we take up what Jacqueline Rose (2021) described as the "unsustainable fantasy of invulnerability", and ask: in what ways can and should we incorporate the vulnerability of the researcher into qualitative research?

To explore researcher vulnerability amongst qualitative research, we organise the book into three sections, foregrounded by two chapters: this introduction and a scene-setting chapter (Chapter 1) around qualitative researcher vulnerability that focuses explicitly on issues of power written by Milli Lake and Alexandra Hartman. The first of the three sections, *Strategies for Negotiating Researcher Vulnerability*, provides different practices and strategies for negotiating, protecting against researcher vulnerability, or working with researcher vulnerability. The second section,

*Experiences of Researcher Vulnerability*, offers several empirical accounts of researchers' experiences with vulnerabilities within a diversity of methodological approaches. The third section, *Embracing Researcher Vulnerability*, focuses on how from the outset researcher vulnerability can be useful, insightful, and productive within research practices. Collectively, these works offer a gradient around researcher vulnerability, shifting from a more protectionist ethos earlier in the three sections towards embracing it in the latter.

## Tools for framing and negotiating researcher vulnerability

Section I of the book includes four chapters that offer practical strategies for protecting against or negotiating researcher vulnerability from several scholars whose work involves vulnerable dimensions. While several strategies herein may be read as forms of guarding against researcher vulnerability, they should also be read as being adaptable, either implicitly or explicitly, for working with and negotiating it in a more productive way. The first of these is Chapter 2 wherein Nicole Brown details how researcher journaling can be used as a practical strategy for negotiating researcher vulnerabilities. In Chapter 3, Olivia Brown, Julie Gore, and Adam Joinson develop a framework for protecting against researcher vulnerabilities in online research, which is especially relevant for research into sensitive topics. Susie Smillie and Julie Riddell in Chapter 4 continue with the foci of the first two chapters by focusing on the process and practice of developing guidance for emotionally demanding research. The final chapter in this section, Chapter 5 from Natalie Edelman, shifts the focus towards including how vulnerabilities, and especially those of the researcher, can be assets of our work. In doing so, she develops a Trauma and Resilience Informed Research Principles and Practice (TRIRPP) framework that aims to empower researchers to work with their vulnerabilities.

## Experiences of researcher vulnerability

Section II of the book includes four in-depth, empirical accounts of scholars working across several methodological approaches whose encounters with their own vulnerability became part of their research practice. The first of these is Kate Woodthorpe in Chapter 6: through auto/biographical work, she considers the ethical implications of writing about family—specifically, her son—and unpacks the emotional work required as well as the vulnerable position in which she is placed. In Chapter 7, Cassie Lowe also focuses on the emotional and ethical aspects of autobiography but within textual analysis methods of the biographies of others. She offers several considerations and the value that researcher vulnerability brings to textual analysis. Moving towards more ethnographic approaches, Zoe John in Chapter 8 assesses her subjection to bullying, sexual husting, and abuse in a mixed martial arts (MMA) club. She explores such instances in relation to her vulnerability, status in the field, coping, and ultimately how recognising and making use of these encounters is important. The final chapter in this section from Devra Waldman,

Michael Dao, Hugo Ceron-Anaya, and Michael D. Giardina, Chapter 9, continues the ethnographic focus across four researchers, each of whom in their own work illustrates the multifaceted nature of vulnerability (including within intersectional and embodied ways) for researchers and participants.

## Embracing researcher vulnerability

Section III, the final section of the book, includes three chapters explicating how authors deliberately set out to embrace researcher vulnerability in their projects. In these works, vulnerability did not just occur to them in their work, but rather was sought out to be productive prior to and throughout the research process. Rhea Ashley Hoskin and Lilith Whiley in Chapter 10 set out to foster vulnerability within research design and institutions. Through Femme-toring, they deliberately challenge the masculinist epistemological centre of the university, seeking to radically shift the gendered construction of the academy towards a form of relational femme praxis. In another institutional challenge, Mark Batterham and Aled Singleton in Chapter 11 reflect on their use of walking therapy and the vulnerabilities this produces within mental health systems that don't typically support or recognise such practices. The final chapter of the book, Chapter 12, is from Dawn Mannay: in her work with care-experienced communities whose 'vulnerable' labelling tends to position them as failing, she explores the roles of reflexivity, emotion, and vulnerability in research relationships so as to make them productive aspects of qualitative research.

For readers of this book, we hope the following questions (in addition to those at the beginning of this introduction) might be useful considerations to you and your work that can be applied to your future thinking, writing, research, projects, grants, and teaching:

- Does researcher vulnerability belong in your work? If so, how?
- How do you conceptualise vulnerability? What might other disciplines or conceptualisations have to offer your thinking here?
- Are there aspects of your research which require you to learn how to manage your vulnerability or emotions? If so, how will you do this?
- Could any of your colleagues' research benefit from embracing researcher vulnerability, and, if so, can you signpost resources to them?
- Can you infuse an awareness of researcher vulnerability when you teach qualitative methods or supervise doctoral students?
- Reflecting on and acknowledging your own sensibilities, sensitivities, or vulnerabilities can be challenging: do you have access to a support network which allows you to discuss them?

Ultimately, we hope this book will help qualitative researchers—no matter their experience or comfort with qualitative research—to consider the ways in which vulnerability is embedded in their work, for participants and themselves. For some, we hope researcher vulnerability comes to resemble less something to be avoided and more so something to think or work with and at times embrace. As we have outlined in this introductory chapter, researcher vulnerability does not exist in isolation; it is intertwined with more commonly accepted understandings of ethics, risk, empathy, positionality, and reflexivity across a plethora of techniques, methods, methodologies, theories, and paradigms. We suggest that researcher vulnerability is indeed productive for thinking through our research practices: it is a potential vehicle through which we might infuse more relationality and humanity into the research process and, in so doing, assist in thinking of participants less as 'data points' from which we extract information and more as 'people' with whom we relate and construct reality/realities.

## Notes

1 This book is an outgrowth of the Qualitative Research Symposium at Bath. It is the fourth edited volume that has been developed through the event and discussions with qualitative peers in the Centre for Qualitative Research (CQR). In prior years, we have focused on positionality (Clift et al., 2018), analysis (Clift et al., 2019), and temporality (Clift et al., 2021).
2 Brené Brown (2006) draws from Shame Resilience Therapy in focusing on emotional responses.
3 Hammersley and Traianou (2012) give an excellent account of the philosophical orientations that have and can be taken towards ethics, including the deontological, consequentialist, situationist, virtuous, relational, and the more radical (pp. 16–34).
4 We are cognizant here that researchers carry a primary responsibility for thinking through research ethics, risk, and vulnerability. We do not wish to suggest that this is not the case, nor that researchers should receive more attention than participants. However, our aim here is to highlight that researchers compared to participants are often less robustly considered in relation to risk, ethics, and vulnerability. Including researchers more substantively can be useful, insightful, and instructive in several respects, which the numerous chapters in this book illustrate.
5 Finlay (2002) details five variants of reflexivity: introspection, intersubjective reflection, mutual collaboration, social critique, and discursive deconstruction.
6 Several ethnographers have turned to the physical aspects of ethnography in the form of embodiment as a means of producing different kinds of work that is more attuned to the sensorial, affective, and emotional life that surrounds researchers and participants (Conquergood, 1991). Part of this involved his advocating for a shift away from the ocular-centric and pseudo-objective notions of observation or speech acts and towards that embodied focus. Doing so runs the risk of placing the researcher in an unfamiliar if not vulnerable position out of which might develop "honesty, humility, self-reflexivity, and an acknowledgement of the interdependence and reciprocal role-playing between knower and known" (p. 182).
7 Such a physical or corporeal turn (Giardina & Newman, 2011a, 2011b) invites researcher vulnerability as an explicit and important aspect of ethnography in the first instance and qualitative research more generally.
8 The body in this way, wrote D. Soyini Madison (2009) in relation to critical ethnography (2006), is more than a feeling/sensing home for our being; it is a site of and for knowledge and knowledge production, through which vulnerability is a source: this requires recognising:

... the vulnerability of how our body must move through the space and time of another—transporting our very being and breath—for the purpose of knowledge, for the purpose of realization and discovery. [...] This is intersubjective vulnerability in existential and ontological order, because bodies rub against one another flesh to flesh in a marked present and where we live on and between the extremes of life and death.

*(2009, p. 191)*

9  Wacquant's (2015) sense of "carnal sociology" or "enactive ethnography," is premised on performing the phenomena of which we study and thus its visceral nature. For Wacquant, this meant engaging in the physical and social practice of boxing in *Body & Soul: Notebooks of an Apprentice Boxer* (2004). Arguing that he could have simply observed boxing as opposed to participating in it, in doing so he embodied his own research, garnering a deeper understanding of pugilism and those involved within the South Side of Chicago, IL. More than a mere wielder of symbols, Wacquant (2015) pointed towards humans also as sensate, suffering, skilled, sedimented, and situated creatures of flesh and blood to which his approach to ethnography might develop a different understanding. We highlight Wacquant here to illustrate how the body is an instrument in his research and carries both risk and vulnerability inherent with the research. However, we also take note of Denzin's (2007) critique that, in focusing so heavily on the body, Wacquant doesn't adequately attend to the politics of representation, reflexivity, and praxis.

10  Whilst cognizant there are multiple ways of doing research *with* participants rather than *for* participants (e.g., participatory action research and community-based participatory research), we will refer to all forms of participatory approaches as 'participatory research'.

11  Denzin (1997, pp. 217–224), for example and in addition to Finlay (2002), outlines six different styles of reflexivity: subjectivist, methodological, intertextual, feminist or standpoint, queer, and feminist materialist (p. 217).

12  Examples of new life story forms included but are not limited to, for example, narrative ethnography, autoethnography, performance ethnography, collaborative ethnography, ethnodrama, sociopoetics, different forms of narrative inquiries, or memory work and collective biography.

## References

Aberasturi-Apraiz, E., Gorospe, J. M. C., & Martínez-Arbelaiz, A. (2020). Researcher vulnerability in doing collaborative autoethnography: Moving to a post-qualitative stance. *Forum: Qualitative Social Research, 21*(3), Art. 8.

Adams, V., Burke, N. J., & Whitmarsh, I. (2014). Slow research: Thoughts for a movement in global health. *Medical Anthropology: Cross Cultural Studies in Health and Illness, 33*(3), 179–197.

Arditti, J. A. (2015). Situating vulnerability in research: Implications for researcher transformation and methodological innovation. *Qualitative Report, 20*(10), 1568–1575.

Ashton, S. (2014). Researcher or nurse? Difficulties of undertaking semi-structured interviews on sensitive topics. *Nurse Researcher, 22*(1), 27–31.

Atkinson, P., Coffey, A., & Delamont, S. (1999). Ethnography: Post, past, and present. *Journal of Contemporary Ethnography, 28*(5), 460–471.

Atkinson, P., Coffey, A., Delamont, S., Lofland, J., & Lofland, L. (Eds.). (2001). *Handbook of ethnography*. London: Sage.

Bashir, N. (2020). The qualitative researcher: The flip side of the research encounter with vulnerable people. *Qualitative Research, 20*(5), 667–683.

Batty, E. (2020). Sorry to say goodbye: The dilemmas of letting go in longitudinal research. *Qualitative Research, 20*(6), 784–799.

Berg, B. L. (2001). *Qualitative research methods for the social sciences* (4th ed.). Boston, MA: Allyn & Bacon.

Behar, R. (1996). *The vulnerable observer: Anthropology that breaks your heart.* Boston, MA: Beacon Press.

Berger, R. (2015). Now I see it, now I don't: Researcher's position and reflexivity in qualitative research. *Qualitative Research, 15*(2), 219–234.

Bloor, M., Fincham, B., & Sampson, H.. (2007). Qualiti (NCRM) commissioned inquiry into the risk to well-being of researchers in qualitative research. *ESRC National Centre for Research Methods, 3*(2), 77–101.

Borgstrom, E., & Ellis, J. (2021). Internalising 'sensitivity': Vulnerability, reflexivity and death research(ers). *International Journal of Social Research Methodology, 24*(5), 589–602.

Bowden, J., & Marton, F. (1998). *The university of learning: Beyond quality and competence in higher education.* London: Kogan Page.

Bradbury-Jones, C., Isham, L., & Taylor, J. (2018). The complexities and contradictions in participatory research with vulnerable children and young people: A qualitative systematic review. *Social Science and Medicine, 215*, 80–91.

Brinkmann, S. (2007). The good qualitative researcher. *Qualitative Research in Psychology, 4*(1–2), 127–144.

Brown, B. (2006). Shame resilience theory: A grounded theory study on women and shame. *Families in Society: The Journal of Contemporary Social Services, 87*(1), 43–52.

Bryman, A. (2012). *Social research methods* (4th ed.). Oxford: Oxford University Press.

Campbell, R. (2002). *Emotionally involved: The impact of researching rape.* New York: Routledge.

Chataway, C. J. (1997). An examination of the constraints on mutual inquiry in a participatory action research project. *Journal of Social Issues, 53*(4), 747–765.

Clift, B. C., Gore, J. Bekker, S., Costas Batlle, I., Chudzikowski, K., & Hatchard, J. (Eds.). (2019). *Myths, methods, and messiness: Insights for qualitative research analysis.* Bath: University of Bath.

Clift, B. C., Gore, J., Gustafsson, S., Bekker, S., Costas Batlle, I., & Hatchard, J. (Eds.). (2021). *Temporality in qualitative inquiry: Theories, methods and practices.* London: Taylor & Francis.

Clift, B. C., Hatchard, J., & Gore, J. (Eds.). (2018). *How do we belong? Researcher positionality within qualitative inquiry.* Bath: University of Bath.

Coffee, A. (1999). *The ethnographic self: Fieldwork and the representation of identity.* Thousand Oaks, CA: Sage.

Conquergood, D. (1991). Rethinking ethnography: Towards a critical cultural politics. *Communications Monographs, 58*(2), 179–194.

Courpasson, D. (2020). Doing ethnography: Walking, talking, and writing. *M@n@gement, 33*(2), 100–105.

Creswell, J. W. (2009). *Research design: Qualitative, quantitative, and mixed methods approaches.* Los Angeles, CA: Sage.

Cross, J. E., Pickering, K., & Hickey, M. (2015). Community-based participatory research, ethics, and institutional review boards: Untying a Gordian knot. *Critical Sociology, 41*(7–8), 1007–1026.

Davison, J. (2004). Dilemmas in research: Issues of vulnerability and disempowered for the social worker/researcher. *Journal of Social Work Practice, 18*(3), 379–393.

Denzin, N. K. (1997). *Interpretive ethnography: Ethnographic practices for the 21st century.* Thousand Oaks, CA: Sage.

Denzin, N. K. (2003). *Performance ethnography: Critical pedagogy and the politics of culture.* London: Sage.

Denzin, N. K. (2007). *Searching for Yellowstone: Race, gender, family, and memory in the postmodern West.* Walnut Creek, CA: Left Coast Press.

Denzin, N. K. (2013). *Interpretive autoethnography*. London: Sage.

Desmond, M. (2014). Relational ethnography. *Theory and Society, 43*(5), 547–579.

Devereux, G. (1967). *From anxiety to method in the behavioral sciences*. Boston, MA: De Gruyter Mouton. https://doi.org/10.1515/9783111667317

Dickson-Swift, V., James, E. L., Kippen, S., & Liamputtong, P. (2006). Blurring boundaries in qualitative health research on sensitive topics. *Qualitative Health Research, 16*(6), 853–871.

Dickson-Swift, V., James, E. L., Kippen, S., & Liamputtong, P. (2007). Doing sensitive research: What challenges do qualitative researchers face? *Qualitative Research, 7*, 327–353.

Dickson-Swift, V., James, E. L., Kippen, S., & Liamputtong, P. (2008). Risk to researchers in qualitative research on sensitive topics: Issues and strategies. *Qualitative Health Research, 18*, 133–144.

Downey, H., Hamilton, K., & Catterall, M. (2007). Researching vulnerability: What about the researcher? *European Journal of Marketing, 41*(7/8), 734–739.

Edwards, R., & Holland, J. (2013). *What is qualitative interviewing?* London: Bloomsbury.

Ellis, C. (2004). *The ethnographic I: A methodological novel about autoethnography*. Walnut Creek, CA: Altamira Press.

Ellis, C., & Berger, L. (2001). Their story/my story/our story: Including the researchers experience in interview research. In J. Gubrium & J. Holstein (Eds.), *Handbook of interview research: Context and method* (pp. 849–873). Thousand Oaks, CA: Sage.

Elmir, R., Schmied, V., Jackson, D., & Wilkes, L. (2011). Interviewing people about potentially sensitive topics. *Nurse Researcher, 19*(1), 12–16.

England, K. V. L. (1994). Getting personal: Reflexivity, positionality, and feminist research. *The Professional Geographer, 46*(1), 80–89.

Fields, J. (2016). The racialized erotics of participatory research: A queer feminist understanding. *Women's Studies Quarterly, 44*(3/4), 31–50.

Finlay, L. (2002a). Negotiating the swamp: The opportunity and challenge of reflexivity in research practice. *Qualitative Research, 2*(2), 209–230.

Finlay, L. (2002b). "Outing" the researcher: The provenance, process, and practice of reflexivity. *Qualitative Health Research, 12*(4), 531–545.

Flicker, S., Travers, R., Guta, A., McDonald, S., & Meagher, A. (2007). Ethical dilemmas in community-based participatory research: Recommendations for institutional review boards. *Journal of Urban Health, 84*(4), 478–493.

Glass, N., & Davis, K. (2004). Reconceptualizing vulnerability: Deconstruction and reconstruction as a postmodern feminist analytical research method. *Advances in Nursing Science, 27*(2), 82–92.

Giardina, M. D., & Newman, J. I. (2011a). What is this "physical" in physical cultural studies? *Sociology of Sport Journal, 28*(1), 36–63.

Giardina, M. D., & Newman, J. I. (2011b). Physical cultural studies and embodied research acts. *Cultural Studies Critical Methodologies, 11*(6), 523–534.

Gilbert, K. R. (2001). *The emotional nature of qualitative research*. London: CRC Press.

Gilson, E. C. (2016). Vulnerability and victimization: Rethinking key concepts in feminist discourses on sexual violence. *Signs: Journal of Women in Culture and Society, 42*(1), 71–98.

Guishard, M. (2009). The false paths, the endless labors, the turns now this way and now that: Participatory Action Research, mutual vulnerability, and the politics of inquiry. *Urban Review, 41*(1), 85–105.

Gunsalus, C. K. (2002). Point of view: Rethinking protections for human subjects. *Chronicle of Higher Education*, November 15, B24.

Hammersly, M., & Atkinson, P. (2007). *Ethnography: Principles in practice* (3rd ed.). New York: Routledge.

Hammersley, M., & Traianou, A. (2012). *Ethics in qualitative research: Controversies and contexts.* London: Sage.

Howard, L. C., & Hammond, S. P. (2019). Researcher vulnerability: Implications for educational research and practice. *International Journal of Qualitative Studies in Education, 32*(4), 411–428.

Hubbard, G., Backett-Milburn, K., & Kemmer, D. (2001). Working with emotion: Issues for the researcher in fieldwork and teamwork. *International Journal of Social Research Methodology, 4*(2), 119–137.

Huckaby, M. F. (2011). Researcher/researched: Relations of vulnerability/relations of power. *International Journal of Qualitative Studies in Education, 24*(2), 165–183.

Jago, B. J. (2011). Shacking up: An autoethnographic tale of cohabitation. *Qualitative Inquiry, 17*(2), 204–219.

Johnson, B., & Clarke, J. M. (2003). Collecting sensitive data: The impact on researchers. *Qualitative Health Research, 13,* 421–434.

Keen, S. (2006). A theory of narrative empathy. *Narrative, 14*(3), 207–236.

Keet, A., Zinn, D., & Porteus, K. (2009). Mutual vulnerability: A key principle in a humanising pedagogy in post-conflict societies. *Perspectives in Education, 27*(2), 109–119.

Kumar, S., & Cavallaro, L. (2018). Researcher self-care in emotionally demanding research: A proposed conceptual framework. *Qualitative Health Research, 28*(4), 648–658.

Kvale, S. (2006). The dominance of dialogical interview research. *Qualitative Inquiry, 12,* 480–500.

Lather, P. (1986). Issues of validity in openly ideological research: Between a rock and a soft place. *Interchange, 17*(4), 63–84.

Lather, P. (2000). Against empathy voice and authenticity. *Kvinder, Køn & Forskning, 4,* 16–25.

Lather, P. (2006). Paradigm proliferation as a good thing to think with: Teaching research in education as a wild profusion. *International Journal of Qualitative Studies in Education, 19*(1), 35–57.

Lather, P. (2012). The ruins of neo-liberalism and the construction of new (scientific) subjectivity. *Cultural Studies of Science Education, 7,* 1021–1025.

Lenette, C., Stavropoulou, N., Nunn, C. A., Kong, S. T., Cook, T., Coddington, K., & Banks, S. (2019). Brushed under the carpet: Examining the complexities of participatory research. *Research for All, 3*(2), 161–179.

Lincoln, Y., & Guba, E. (2000). Paradigmatic controversies, contradictions, and emerging confluences. In N. K. Denzin & Y. S. Lincoln (Eds.), *Handbook of qualitative research* (2nd ed., pp. 163–188). California: Sage Publications.

Luna, F. (2009). Elucidating the concept of vulnerability: Layers not labels. *International Journal of Feminist Approaches to Bioethics, 2*(1), 121–139.

Madison, D. S. (2006). The dialogic performative in critical ethnography. *Text and Performance Quarterly, 26*(4), 320–324.

Madison, D. S. (2009). Dangerous ethnography. In N. K. Denzin & M. D. Giardina (Eds.), *Qualitative inquiry and social justice* (pp. 187–197). Walnut Creek, CA: Left Coast Press.

Madison, D. S. (2011). *Critical ethnography: Method, ethics, and performance.* London: Sage.

Martell, L. (2014). The slow university: Inequality, power and alternatives. *Forum: Qualitative Social Research, 15*(3), 2–17.

McClelland, S. I. (2017). Vulnerable listening: Possibilities and challenges of doing qualitative research. *Qualitative Psychology, 4*(3), 1–15.

Muhammad, M., Wallerstein, N., Sussman, A. L., Avila, M., Belone, L., & Duran, B. (2015). Reflections on researcher identity and power: The impact of positionality on Community Based Participatory Research (CBPR) processes and outcomes. *Critical Sociology, 41*(7–8), 1045–1063.

Ospina, S. M., Burns, D., & Howard, J. (2021). Introduction to the handbook: Navigating the complex and dynamic landscape of participatory research and inquiry. In D. Burns,

J. Howard, & S. M. Ospina (Eds.), *The SAGE handbook of participatory research and inquiry* (pp. 3–16). London: Sage.

Punch. K. F. (2005). *Introduction to social research: Quantitative and qualitative approaches* (2nd ed.). London: Sage.

Rager, K. B. (2005). Compassion stress and the qualitative researcher. *Qualitative Health Research, 15*(3), 423–430.

Råheim, M., Magnussen, L. H., Sekse, R. J. T., Lunde, Å., Jacobsen, T., & Blystad, A. (2016). Researcher-researched relationship in qualitative research: Shifts in positions and researcher vulnerability. *International Journal of Qualitative Studies on Health and Well-Being, 11*(1), 1–12.

Lee, R. M., & Renzetti, C. M. (1990). The problems of researching sensitive topics: An overview and introduction. *American Behavioral Scientist, 33*(5), 510–528.

Richardson, L. (1994). Writing as a method of inquiry. In N. Denzin & Y. Lincoln (Eds.), *Handbook of qualitative research* (pp. 516–529). Thousand Oaks, CA: Sage.

Richardson, L. (2000). Evaluating ethnography. *Qualitative Inquiry, 6*, 253–255.

Ritchie, J., Lewis, J., Nicholls, C. M., Ormston, R. (Eds.). (2014). *Qualitative research practice: A guide for social science students and researchers.* London: Sage.

Rogers, W., Mackenzie, C., & Dodds, S. (2012). Why bioethics needs a concept of vulnerability. *International Journal of Feminist Approaches to Bioethics, 5*(2), Special Issue on Vulnerability, 11–38.

Ronai, C. R. (1995). Multiple reflections of child sex abuse: An argument for a layered account. *Journal of Contemporary Ethnography, 23*(4), 395–426.

Rose, J. (2021). *On violence and violence against women.* London: Faber & Faber.

Shahjahan, R. A. (2015). Being 'lazy' and slowing down: Toward decolonizing time, our body, and pedagogy. *Educational Philosophy and Theory, 47*(5), 488–501.

Sherry, E. (2013). The vulnerable researcher: Facing the challenges of sensitive research. *Qualitative Research Journal, 13*(3), pp. 278–288.

Silverio, S. A., Sheen, K. S., Bramante, A., Knighting, K., Koops, T. U., Montgomery, E., … Sandall, J. (2022). Sensitive, challenging, and difficult topics: Experiences and practical considerations for qualitative researchers. *International Journal of Qualitative Methods, 21*, 1–16.

Silverman, D. (2010). *Doing qualitative research* (3rd ed.). London: Sage.

Stout, R. (2019). Empathy, vulnerability and anxiety. *International Journal of Philosophical Studies, 27*(2), 347–357.

Wacquant, L. (2004). *Body & soul: Notebooks of an apprentice boxer.* New York: Oxford University Press.

Wacquant, L. (2015). For a sociology of flesh and blood. *Qualitative Sociology, 38*, 1–11.

Watson, C. (2009). The 'impossible vanity': Uses and abuses of empathy in qualitative inquiry. *Qualitative Research, 9*(1), 105–117.

Wilson, E., Kenny, A., & Dickson-Swift, V. (2018). Ethical challenges in community-based participatory research: A scoping review. *Qualitative Health Research, 28*(2), 189–199.

Wisner, B. (2016). Vulnerability as concept, model, metric, and tool. In D. Benouar (Ed.) *Oxford research encyclopedia of natural hazard science.* Oxford University Press. https://doi.org/10.1093/acrefore/9780199389407.013.25

Wolcott, H. F. (2008). *Ethnography: A way of seeing.* Lanham, MD: Alta Mira Press.

Woodby, L. L., Williams, B. R., Wittich, A. R., & Burgio, K. L. (2011). Expanding the notion of researcher distress: The cumulative effects of coding. *Qualitative Health Research, 21*, 830–838.

# 1

# VULNERABILITY, THE PURSUIT OF KNOWLEDGE, AND THE HUMANITY OF DOING RESEARCH*

*Milli Lake and Alexandra C. Hartman*

## Introduction

The first few in-person interactions following months of lockdown resulting from the COVID-19 pandemic were world-shifting. I (Milli) recall two chance encounters in particular: one with a friend and one with a group of students. The conversations were not noteworthy in their substance. What made them so memorable was the experience of sharing air and space with other human beings; it was like being jolted awake by the extraordinary life force that is human connection. After months of deprivation and isolation, entering into someone else's world, even just for a moment, and connecting through a story, an idea, an experience, or an emotion, felt transporting. Such encounters were not impossible to recreate online, but making them took so much more work that they were almost entirely out of reach. The power of embodied connection (Sikka, 2021, pp. 52–53) of breathing the same air as someone else and of truly being present, even for just a moment, with another human being and knowing that some part of what they are feeling or expressing is shared in what you are feeling and expressing, brings us to life. The energy, mutual recognition, and power created in and by those connections are what psychologists have sometimes called empathy. It can feel like love.

These encounters offered a number of lessons for the practice of doing research. Importantly, they demonstrate the power of briefly inhabiting the same world as someone in order to communicate instinctively and intuitively. It is this slightly intangible quality of human interaction that can make research and especially qualitative research so valuable; when researchers create shared experience and meaning through embodied connection, they become more attuned to the unspoken cues that aid interpretation (Ansoms et al., 2021; Fujii, 2015, 2018; Thomson et al., 2013). Perhaps even more pertinent, though, is the pursuit of equality, humanity, and embodied connection as a *political* project. Working within a feminist tradition,

---

* This reflection is taken from a keynote address given by Milli Lake at the Seventh Annual *Qualitative Research Symposium* on researcher vulnerability, hosted by the University of Bath's Centre for Qualitative Research in 2022. The keynote has been adapted for publication in collaboration with Alexandra C. Hartman.

DOI: 10.4324/9781003349266-2

we emphasize the importance of centering the agency, autonomy, and fundamental equality of those we are working with in the course of our research, even in spite of structural inequalities that may exist (e.g. Kulick & Rydström, 2005). We posit that treating people as equals – and indeed being fully present in interactions with other human beings – *requires* some degree of introspection, reflexivity, and in touch-ness with ourselves (Bond, 2018; Thomas, 2018). Following others who have written on these themes (e.g. Butler & Athanasiou, 2013; Clark, 2019), we understand this as vulnerability. We suggest that vulnerability offers more than mere self-reflection. Vulnerability demands an understanding of one's own precariousness and the precariousness of others, as well as submission to the full range of human emotions (Clark, 2019).[1] These practices are preconditions for empathy and congruence and, as such, are invaluable tools for centering shared humanity in the research process.

We come to this piece as researchers actively thinking through how to foster empathy and congruence in research interactions that are, by design, extractive and hierarchical. The reflections we present here are in-process and incomplete. Rather than assuming answers, we share our evolving thoughts in the spirit of dialogue and conversation. We use this space to document our ongoing exploration of these themes as we are currently navigating them in our own qualitative research practices.

By way of background, we write this piece after many years of teaching – and employing – qualitative research methods in contexts of violence, inequality, and extreme trauma. We integrate Milli's experience running the Advancing Research on Conflict (ARC) consortium, which focuses on trauma-informed qualitative research practices in environments affected by violence and conflict, and Alex's work as a researcher and humanitarian practitioner working with displaced communities to access their legal rights and teaching of qualitative research methods to students of all levels. Perhaps most importantly, these reflections are deeply informed by our joint and ongoing voluntary work as trauma counsellors supporting survivors of sexual violence, which is situated within a person-centered therapeutic tradition (Cornelius-White, 2014; Rogers, 1959).[2]

We draw on these experiences to dissect what it means to navigate power and hierarchy in research interactions that are historically hierarchical; how to foster ethical research practices in contexts laden with power asymmetries; and how to honor equality, agency, and humanity throughout the research process (Thomson et al., 2013). We posit that embracing real human connection in our research – through practices of empathy and congruence – enhances its richness, insights, and methodological rigor. In doing so, we argue that the concepts of empathy and congruence – and, as a precondition for these, vulnerability – developed within the tradition of person-centered therapy and trauma-informed care provide a practical way of thinking about and doing ethical research that pushes the boundaries of the current state of the art.[3] Finally, we call attention to some potential limitations of our approach and highlight risks that can emerge from centering vulnerability in our practices as researchers.

## Our backgrounds

I, Milli, grew up in London in the 1980s and 1990s and arrived in academia entirely by accident. My background in activism and human rights work meant that I was first drawn to research and writing as forms of political activism. Throughout graduate school in the United States, it felt hard at times to keep sight of the relationship between academia and activism, but over the years, I have sought to (re)center these commitments in my work.

I, Alexandra, grew up in New York City in the 1980s and 1990s in a Jewish-Quaker community that valued pacificism and service. I could not have imagined academia as a possibility without the support of numerous mentors and supporters and my failure to secure a humanitarian job at the right time and place. Research whether for academic or other purposes at first seemed (and sometimes still is) a way to try to understand things that do not make sense.

We share these details not just for context, but because we believe that understanding researchers, as with research participants, as human beings allows for a more authentic interrogation of positionality, while fostering conditions for connection.

We have long been reflecting on the ethical responsibilities of academic researchers working in conflict-affected contexts, often away from home and researching communities in which we are not rooted. It was for this reason that Milli first founded the ARC consortium, together with Sarah Parkinson, and later with Kanisha Bond and Kate Cronin Furman. I, Milli's, own experience as a PhD student embarking on fieldwork in the Democratic Republic of Congo for the first time was in many ways one of woeful under-preparedness. Despite outstanding mentorship, I left for "the field,"[4] as so many PhD students do with little idea of what to expect from the practicalities of doing research. While I had received ample preparation for how to select and justify my cases, few instructors had discussed with me how I might feel when my research participants asked me to help them travel to a nearby hospital to receive treatment, or for support with a pregnancy born from rape. While my instincts were always to provide support where I could, sometimes these requests muddied my perceptions of informed consent and my own position within the research, creating a very real concern that often people were only agreeing to talk to me because they needed help (Lewis et al., 2019).

I, Alex, encountered similarly ethically fraught interactions as a paralegal working with displaced people in Cairo, Egypt, that pushed me to interrogate what it means to engage with others in safe, loving, and mutually beneficial ways. The complexities of providing basic legal and administrative support to people with less power and agency within an international legal system that incentivizes suffering posed ethical questions that I continue to grapple with, including how to assess the place for outside intervention (as opposed to community-based solutions) in humanitarian crises, and what agency means in systems of oppression where helplessness is strategic. My experience as a practitioner led me to emphasize mutual benefit as a critical aspirational goal of the research process, albeit one that is in tension with a key tenet of much political science research that assumes researcher neutrality.

## Time and place: problematizing ethics in political science

Fraught research interactions pushed a number of junior scholars trained predominantly in the global north and embarking on fieldwork in conflict and violence-affected research sites for the first time to come together to talk through some of the intersecting ethical, methodological, and logistical challenges and decisions PhD researchers were likely to face over the course of their fieldwork. Creating the ARC summer program and consortium, Milli, in collaboration with Sarah Parkinson, brought together a collection of researchers, practitioners, and PhD students to discuss the realities of implementing research projects in contexts affected by violence, to explore what it meant to integrate an ethical sensibility, and to unpack the relationship between method, practicalities, and ethics.

While feminists and postcolonial scholars, as well as qualitative researchers within political science and beyond, have offered a number of powerful insights on extractive research practices, political science as a discipline has historically fallen behind the curve in prioritizing these conversations. We have instead observed a sense of entitlement on the part of predominantly white global north academics entering spaces that are not their own and extracting knowledge to serve their own professional ends (Lake & Parkinson, 2017; Mwambari, 2019; Mwambari & Owor, 2019; Parkinson, 2019). Indeed, there are a number of ethical pitfalls beyond those mentioned above that may arise, and most political science PhD programs in Europe and North America have left PhD students to navigate these dilemmas and pitfalls on their own, through trial by fire once they "land" in their field sites.

The result has been that many PhD students arrive or depart for fieldwork amidst violence or in contexts laden with structural inequalities facing considerable mental health challenges, alongside other obstacles to their research. Milli's experience with the ARC summer program revealed large numbers of students feeling ill-equipped to deal with ethical, logistical, practical, and research challenges they might face in field sites they previously had little prior familiarity with. While this may be true of all qualitative research within political science, in the midst of a war, when working amidst populations living in grave precarity and often in desperate need of material and humanitarian assistance, the weight of this realization can be exceptionally heavy. In the early years of the ARC summer program, we encouraged students to weigh the importance of their work with the demands – and risks – it placed on people's time, rather than assuming because the empirical or theoretical contribution would be valuable, the research was necessarily justified. Working in close proximity to violence, decisions researchers make on a day-to-day basis, such as how to securely store sensitive or incriminating fieldnotes, or whether or not to travel to an insecure location with a translator positioned differently in their exit options or access to support networks, can feel – and often are – particularly consequential, sometimes touching on life or death (Parkinson, 2015). However, the university's – and the discipline's – duty of care to researchers extends not only to those touched by the research, as interlocutors, translators, or simply as members of researched communities, but also to training and supporting researchers to make ethical choices and face the emotional and political – as well as the intellectual – repercussions of their work (Ansoms et al., 2021).

As discussed so eloquently by Richa Nagar and co-authors (2002), structural asymmetries grant metropolitan, global north universities access to more resources, and therefore richer rewards, as well as disproportionate control and authority over what constitutes legitimate knowledge (Tilley, 2017). These dynamics perpetuate the same epistemic hierarchies that lead us to see some forms of knowledge creation and data extraction as valuable and legitimate, while other forms of knowledge and expertise are conceptualized simply as raw data to be extracted (Bahati, 2019; Baganda, 2019; Mwambari, 2019; Tilley, 2017).

This reckoning among conflict researchers (see Wood, 2006, 2007; and Fujii, 2010 for visionary contributions) provoked a number of field-wide changes and conversations concerning the ethics of doing research in political science (APSA Guidance, 2020). Over the last 30–40 years, there have been a number of efforts, following examples set in anthropology, sociology, psychology, and other social sciences, to redress these imbalances and to grapple with the ways that research and knowledge production are infused with the extractive logics of colonial institutions, where research participants serve primarily as a means for already privileged researchers to succeed within their discipline. A commitment to push back against the coloniality of academic research within social sciences has co-evolved with several other troubling trends that have fundamentally shaped the space where the norms of what is acceptable, high quality, and "good" research in political science are created, lived, and reproduced.

First, an effort to understand the colonial logic of research has unfolded within a larger critical effort to expose the deeply problematic and distressing antecedents of both medical research and social science research (e.g. the Nuremberg Code, 1996). Second, in the past 20 years institutions of higher education have become ever more sensitive to the legal liability they face for actions researchers take. While most pronounced in the United States, a mindset of liability management has spread to institutions in the United Kingdom, and increasingly, globally. The result has been an increased emphasis on highly bureaucratized ethics review processes (referred to in the United States as Institutional Review Boards, or IRBs), alongside immense caution around the language and idea of "safeguarding human subjects" (Tapscott & Rincón Machón, 2022).

Yet, in a push to acknowledge structural inequalities, guard against possibilities for exploitation, violence, harm and retraumatization, and grapple more seriously with power dynamics and coloniality as they manifest in extractive research relationships, scholars have often overlooked what it means to actively challenge – rather than reproduce – hierarchies in our research processes. The environment we describe above, while placing a welcome emphasis on what it means to do ethical research, faces a real obstacle, which – outside of feminist and decolonial circles – remains woefully unchallenged: a paternalistic force that situates researchers as embodiments of the institutions they represent and their participants as no more than victims of potential exploitation. These dynamics can create new power asymmetries that similarly inflect our research relationships and infuse the data we gather. When we privilege highly bureaucratized safeguarding protocols over human-to-human communication, we risk an erasure of the humanity of everyone involved in the research process (Cunniff Gilson, 2016, p. 74; Rogers et al., 2012). Thus, in an effort to recognize and attend to structural inequalities and imbalances, we can overlook points of synergy, equality, similarity, and connection.

In the past decade of working with PhD students conducting research in contexts where structural inequalities are hyper-visible, we have observed the field gravitate toward an institutional – and often paternalistic – approach to ensuring the safety of those we engage with in our research. Even with the best of intentions, such an approach can lead researchers to deny research participants of their agency and power, and to reject their participation or co-creation of the research space (Blee & Currier, 2011).[5]

How can we advocate for a discipline-wide ethical sensibility without reifying the hierarchies and bureaucracies of the institutions complicit in this structural disempowerment? By way of a very simple example, while the signed consent forms so often promoted by institutional review boards may be appropriate in some contexts, they are almost immediately alienating to any research participant in a position of structural vulnerability. Cultures of litigation at US and UK universities render anyone unaccustomed to institutional formalities alienated from the processes proclaimed to ensure their protection and safety. The fact that inclusion and exclusion criteria, alongside stringent recruitment protocols, so often fail to match the realities of the research contexts we are working in, privilege process over practice in ways that can leave researchers *and* their participants subservient to structures entirely devoid of real communication.

Rigid adherence to institutional ethics protocols can result in real human costs, ranging from an erasure of the agency and power of research participants to tangible physical danger when researchers are instructed to collect signatures from those whose identities should not be recorded, let alone transported across borders.[6] Beginning a research interaction with someone who already has little reason to trust a researcher with a notepad by reading them a wordy consent script puts the researcher's institutional power on full display and into effect. Such an act can reproduce, reify, and pedestal epistemic and material hierarchies, wherein the researcher's expertise is branded with institutional approval, and the participant's lived experience is simply a data point for consumption and interpretation by those with power (Bouka, 2019; Mwambari, 2019). These micro-interactions serve to reproduce the very forms of structural and epistemic violence they were ostensibly created to guard against. When researchers seek to establish equality, coproduction, and collaboration in their research interactions, on the other hand, they are frequently accused of glossing over or invisibilizing structural power imbalances that are clearly present. Efforts to "return data" to research participants or collaborators strike an unrealistic note, or are quickly de-prioritized when funding and time run out. These efforts, if they do occur, rarely make their way into the publications that remain the currency of academic credibility.

Drawing on insights from research on congruence and empathy within relational psychotherapy and person-centered therapeutic traditions (Greenberg & Geller, 2001), we have been exploring the potential role that researcher vulnerability, as a precondition for empathy, human connection, and congruence, can play in navigating an emerging dichotomy between the extractive researcher (the persecutor) and the paternalistic researcher (the rescuer).[7] Simply ignoring power asymmetries that clearly exist would be deeply unethical. How, then, can researchers honor the foundational principles of equality and dignity within our processes and interactions, and actively work to challenge rather than reproduce structural manifestations of violence, while acknowledging and taking responsibility for their own power in the context of extractive research relationships? For those of us situated within feminist research traditions, who are committed to dismantling rather than reproducing such hierarchies, we ask how we might embrace principles of equality and shared humanity in order to hold these two realities that are so often positioned in tension, together?

## Empathy, congruence, and vulnerability as a foundation for ethical research

We suggest that embracing principles of empathy and congruence can create entry points that aid researchers in straddling what is often presented dichotomously: honoring the power and agency of researched communities and trusting research participants to make their own decisions, while acknowledging that structural power asymmetries often overshadow and constrain those choices. Too often, researchers, under the weight of institutional directives, gravitate toward one of these orientations at the expense of the other, either assuming full responsibility over the research space, or glossing over the researcher's structural power altogether in pursuit of more equal collaboration. We have found in our work as researchers and practitioners that moving through interactions with attention to our own and others' vulnerability has been both the most practical way to try to grapple with the inevitable ethical challenges of conducting empathetic research with other human beings and a way to make research the cite of curiosity, generation, and joy. We draw on feminist epistemology and feminist new materialism to propose how subtle attention to the embodied research experience might serve as a foundation for ethical research that operates on a different plane to that of institutional review processes and assessments of liability.

By vulnerability, we do not mean self-disclosure or displays of weakness before others. Rather than conceiving of vulnerability as weakness, we follow Cunniff Gilson (2016, p. 76), Brown (2012), and others in understanding vulnerability across at least two dimensions. First, we conceive of vulnerability as a shared human experience of interdependence, ebbing and flowing situationally rather than manifesting as a fixed or immutable trait determined by one's circumstance, identity, or position in a hierarchy. Put differently, one's vulnerability is not a function of who or where they are. Second, while vulnerability shares an awareness of self with practices of reflexivity, it demands a recognition of mutuality and human interdependence, even against the backdrop of a wide range of structural power asymmetries.[8] Finally, we understand vulnerability as a willingness to recognize one's own precariousness and connect with our own ability to feel a full range of human emotions, including shame, grief, and joy, as a precondition for engaging in empathetic interactions with others. It demands us as researchers to connect with times we have felt shame, grief, pain, and joy, as well as to recall in ourselves the emotions that make us human. This openness and ability to feel is the basis of our equality as human beings, and the entry point for genuine empathy and communication. When a research participant is describing an experience to a researcher, the researcher's ability to relate to or connect with the feelings, if not the experience itself, creates the connection that is the foundation of qualitative research.

In centering the embodied research experience, we emphasize a distinction between power within *relationships* and power within *interactions*. We argue that everyday, micro-interactions can *either* strive to undo, resist, or challenge hierarchy, or can reaffirm, reinforce, and reproduce it. Trauma-informed modes of care have shown that for someone who has been a victim of violence, coercion, or abuse, removing their control – for example, by treating them bureaucratically (e.g. as a "number" in a study, or through a dispassionate reading of a formal consent script); by using language that alienates or distances; or by taking sole ownership of the space through a set of rigid research protocols – can recall other experiences of having power denied to them (Becker-Blease, 2017). For those who have experienced sexual abuse, state violence, torture, or intimidation, these can be particularly damaging triggers. Research on sexual abuse demonstrates that the reproduction of hierarchy that is created by placing one party's power visibly on display – an experience that is often reproduced in interactions of police reporting or medical examinations – can easily create conditions for retraumatization, replicating the ways power has been denied to survivors of sexual assault in the past. While we do not contest that preventing coercive, non-consensual, exploitative relationship forms should be a priority for universities, we do argue for attention to the ways researchers communicate and relate to research participants (how they *interact* with participants). We also strive to acknowledge the inevitable ebb and flow of power between participations, which creates the conditions for truly generative research (Kostovicova & Knott, 2022).

This implies that striving for neutrality, objectivity, and impartiality by treating all research participants exactly the same, using identical consent scripts, or reading out formal interview questions, can create distance rather than connection between the researcher and the researched. Rather than entering into an interaction organically and relating to someone as an equal and as a human being, the formality of the types of research interactions that seek to minimize instead of embrace humanity can tap into perceptions that the research participant is not being seen or heard. Moreover, research formalities can inadvertently serve the purpose of carving out the researcher's "right" to be in a particular space, and their entitlement to people's time. When researchers *perform* their researcher role, privileging this identity over their identity as a human being and an equal, the fragmentation and assertion of difference that results can do immense harm.

There are a number of concrete ways that researchers can actively avoid these triggers, and co-create ownership and safety within a research space even in the context of extractive or otherwise asymmetric research relationships. However, while the actions we take are important, fostering authentic ways of being that allow us to enter into spaces as our full selves rather than as representatives of face-less projects and institutions can be far more powerful than the precise words and practices we employ.

Very practically, feminist epistemology has long taught us of the value of bring-ing our full selves into the research space in ways that permit communication, connection, dignity, and authenticity (Harding, 2004; Krystalli, 2019). Insights from radical clinical psychology, feminist ethics of care, and from trauma and crisis support work teach us that empathy is foundational to human connection (Barad, 2007; Rogers, 1959; Sikka, 2021, p. 53). The core principles of feminist care ethics reveal that radical empathy, which we conceptualize as the ability to be present with someone and to meet and hold their pain, complexity, or emotion as if it is our own, is what allows us to connect with other human beings (Jordan & Schwartz, 2018). In contrast to sympathy or mere observation, empathy allows us to feel with someone, rather than simply observe and honor their experiences from the outside (Brown, 2012; Rogers, 1959). While sympathy is an act of pity generated from afar, empathy – being present with someone in their pain and opening oneself to the underlying emotions shared among all humans – is the pursuit of solidarity, connection, and shared meaning. Put differently, where sympathy inserts distance, empathy creates connection.[9]

One reason that radical social work, relational psychotherapy, and person-cen-tered psychosocial care value empathy so highly is that it provides the ability to be present with someone (rather than judging or pitying them from the outside) that can create the spaces of trust and validation that allow for disclosure. Because of its foundation in shared human emotion, empathy permits a space of relative safety where someone can feel comfortable talking without fear of judgment. Without claiming to know exactly how someone feels, this praxis is based on the premise that all human beings – regardless of their formal power or divergent life experi-ences – have access to a shared range of human emotions that sit at the core of our fundamental equality as human beings, allowing us to feel with one another.

Yet empathy is about more than just creating conditions for disclosure. In addi-tion to fostering solidarity and recognizing all people's equal humanity, empathetic interactions are also what enable genuine communication. We thus argue that researchers can benefit from entering into data generation spaces not only with empathy, but also with congruence. Congruence can be broken down into two parts: "1) The ability to be aware of one's own internal experience, and 2) transpar-ency, the willingness to communicate to the other person what is going on within" (Greenberg & Geller, 2001, p. 148). While empathy has a (we would argue still too limited) place in what is often described as good qualitative data collection practice, we focus on congruence, and the vulnerability that true empathic and congruent interaction rests on, as crucial "ways of being" when conducting ethical research.[10]

We follow psychologists, scholars, and activists in this space to unpack the role that being empathetic and congruent has on doing the work of research, and the vulnerability that each of these ways of being necessitates. Our lived experience is that vulnerability plays a key role in fostering human connection, and that it is, in fact, vulnerability that creates the conditions for deep knowing.

Building empathy – the process of entering into someone else's world to access shared human emotion – necessarily means attuning to our own emotional registers. Researchers, like research participants, exhibit weakness, strength, uncertainty, complexity, contradiction, insecurity, shame, and joy. These human emotions affect all human beings, regardless of our positionality. Because empathy requires sharing emotional space with others, it requires that we let ourselves feel fully. For this reason, our ability to tap into these emotions – which requires a form of internal vulnerability or being vulnerable with one's self – are preconditions for fostering empathetic interactions. Being congruent similarly requires that we are aware of our own internal experiences in the research process, in order to be real with others engaged in our research. We do not conceptualize vulnerability as extreme self-disclosure or oversharing with research participants. However, we do understand it as internal consistency, honesty, self-reflection, and openness, which permits us to be fully present and genuinely communicative in our interactions. Attuning to and centering our humanity over the bureaucracies of research helps us to build relationships and spaces of equality, trust, and safety.

## Vulnerability and methodological rigor

In this final section, we reflect on the importance of empathy and congruence, which we believe necessitate vulnerability and self-knowing, for genuine communication, and, therefore, for methodological rigor (Harding, 1992; Nagar et al., 2002). Indeed, without letting ourselves into someone's world, if we are fortunate enough to be allowed to share in that world, we have little capacity to receive, hear, or understand the "data" we are gifted. Without sharing in the world our research participants reveal to us, our ability to analyze or interpret the information they are imparting is severely compromised. If we are preoccupied with performing the role of a good researcher, rather than being truly present with the participants in our research, we potentially miss out on the meaning, nuance and subtlety behind their words, the metadata that can inform our interpretations of their experiences, and the complexities and contradictions that they might be communicating with us (Fujii, 2010). Quite simply, communication occurs relationally in and through interaction.

Rather than compromising our research, decades of feminist scholarship has taught us that departing from the rigid pursuit of objectivity or neutrality is crucial for generating rigorous and genuine research insights (Enloe, 2004; Lather, 1986, 1993). Being fully human in our interactions with others – and thereby understanding the information, perspectives, and experiences imparted by other human beings – is the methodological praxis that allow us to access what Harding (2004) calls "situated knowledge." Researcher vulnerability, therefore, as a precondition for empathy, congruence, and connection, is indispensable for qualitative researchers, offering us a toolkit – through sharing universal human emotions – to be fully receptive to what our research participants have and are able to communicate. While we may never be able to fully access someone else's meaning or life experience, the intimacy of qualitative research and its ability to produce situated knowledge through glimmers of someone else's reality is precisely its rigor and strength.

Indeed, if we are not vulnerable, we risk playing the role of the researcher, rigidly reproducing hierarchies of knowledge production while embodying the institutions we represent. Such ways of being insert distance and erect barriers that at best compromise our data or prevent us from fully seeing, hearing, contextualizing, or analyzing (Ansoms et al., 2021; Enloe, 2004), and at worst do violence and harm. On the contrary, actively choosing to dismantle these hierarchies by instead meeting our research participants as equals and agents of their own fates can honor our shared humanity and enrich our knowledge in myriad ways. Trusting our research participants as equals and as human beings with agency and power allows us to situate our so-called "subjects" as participants in our research and the experts in their own lived experiences. While researchers cannot redress systemic power imbalances embodied by universities and manifest in hierarchies of global knowledge production, our ways of being can actively challenge and dismantle the harmful reproduction of these hierarchies in our micro-interactions.

## Conclusion

We do not advocate for vulnerability as self-disclosure. Rather, we suggest that internal vulnerability and self-reflection – a willingness to be aware of our own internal experiences and interdependencies, and to be genuine and transparent in our research interactions – are the bedrocks of empathetic and congruent communication.

There is no script for this. Vulnerability emerges precisely because researchers must figure out what this means for themselves. This process is one of honesty, self-reflection, and a willingness to enter into a space authentically, in full recognition of our weaknesses and strengths. It involves a willingness to feel, to affect and be affected by, and to be fully present with other human beings, rather than being preoccupied with processes, appearances, outward-facing credibility, credentials, or research competencies.

There has long been a tendency, heralded by litigation-conscious institutional review boards within global north universities, to use bureaucracy to provide structure and predictability to research interactions. Those entering new research terrain may face different incentives and feel the pull of security, and safety-nets of formality and process, to compensate for feelings of insecurity, inadequacy, or imposter syndrome. Yet we have shown that performing the role of the researcher instead of entering into research spaces with humanity provides a barrier rather than a crutch for meaningful qualitative research. In addition to being triggering for some research participants, an inflexible approach obstructs genuine and open communication and impedes understanding. We urge researchers to integrate an ethical sensibility in their research practices, but to do so while trusting themselves and their participants to co-create safe research spaces, sharing in each other's vulnerability, and to foreground participants' own knowledge as experts in their own lives. It is instructive to reflect on our own identities, obstacles, and insecurities as they emerge in our research relationships, and to explore how being vulnerable and congruent with ourselves and with others can open the door to new planes of communication.

## Notes

1 See also Gilson (2011 and 2016) (74–77) on vulnerability as interdependence. There is a wealth of literature pushing back against the idea of vulnerability as a fixed or immutable trait, instead perceiving vulnerability as fluid, relational, and shared universally (Brown, 2012; Rogers et al., 2012). Gilson (2011, 75) understands vulnerability "first, as a condition of potential (rather than fixity); second, as fundamental and shared (rather than inequitably and hierarchically attributed); third, as having a diversity of manifestations (rather than homogenous ones); and, finally, as experienced in ambivalent and ambiguous ways and as having ambivalent and ambiguous value (rather than being inherently negative)."

2 We wish to acknowledge our gratitude and debt to the training we have received, without which the insights we describe here would have taken different forms. To protect our confidential and anonymous way of working with survivors, we do not disclose the organization that trained us or key details from the training program that would compromise our ability to work. Nonetheless, many of the practices we discuss, which we have been working with for many years through the lens of trauma-informed research, have been deepened and enriched by this skills-based training and work.

3 Here we follow decades of feminist scholarship, including within the field of conflict research. See Thomson et al. (2013) and Ansoms et al. (2021) for pioneering contributions.

4 Various scholars have discussed the racially inflected terminology of "the field," which implicitly exoticizes and assumes outsider-ness, positioning "the field" as always "over there." The use of this language discursively precludes the possibility that legitimate knowledge can be produced by those who call "the field" home (see Bisoka 2022 in Ansoms et al. 2021; Mitchell 2013; Nhemachena et al. 2016).

5 Indeed, the language of the "human subject" preferred by institutional review processes neatly reflects this dynamic.

6 This is why many researchers working in conflict contexts will only consent to oral consent processes and complete anonymity.

7 Our model is informed by a heuristic used in clinical psychological practice called the Drama Triangle (Karpman, 1968; see also L'Abate, 2009).

8 We are cognizant that researchers – particularly those working in violent and authoritarian contexts – may face pressures to embody strength and downplay their own vulnerability. We do not suggest that exhibiting strength, authority, and confidence (and downplaying our own vulnerability) is misguided in such interactions; rather, we suggest that the internal congruence, empathy, and openness that vulnerability provides permits us to more fully access and interpret the metadata that can inform our reading of the broader research and security context. It also enables us to understand and connect with the humanity and motivations of those in positions of greater structural power. In this sense, our framework is not only relevant for engaging with research participants

in positions of structural vulnerability, but also carries resonance for research across a range of contexts and power hierarchies. In short, vulnerability, whether communicated outwards or not, creates the conditions for tuning in to our circumstances, and to the emotions of others, making us safer, more empathetic, and better and more rigorous researchers.

9  This perspective diverges slightly from Arendt's celebration of distance as a fundamental component of human interaction (Arendt, 1958).

10  We acknowledge that congruence is not always beneficial to every research interaction. Indeed, even when centering congruence in our research interactions, congruence must remain boundaried. Further, under some circumstances it can be dangerous or inappropriate to communicate "what is going on within."

## References

Ansoms, A., Bisoka, A. N., & Thomson, S. (Eds.). (2021). *Field Research in Africa: The Ethics of Researcher Vulnerabilities*. Rodchester, NY: Boydell & Brewer.

APSA. (2020). Principles and guidance for human subjects research. *American Political Science Association*. Retrieved from: https://connect.apsanet.org/hsr/principles-and-guidance/

Arendt, H. (1958). *The Human Condition*. Chicago, IL: University of Chicago Press.

Baganda, S. B. (2019). The 'Local' Researcher – Merely a Data Collector? *Oxfam Blogs: From Poverty to Power*. August 20, 2019. Retrieved from: https://frompoverty.oxfam.org.uk/the-local-researcher-merely-a-data-collector/

Bahati, I. (2019). Le Robot Producteur Sud: Quel Avenir Dans Les Zones Rouges? *Rift Valley Institute*. May 23, 2019. Retrieved from: https://riftvalley.net/news/le-robot-producteur-sud-quel-avenir-dans-les-zones-rouges

Barad, K. (2007). *Meeting the Universe Halfway: Quantum Physics and the Entanglement of Matter and Meaning*. Durham, NC: Duke University Press.

Becker-Blease, K. A. (2017). As the World Becomes Trauma-Informed, Work to Do. *Journal of Trauma & Dissociation*, 18(2), 131–138.

Blee, K. M., & Currier, A. (2011). Ethics Beyond the IRB: An Introductory Essay. *Qualitative Sociology*, 34(3), 401–413.

Bond, Kanisha D. (2018). Reflexivity and Revelation. *Qualitative & Multi-Method Research*, 16(1), 45–47.

Bouka, Y. (2019). Considering Power Imbalances in Collaborative Research. *Rift Valley Institute*. May 15, 2019. Retrieved from: https://riftvalley.net/node/1007

Brown, B. (2012). *The Power of Vulnerability: Teachings on Authenticity, Connection and Courage*. Lousiville, CO: Sounds True.

Butler, Judith, & Athanasiou, Athena (2013). *Dispossession: The Performative in the Political*. John Wiley & Sons.

Clark, J. H. (2019). With You, Time Flowed Like Water: Geographies of Grief across International Research Collaborations. In *Vulnerable Witness: The Politics of Grief in the Field*, K. Gillespie, & P. Lopez (Eds.). Oakland: University of California Press.

Cornelius-White, J. H. (2014). *Person-Centered Approaches for Counselors*. London: Sage.

Cunniff Gilson, E. (2016). Vulnerability and Victimization: Rethinking Key Concepts in Feminist Discourses on Sexual Violence. *Signs: Journal of Women in Culture and Society*, 42(1), 71–98.

Enloe, C. (2004). *The Curious Feminist: Searching for Women in a New Age of Empire*. Oakland: University of California Press.

Fujii, L. A. (2010). Shades of Truth and Lies: Interpreting Testimonies of War and Violence. *Journal of Peace Research*, 47(2), 231–241.

Fujii, L. A. (2015). Five Stories of Accidental Ethnography: Turning Unplanned Moments in the Field into Data. *Qualitative Research*, 15(4), 525–539.

Fujii, L. A. (2018). *Interviewing in Social Science Research: A Relational Approach*. New York and London: Routledge.

Gilson, E. (2011). Vulnerability, Ignorance, and Oppression. *Hypatia*, 26, 308–332.

Greenberg, L. S., & Geller, S. (2001). Congruence and Therapeutic Presence. *Rogers' Therapeutic Conditions: Evolution, Theory and Practice*, 1, 131–149.

Harding, S. (1992). Rethinking Standpoint Epistemology: What Is "Strong Objectivity?" *Centennial Review*, 36, 3.

Harding, S. G. (2004). *The Feminist Standpoint Theory Reader: Intellectual and Political Controversies*. Edited by S. Harding. New York: Routledge.

Hayward, Clarissa, Kadera, Kelly, & Novkov, Julie. (2021). American Political Science Review Editorial Report: Executive Summary (Spring 2021). *Political Science Today*, 1(3), 46–53.

Jordan, J. V., & Schwartz, H. L. (2018). Radical Empathy in Teaching. *New Directions for Teaching and Learning*, 153, 25–35.

Karpman, S. (1968). Fairy Tales and Script Drama Analysis. *Transactional Analysis Bulletin*, 7(26), 39–43.

Krystalli, R. (2019). Narrating Violence: Feminist Dilemmas and Approaches. In *Handbook on Gender and Violence*, L. J. Shephard (Ed.). Elgar Online, 173–188.

Knott, E. (2019). Beyond the Field: Ethics after Fieldwork in Politically Dynamic Contexts. *Perspectives on Politics*, 17(1), 140–153.

Kostovicova, D., & Knott, E. (2022). Harm, Change and Unpredictability: The Ethics of Interviews in Conflict Research. *Qualitative Research*, 22(1), 56–73.

Kulick, D., & Rydström, J. (2005). In *Loneliness and Its Opposite*. Durham, NC: Duke University Press.

L'Abate, Luciano. (2009). The Drama Triangle: An Attempt to Resurrect a Neglected Pathogenic Model in Family Therapy Theory and Practice. *The American Journal of Family Therapy*, 37(1), 1–11.

Lather, P. (1986). Issues of Validity in Openly Ideological Research: Between a Rock and a Soft Place. *Interchange*, 17(4), 63–84.

Lather, P. (1993). Fertile Obsession: Validity after Poststructuralism. *The Sociological Quarterly*, 34(4), 673–693.

Lake, M., & Parkinson, S. (2017). The Ethics of Fieldwork Preparedness. *Political Violence at a Glance*. June 5, 2017. Retrieved from: https://politicalviolenceataglance.org/2017/06/05/the-ethics-of-fieldwork-preparedness/

Lewis, C., Banga, A., Cimuka, G., Hategekimana, J., Lake, M., & Pierotti, R. (2019). Walking the Line: Brokering Humanitarian Identity in Conflict Research, *Civil Wars*, 21(2), 200–227.

Mitchell, A. (2013). Escaping the 'Field Trap': Exploitation and the Global Politics of Educational Fieldwork in 'Conflict Zones'. *Third World Quarterly*, 34(7), 1247–1264.

Mwambari, D. (2019). Local Positionality in the Production of Knowledge in Northern Uganda. *International Journal of Qualitative Methods*, 18, 1–12.

Mwambari, D., & Owor, A. (2019). The Black Market of Knowledge Production. *Governance in Conflict Network* (blog). Retrieved from: convivialthinking.org.

Nagar, R. (2002). Footloose Researchers, 'Traveling' Theories, and the Politics of Transnational Feminist Praxis. *Gender, Place and Culture: A Journal of Feminist Geography*, 9(2), 179–186.

Nagar, R. (2014). *Muddying the Waters: Coauthoring Feminisms across Scholarship and Activism*. Urbana-Champaign: University of Illinois Press.

Nagar, R., Lawson, V., McDowell, L., & Hanson, S. (2002). Locating Globalization: Feminist (Re)Readings of the Subjects and Spaces of Globalization. *Economic Geography*, 78(3), 257–284.

Nhemachena, A., Mlambo, N., & Kaundjua, M. (2016). The Notion of the "Field" and the Practices of Researching and Writing Africa: Towards Decolonial Praxis. *Africology: The Journal of Pan African Studies*, 9(7), 15–36.

Parkinson, S. E. (2015). Towards an Ethics of Sight: Violence Scholarship and the Arab Uprisings. *LSE Middle East Center Blog*, August 26, 2015. Retrieved from: https://blogs.lse.ac.uk/mec/2015/08/26/towards-an-ethics-of-sight-violence-scholarship-and-the-arab-uprisings/

Parkinson, S. (2019). Humanitarian Crisis Research as Intervention. *Middle East Report*, 290(2019), 29–37.

Rogers, C. R. (1959). The Essence of Psychotherapy: A Client-Centered View. *Annals of Psychotherapy*, 1, 51–57.

Rogers, W., Mackenzie, S., & Dodds, S. (2012). Why Bioethics Needs a Concept of Vulnerability. *International Journal of Feminist Approaches to Bioethics*, 5(2), Special Issue on Vulnerability (Fall 2012), 11–38.

Sikka, T. (2021). *Sex, Consent, and Justice: A New Feminist Framework*. Edinburgh: Edinburgh University Press.

Tapscott, R., & Rincón Machón, D. (2022). Introducing the Research Ethics Dataset. https://governingresearchethics.com/reg/

Thomson, S., Ansoms, A., & Murison, J. (Eds.). 2013. *Emotional and Ethical Challenges for Field Research in Africa: The Story Behind the Findings*. Basingstoke: Palgrave Macmillan.

Tilley, L. (2017). Resisting Piratic Method by Doing Research Otherwise. *Sociology*, 51(1), 27–42.

The Nuremberg Code. British Medical Journal No 7070 Volume 313: Page 1448, 7 December 1996.

Thomas, L. (2018). Unmasking: The Role of Reflexivity in Political Science. *Qualitative and Multi-Method Research*, 16, 42–44.

Wood, E. (2006). The Ethical Challenges of Field Research in Conflict Zones. *Qualitative Sociology*, 29, 373–386.

Wood, E. (2007). Field Research during War: Ethical Dilemmas. In *New Perspectives in Political Ethnography*, L. Joseph, M. Mahler, & J. Auyero (Eds.), 205–223. New York: Springer New York.

# SECTION I

# Strategies for Negotiating Researcher Vulnerability

# 2

# RESEARCH JOURNALING TO DEAL WITH VULNERABILITIES IN RESEARCH

*Nicole Brown*

## Setting the scene

Since the dawn of qualitative research, researchers have explored key themes such as positionality and reflexivity, as they have been painfully aware of the roles they play in a research process. Research methods textbooks and articles have long highlighted significant tensions of being an insider researcher (e.g. Elliott, 1988; Zinn, 1979), researching sensitive topics (e.g. Lee and Renzetti, 1990; Sieber and Stanley, 1988), and/or getting involved with vulnerable groups (e.g. Goodin, 1986; Weil, 1989). At the time, vulnerability was discussed under the umbrella of ethnographic fieldwork, in anthropology for example, where individuals spend substantial amounts of time researching communities by navigating, working, and living with them. As researchers get involved in, engage with, observe, and analyse ways of working and living that differ from their own, they encounter so-called culture bumps. Culture bump theory posits that individuals experience disconnects, tensions, and discrepancies caused by the difference between expectations and actual, real-life developments (Archer, 1991). Whilst people learn to cope and deal with culture bumps by engaging in critical self-reflection to uncover personal thoughts, beliefs, and prejudices, the initial responses tend to be complex and emotional in nature. It is this complex, emotional involvement that is referred to when vulnerability is described as a condition that manifests in the witnessing of and writing about social and cultural phenomena (Behar, 1996).

As qualitative research moved on, however, discussions around vulnerability became more significantly focussed on research participants, even though being involved with communities throughout the research process may impact individuals to such an extent that they experience vicarious trauma, compassion fatigue, and burnout (e.g. Hendron et al., 2012; Newell and MacNeil, 2010). Particularly in the contexts of stressful, private, sensitive topics, research becomes threatening or

DOI: 10.4324/9781003349266-4

damaging (e.g. Gibson, 1996; Johnson and Clarke, 2003). Vulnerability then is no longer an emotional response, but distress and risk (e.g. Ballamingie and Johnson, 2011; Davison, 2004).

Whilst vulnerability is discussed and highlighted, there is a noticeable absence of guidelines on how researchers should be approaching their vulnerability and/or exploring their emotional responses. This chapter seeks to redress this gap by offering an insight into how research journaling may be a practical tool to support researchers. I do not wish to suggest that research journaling is the only means to deal with vulnerability, nor do I suggest that research journaling is an appropriate measure for all contexts and situations. However, drawing on my experiences as a researcher and research supervisor, I offer some practical strategies and examples for the role a research journal can effectively play. I begin this chapter with an overview of how literature describes vulnerabilities in research, along with a critique of vulnerability in those contexts. I then explore research journaling as a form of writing before I share two examples from my own research journaling practice. Subsequently, I show what may be possible when we move on from research journaling into a creative, arts-based approach to research, whilst also outlining future opportunities for researchers to engage with research journaling in the context of their own vulnerability. The conclusion reiterates key messages from the chapter.

## Vulnerable researchers

Within the context of social sciences research, vulnerability is widely discussed as a topic with some scholars emphasising the role of participants, whereas others focus on the researcher experience, which is not limited to the relationship with participants, but also includes collaborations within colleagues (Laar, 2014). Commentators outline that the feeling of vulnerability stems from relations of power within the research process (e.g. Huckaby, 2011), as well as from life experiences relating to the topics under exploration and regarding the individual's personal characteristics such as gender, race, sexual orientation, or political and ideological viewpoints (e.g. Howard and Hammond, 2019), whereby, of course, such personal characteristics may coincide with power dynamics at play. Without formally acknowledging the theory, these commentators reiterate Archer's (1991) concept of culture bumps, the discrepancy between one's own stance and somebody else's opinions and thoughts.

Unfortunately, however, this discourse of vulnerability does not take into account that the terms "vulnerable" and "vulnerability" themselves are the result of power dynamics, as it is within the eye of the beholder as to who is to be seen vulnerable (Brown and Quickfall, 2022). Let us consider a researcher exploring the sensitive topics of bullying and harassment in an educational research study with participants who are aged 8–13 years. Most ethical review boards, grant funders, and publishing companies will see the participants as vulnerable, as they are underage, and that may well be the case. However, what if the researcher is an early career researcher, or is an experienced researcher but new to the methodological instruments to be used in this study, or is someone who has themselves been subjected to bullying and harassment throughout their own educational career or who is a teacher-researcher working in the school context that is to be studied? In such situations, it is the researcher – along with the participants – whose vulnerability should be recognised formally. In practice, therefore, vulnerability is not a simple black-and-white situation, as the context, circumstances, and even the project details matter in whether or not a person is vulnerable. Irene Zempi's (2016) account of researching Muslim women's experiences of wearing the niqab (face veil) in public in the United Kingdom exemplifies this previous point. Zempi herself identifies as a non-Muslim woman, who was encouraged by her research participants to step into their shoes by wearing the niqab herself. Zempi, very aware of her own privilege of being able to step out of the niqab at any point, had not realised what she had let herself in for when she agreed to this aspect of her research. Her harrowing account of name-calling, swearing, threats of physical violence, and derogatory forms of humour (Zempi, 2019) demonstrates a vulnerability acquired for that specific period of time that she had not anticipated. A particularly controversial example of a researcher entering a risky space and making themselves vulnerable is Alice Goffman's (2014) *On the Run: Fugitive Life in an American City*, an ethnographic study of a Philadelphia neighbourhood. In this particular case, critics emphasise that a young white woman fresh out of university would sincerely not have been able to judge the potential risks and vulnerabilities at play, when she entered the socially deprived, Black neighbourhood in Philadelphia, and that therefore she should not have been allowed to engage in that research. Irrespective of the wider criticism of accuracy, transparency, and morality, the fact remains: vulnerability is ambiguous and ambivalent.

Another important aspect lies within the wider context of contemporary higher education, and the ways of working this wider context brings. Without delving into the details of the neoliberal academy (see Tight, 2019), I do wish to highlight the vulnerability individuals experience. Amongst the general public, higher education continues to be seen as a working environment, where flexibility, privilege, and autonomy prevail. In fact, even academics themselves continue to romanticise their working environment (Lovin, 2018). Unfortunately, this idealised image of working within the academy could not be further from the truth of contemporary higher education. Precarious contracts, job insecurity, pressures from teaching and research excellence frameworks, and highly competitive grant applications are making researchers' lives and careers difficult (e.g. Evans, 2016; Naidoo-Chetty and du Plessis, 2021). University-wide cost-cutting measures in the wake of the COVID-19 pandemic have significantly increased individuals' fear over their roles and positions (Gilbert, 2021). Vulnerability in this context is inextricably linked to being able to afford the basics: housing, food, and a good work-life balance. The reality of contemporary higher education is one of stress, depression, and burnout (Darabi et al., 2017; Mudrak et al., 2018; Opstrup and Pihl-Thingvad, 2016). Of course, not all early career researchers find themselves in such dire circumstances, yet, even if a researcher is able to secure a post-doctoral position after another, there is hardly every sufficient continuity to settle down properly at one location, which again coincides with poor overall health and wellbeing, and also impact relationships (Lashuel, 2020).

## Role of writing in research

Depending on the disciplinary conventions, philosophical standpoints and research approaches, research journals or fieldnotes are more or less integral to the research process. The tradition of keeping field notes dates back to studies within ethnographic anthropology and other disciplines influenced by positivism, where observations needed to be recorded systematically and in as great detail as possible (e.g. Emerson et al., 2011; Remsen, 1977). Field notes then were an opportunity to record information objectively, accurately, and immediately (Ottenberg, 1990). The aim and purpose of those field notes was to enable the analysis and interpretation in the moment, but also later in the research process. However, impressions and personal experiences were not usually included in such note-taking, a way of working that Ottenberg (1990), for example, genuinely regrets. Ottenberg (1990) talks about how recording memories and experiences would have added an interesting layer of data and meaning, had he recorded what he calls his "headnotes", the "notes" he holds in his mind. Grounded theory, by contrast, advocates detailed memo-writing as an intermediary step of sense-making between coding and writing (Charmaz, 2012, 2014). As a method, grounded theory has developed over the course of time and is often misunderstood (Charmaz, 2012), but the strong emphasis on writing notes and memos has remained a constant throughout. "Memo-ing" is not related to maintaining immediate field notes but is already a layer of analysis that enables the researcher to formulate initial interpretations based on the codes generated from interview transcripts. Through reflexivity work, the researcher knows about their role in the conceptualisations as they occur. However, other than that, the researcher largely remains an unseen entity in this process. Whilst this extra layer of information and potential for analysis may well be an important factor regarding diary-keeping and research journaling, Ottenberg (1990) and Charmaz (2012, 2014) are not fully transparent about the power of writing.

In her work, Laurel Richardson, for example, highlights that writing is the main element of research and indeed is the inquiry (e.g. Richardson, 2000, 2001, 2002; Richardson and St Pierre, 2000). As we are recording our thoughts, experiences, and observations in field notes, diaries, and research journal entries, we engage in writing throughout the research process, not merely afterwards at the end of the journey (Gibbs, 2007). Writing is also not only a solitary endeavour but works as a collaborative inquiry (Gale and Wyatt, 2017). It is through writing that we uncover, discover, and rediscover experiences and indeed, our selves. We make sense, interpret, and reinterpret our position vis-à-vis others and the world. Of course, our writing is contextualised in the specificities and particularities of the moment when the writing occurs. We shape and are shaped in writing, and through writing we can link ourselves to the other and the world, which, in turn, enables us to process our positionality, our sense of belonging, and our identities.

It is this power of writing that is tapped into in therapeutic contexts. In our contemporary society, writing therapy has long been recognised as a meaningful approach to support individuals with mental health illnesses, post-traumatic stress disorders, pain conditions, and stress-related diagnoses. Early studies suggest that through writing individuals become more reflective and deliberate (McKinney, 1976), which spills into their everyday life experiences and thereby fosters better symptom management. It has also been observed that the process of writing, thus externalising one's emotions, is often sufficient for individuals to learn cope with their experiences so that no further therapeutic support would actually be needed (Murphy and Mitchell, 1998). This does not mean that counselling or therapies should be replaced by writing as therapy, but it does show that writing offers significant support in dealing with difficult circumstances and experiences.

If as researchers we accept that journaling personal experiences may offer an additional layer of information and analysis, but also that engaging in writing itself may be experienced as therapeutic and cathartic, then it should not come as a surprise that journaling may help us deal with our vulnerability. At a first level, writing about our vulnerability leads to us externalising our experience of vulnerability and any associated emotional responses. At a second level, revisiting our own writing about vulnerability, enables us to engage with the experience and emotions in a more rational, scholarly manner as if we were dealing with research data. Together, the initial externalisation and subsequent rationalisation allow us to distance ourselves somewhat from the immediate experience and feelings. It is at this stage that the cathartic effect of having journaled truly sets in. In the following, I would like to share examples of research journaling from my own journaling practice: the poem "This is just to say" and two images entitled "Two parts of a whole".

I should say here that I have many exercise books, ring binders, loose papers, computer documents, arts projects, and files that make up my compendium of research journaling. What I have chosen to share in this chapter are examples of where I used research journaling for specific purposes, and in particular ways, in order to deal with what I found difficult to process at the time.

The poem "This is just to say" came out of several very painful experiences, where other academics used my work and presented that as theirs. Unfortunately, this unethical behaviour is not uncommon in the context of contemporary higher education, and may even be a sign of the times in that we see competitiveness play out, with the more junior members of the academy suffering the results the most.

### *This is just to say*

> I have taken
> the thoughts
> you voiced in
> our meeting
>
> and which
> you were probably
> saving
> for writing

> Forgive me
> they were ingenious
> so noble
> and so bold.
>     (Brown, 2021a)

Although rarely talked about, plagiarism, academic, and research misconduct are rampant in higher education (Dubois et al., 2013; Hausmann et al., 2016; Tolsgaard et al., 2019), which, given the competitive situation described earlier, should not come as a surprise. At a rational, scholarly level, I even understood, when the situations occurred that other people used my work for their purposes and presented it as theirs. However, at a personal level, I felt angry and hurt that someone would do this to me, and I became worried and anxious about the impact and consequences. After all, I also needed to establish myself as an academic, and if other people presented my ideas as theirs, how would I then be able to gain sufficient evidence for my own career developments? I felt vulnerable. I realised that I would need to offload these emotions as otherwise I would not be able to let go, which would result in even poorer wellbeing. I set to writing an apology that would be half-hearted and not completely meant. Using the "This is just to say" poem by William Carlos Williams as a template, I crafted my own version of the three-versed 28-word non-apology. I took true pleasure in playing with words and syllables, as well as the irony of having "stolen" the poem format to express someone "stealing" ideas from another person.

It would be wrong to say that as soon as the poem was completed, my anger, hurt, and fear dissolved. Yet, focussing my mind on producing something to come out of the experience that would be an impactful statement, did help me process my emotions. Very soon, I wanted to share my poetry to see whether the experience would resonate with others and perhaps trigger a response of laughing-crying amongst those who work in higher education. However, not all of my journaling is always meant to be shared, as the next example "Two parts of a whole" will show:

## Two parts of a whole

These images (Figures 2.1 and 2.2) are two of a series of paintings, collages, and installations. For several years now, I have worked on ableism in academia and have researched academics' lived experience of disability, chronic illness, and/or neurodivergence as they navigate the higher education context. My data collection approaches included delivering arts-based workshops, holding interviews, and recording focus group conversations. The constant narrative throughout the different projects with all the participants was that of "two faces" (e.g. Brown, 2019, 2020, 2021d, 2021e, 2022). Participants always explain that they have a public academic self that is well-curated to foster the image of an accomplished, successful researcher and teacher, along with a private self that deals with the fall-outs of needing to be that accomplished, successful researcher and teacher. I was particularly

**FIGURE 2.1**   Two parts of a whole.

**FIGURE 2.2**   Two parts of a whole 2.

affected by my participants' stories of having to hide parts of themselves, as that would not be tolerated, least welcome in their workplaces. A level of connection and empathy ensued, but I realised I needed to explore these "two faces", if I was to be able to move on from these conversations. Through doodling, painting, and collage-making, I became better acquainted with my participants' plight, and connected more closely with my participants' experiences of higher education, but I was also able to externalise my own feelings of distress. The interviews and conversations collapsed the protective walls I had built around me to ensure I would not become overly invested and emotionally involved. Using the arts-based forms of expression was a form of "emotion dump" that enabled me to rebuild those protective walls. Obviously, by sharing my humble attempts at creating something meaningful, and powerful, I am making myself vulnerable again, now. But I think it is important, especially for early career researchers, to see that research journaling does not necessarily need to be aesthetically pleasing and also that not all entries in that research journal must be shared.

## Ideas for research journaling

Many researchers feel that they do not have the time to write detailed notes and use that as an excuse for not journaling at all (Remsen, 1977). In my experience, I have also seen that researchers worry about getting the journaling wrong, or they do not really know where they should start and how (Brown, 2021b). Consequently, journaling becomes this all-encompassing exercise that we must work towards and that should be attained. Thus, journaling becomes connected with "should" and "must" statements and becomes seen as a chore. I argue that for research journaling to be meaningful, helpful, and effective, we need to approach it far more pragmatically, for example, by using templates for specific activities.

So far, throughout this chapter, I have focussed on the vulnerabilities in the sense of distress and risk, the affective aspects of research. However, as was mentioned earlier, vulnerability amongst researchers is not merely about emotional responses, worries, and anxieties, it is also about developing careers, preparing for promotions, and planning for grant applications, as all of these are necessary to position oneself within a labour market that is characterised by instability, insecurity and precarity.

As I mentioned earlier, I do not have one research journal, but a collection of exercise books, papers, ring binders, and the like. This is because I use many different trackers, that is templates which help me keep track of particular aspects of my work. In my book *Making the Most of Your Research Journal* I offer many practical strategies, tools, and ideas for using research journaling effectively. However, at this stage I would like to share two ideas for research journaling from Chapter 3 (Brown, 2021b) to proactively support researchers within the context of contemporary higher education: the research tracker and the full CV. These are two particularly important tools that enable academics, and more specifically those at earlier career stages, to build stronger career trajectories and narratives. The researcher tracker and the full CV therefore are dissimilar to the tools presented earlier in this chapter, but they are practical strategies that enable individuals to combat vulnerability when it comes to standing out against the competition in job interviews, grant applications, and the like.

### Research tracker

Essentially, this is a document or handwritten record to keep track of research projects and publications. Some colleagues also call it the research pipeline. The layout of a research tracker often depends on whether the researcher is planning for a big project, such as a doctoral thesis or books, or if the researcher is working on their publication strategy, as is commonly required. The research tracker for bigger projects lists different stages of research and the chapters that need to be written, whereas the research tracker for the overall publication strategy lists the status of each publication, as it moves from conceptualisation, through writing, submitting, revising, and resubmitting to publication. Some researchers may even have both trackers alongside one another. For a research tracker template and more guidance on maintaining such a research pipeline, see Brown (2021c).

The main advantage of these trackers is that the researcher can keep an oversight of all works in progress, which, in turn, helps prioritise what needs to be done in the short-, mid-, and long-term. If it becomes evident that there are no articles or chapters under review, for example, writing a new article or chapter should be taking priority over finishing a chapter of a bigger project, as the review process in academia is rather lengthy. Ultimately, we should all have an article or chapter, or more, under review at any one time for our publication strategy to continuously move forward instead of stagnating. Naturally, the information from the research tracker will also become helpful when applying for new positions, roles, or grants. Many grant or job applications do not necessarily allow for listing "publications in progress". Yet, within the narratives of expressions of interest or during interviews, a researcher's progression, research vision, and productivity will be tested, and extracting the information from the researcher tracker will enable the applicant to provide irrefutable evidence.

## The full CV

A full CV is exactly what it says: a document that lists every aspect of a researcher's working life. Just like the researcher tracker, a full CV also serves several purposes. On a very basic level, the full CV is an opportunity to simply keep a record of what a researcher has done, as in the throes of our work we tend to forget which conferences we presented at, which websites we contributed to with a blog post, or which research engagement activities we were involved in when we agreed to a podcast interview. Secondly, this record of what a researcher has done enables us to keep track of our achievements. Again, when life is busy with researching, writing, teaching, marking, grant applications, administrative duties, and whatever else we do, we are often unable to formulate for ourselves what we have achieved in a particular period of time. By regularly updating a document that is a full CV, we have a tracker of all the tasks and duties we have completed. The full CV is not about presenting ourselves in the best possible light, it is about having an as a detailed record of our work as possible, with all of the failed grant bids included, which leads me to the third purpose of the full CV: a full CV is an incredibly useful starting point for any job or grant applications, as we can easily extract the information that is relevant for the role or bid we apply for. Instead, of having to recreate a CV from memory, which tends to fail us under the pressure of needing to reconstruct milestones and events, researchers can simply adapt their full CV to speak to any specific criteria, which, in some cases, may relate to demonstrating willingness. For example, interviewers will recognise a researcher's willingness to apply for grants, even if they were unsuccessful; hence, my advice to include all information within the full CV document. Should you wish to begin a full CV, please, download a template from the companion website to my book: https://policy.bristoluniversitypress.co.uk/asset/9868/3.x-nb-full-cv.docx.

At this point, I would like to return to what I mentioned in the introductory sections about contemporary higher education regarding job insecurity, precarious contracts, competitiveness in the academy, as well as the emphasis on productivity and effectiveness. Naturally, maintaining a full CV and a research tracker does not automatically result in improved roles or more secure contracts. However, even the mundane tasks of tracking one's progress does offer a sense of achievement and success, which would otherwise become lost. The benefit of the full CV and research tracker derives from the fact that as researchers we can see our professional growth in front of us, in black on white, or colour. For many academia is a lonely environment, where criticism, negative feedback, and disappointing module evaluations are all-too-common, whereas positive reinforcement and praise are hard to come by. Tracking activities and milestones with strategies like the full CV and the research pipeline offer an opportunity for the individual to positively reinforce their work, to praise themselves. Vulnerability cannot automatically be countered; but just like using writing as an "emotion dump", the "brain dump" that is the recording and tracking may be experienced as cathartic.

## Research journaling: to infinity and beyond

Thus far, I have discussed writing as an act of sense-making of one's experiences or as an opportunity to prepare systematically for further career development to show how research journaling may help us deal with our vulnerability. I have also reiterated that this kind of research journaling does not need to be a public endeavour and can remain purely private. In fact, many journalers do not even revisit their own entries. Instead, they externalise their experiences through writing, and once they feel they have finished that process of externalisation, they shred and dispose of the pieces of paper. I am known to have burned the odd piece of paper as a symbolic act of cleansing and completing a particular research journey. Most notable is the episode after I had finished my undergraduate thesis and Viva. Theoretically, I would have wanted to burn all my books, but obviously, me being me, I did not feel I could get rid of, let alone burn a single book. So, in the presence of friends and family, at the foot of an Inuksuk (an Inuit man-made landmark of stone that was traditionally used for navigation) that adorned the university campus, I set fire to the reading list of American and Canadian literature.

Although the "getting rid" felt cathartic in its own right, my instinct to hold on to all research entries and journals has enabled many avenues I had not envisaged or planned for. The more I experimented with form and media, the more experienced I became in research journaling, and the more opportunities I saw arising. Not every journal entry offers new opportunities for analysis and extra layers of interpretation, but the aggregate of journaling allows for experimentation with the entries through revisiting. One such example is "An academic lament", a poem written in villanelle form for a collaborative Poetic Inquiry project (Brown et al., 2023):

## An academic lament

Academia's a lonely place
for us hamsters in the wheel
spin, spin, spinning in this rat-race.

Chasing promotions to face
precarity with a heart of steel.
Academia's a lonely place.

You depend on others' grace
to overcome rejection, to heal.
Spin, spin, spinning in this rat-race.

Successes are hard to trace
on your own. It feels
academia's a lonely place.

We're trapped to compete, to brave-face
the loneliness we feel
spin, spin, spinning in this rat-race.

And so, we hamsters continue to pace
the bars of the academic cage and wheel.
Academia's a lonely place
spin, spin, spinning this rat-race.

Once I had used my journals as an "emotion dump" regarding my own experiences of the neoliberal academy, I began to analyse interview transcripts from various projects in relation to my own experiences. Rather than be guided by the interview data, I specifically looked for thematic links. As I observed conversations and email communications reflecting the same thematic links, I began journaling by taking notes. All of this information resulted in an image of a hamster perpetually trapped in a wheel. I deliberately select the villanelle structure to replicate the continuous recurrence with its repetitive verses. This carefully crafted poem has moved on drastically from the initial ramblings and random notes, it has developed into an output as part of a Poetic Inquiry. As is often the case with research methods, the definition of what constitutes of Poetic Inquiry varies greatly, but commonly relates to the researcher's "use of poetry as/in/for inquiry" (Faulkner, 2017, p. 210). In the case of "An academic lament", I started out with the particulars and specificities of my own experiences as a researcher and academic, which I then set against more universal ideas and realities. In collaboration with other poetic inquirers, it emerged how relatable the experienced reflected in my villanelle were. Through its emotional and emotive connection, Poetic Inquiry offers an opportunity to raise awareness of social justice matters, to call for change, and to demand transformation, in the individual and society as a whole. Naturally, we may be critical regarding the power of poetry, but to do so would mean we would have to be critical of the powers of all qualitative research, more generally. It is not my aim to critique nor to defend the role and purpose of Poetic Inquiry. I am merely demonstrating that research journaling offers opportunities far beyond what Ottenberg (1990) imagined, when he bemoaned the fact that he had not recorded certain experiences, as they felt to be outside the scope of anthropological field notes. Whilst there is no particular need that forces us to share the research journaling we did as part of dealing with our vulnerabilities, we may find that there are important messages and experiences that are more universal and therefore should be shared. For some researchers, like myself, the Poetic Inquiry may offer this space, others may turn to drawing, painting, collaging, photography, videography, or indeed any other form of expression. To infinity and beyond.

## Conclusion

For this conclusion, let me return to the beginning of this chapter: my emphasis on understanding and exploring vulnerability. All researchers are more or less vulnerable at some point in their careers. Being vulnerable does not mean being weak, with the inverse also true: not being vulnerable does not mean being strong. Being vulnerable, therefore, is not necessarily something that we should avoid. Indeed, in many cases we become vulnerable because we were unable to predict potential risk and distress accurately, and so stumble into this feeling of vulnerability. What is important is that we have mechanisms and strategies to deal with any vulnerability that may arise throughout the research process.

Research journaling is one such tool. When we need to make sense of our experiences the research journal can become a loyal friend, attentive listener, and caring coach. Ultimately, the research journal is not actually a therapist, though, and in more serious circumstances it is imperative to seek professional help, which may well exacerbate our feeling of vulnerability.

I have discussed the benefits of writing in the context of therapy, but I would like to add to that here that "writing" does not necessarily mean "physically, literally writing". Research journaling can take many forms and should suit the individual. For some research journaling will take the written form, as it does for me for the most part. For others, though, research journaling is doing arts and crafts, or recording themselves on video or audio. The therapeutic effect of externalisation and rationalisation is not diminished by form or media, it is, however, impacted by a form or medium that does not suit the researcher. As we begin research journaling, therefore, we may need to experiment with different modes and media to identify what suits us best, and how we can best harness the cathartic effect of research journaling. I felt incredibly self-conscious the first time I recorded myself on video talking about my experiences, although I kept an open mind. In the end, the recordings did not work for me, and instead, writing, fictionalisation, and Poetic Inquiry have become my preferred modes for research journaling, although I am often anxious when I share some of my works in progress. Even the process of research journaling is characterised by our vulnerability: we begin our journey to dealing with vulnerability through research journaling by making ourselves vulnerable and trying out new approaches; and when we share our journal entries, we make ourselves vulnerable again as we open our offerings to the world. In sum, vulnerability remains with us, but the research journal is a patient companion.

# References

Archer, C. M. (1991). *Living with Strangers in the USA: Communicating Beyond Culture.* Englewood Cliffs, NJ: Prentice-Hall.

Ballamingie, P., & Johnson, S. (2011). The vulnerable researcher: Some unanticipated challenges of doctoral fieldwork. *The Qualitative Report, 16*(3), 711–729.

Behar, R. (1996). *The Vulnerable Observer: Anthropology That Breaks Your Heart.* Boston, MA: Beacon Press.

Brown, N. (2019). The embodied academic: Body work in teacher education. In: Leigh, J. S. (ed.) *Conversations on Embodiment across Higher Education: Teaching, Practice and Research.* London: Routledge, 86–95.

Brown, N. (2020). Disclosure in academia: A sensitive issue. In: Brown, N., & Leigh, J. S. (eds.) *Ableism in Academia: Theorising Experiences of Disabilities and Chronic Illnesses in Higher Education.* London: UCL Press. DOI: 10.2307/j.ctv13xprjr.9.

Brown, N. (2021a). This is just to say. *So Fi Zine, 9,* 11.

Brown, N. (2021b). *Making the Most of Your Research Journal.* Bristol: Policy Press.

Brown, N. (2021c). Making the most of your research journal: Research pipeline. https:// policy.bristoluniversitypress.co.uk/making-the-most-of-your-research-journal/ online-resources/supplementary-materials/research-pipeline

Brown, N. (2021d). Introduction: Being "different" in academia. In: Brown, N. (ed.) *Lived Experiences of Ableism in Academia: Strategies for Inclusion in Higher Education.* Bristol: Policy Press, 1–14.

Brown, N. (2021e). Deafness and hearing loss in higher education. In: Brown, N. (ed.) *Lived Experiences of Ableism in Academia: Strategies for Inclusion in Higher Education.* Bristol: Policy Press, 141–158.

Brown, N. (2022). The social course of fibromyalgia: Resisting processes of marginalisation. *International Journal of Environmental Research and Public Health, 19*(1) [Special Issue: Chronic Disease, Disability, and Community Care], 333–346. DOI: 10.3390/ijerph19010333.

Brown, N., & Quickfall, A. (2022). Sensitive topics and vulnerable groups: Position paper for the British Educational Research Association. https://www.nicole-brown.co.uk/ Downloads/PositionPaperSensitiveTopicsVulnerableGroups.pdf

Brown, N., McAllister, A., Haggith, M., Buchanan, M., Katt, E. S., Kuri, E., Peterson-Hilleque, V. L., van der Aa, J., & Warner, L. (2023). In: van Rooyen, H., & Pithouse-Morgan, K. (eds.) *Voices and Silences: Poetry as Knowing and Learning in Social Research.*

Charmaz, K. (2012). The power and potential of grounded theory. *Medical Sociology Online, 6*(3), 2–15.

Charmaz, K. (2014). *Constructing Grounded Theory.* 2nd ed. London, Thousand Oaks, California, New Delhi, Singapore: Sage.

Darabi, M., Macaskill, A., & Reidy, L. (2017). Stress among UK academics: Identifying who copes best. *Journal of Further and Higher Education, 41*(3), 393–412.

Davison, J. (2004). Dilemmas in research: Issues of vulnerability and disempowerment for the social worker/researcher. *Journal of Social Work Practice, 18*(3), 379–393. DOI: 10.1080/0265053042000314447.

Dubois, J. M., Anderson, E. E., Chibnall, J., Carroll, K., Gibb, T., Ogbuka, C., & Rubbelke, T. (2013). Understanding research misconduct: A comparative analysis of 120 cases of professional wrongdoing. *Accountability in Research, 20*(5–6), 320–338.

Elliott, J. (1988). Educational research and outsider-insider relations. *International Journal of Qualitative Studies in Education, 1*(2), 155–166.

Emerson, R. M., Fretz, R. I., & Shaw, L. L. (2011). *Writing Ethnographic Fieldnotes.* 2nd ed. Chicago, London: University of Chicago Press.

Evans, M. (2016). Job security: A fair go for university staff. *Advocate: Journal of the National Tertiary Education Union, 23*(3), 18–21.

Faulkner, S. L. (2017). Poetic inquiry. In: Leavy, P. (ed.) *Handbook of Arts-Based Research.* New York, London: The Guilford Press, 208–230.

Gale, K., & Wyatt, J. (2017). Working at the wonder: Collaborative writing as method of inquiry. *Qualitative Inquiry, 23*(5), 355–364.

Gibbs, A. (2007). Writing as method: Attunement, resonance, and rhythm. In Knudsen, B. T., & Stage, C. (eds.) *Affective Methodologies: Developing Cultural Research Strategies for the Study of Affect.* Basingstoke, New York: Palgrave Macmillan, 222–236.

Gibson, V. (1996). The problems of researching sensitive topics in health care. *Nurse Researcher, 4*(2), 65–74. DOI: 10.7748/nr.4.2.65.s7.

Gilbert, N. (2021, August 9). UK academics seethe over universities' cost-cutting moves. *Nature.* https://www.nature.com/articles/d41586-021-02163-9. Last accessed: 13 June 2022.

Goffman, A. (2014). *On the Run: Fugitive Life in an American City.* Chicago, London: The University of Chicago Press.

Goodin, R. E. (1986). *Protecting the Vulnerable: A Re-analysis of Our Social Responsibilities.* Chicago, London: University of Chicago Press.

Hausmann, L., Murphy, S. P., & Publication Committee of the International Society for Neurochemistry (ISN). (2016). The challenges for scientific publishing, 60 years on. *Journal of Neurochemistry, 139,* 280–287.

Hendron, J. A., Irving, P., & Taylor, B. (2012). The unseen cost: A discussion of secondary traumatization experience of the clergy. *Pastoral Psychology, 61*(2), 221–231. DOI: 10.1007/s11089-011-0378-z.

Howard, L. C., & Hammond, S. P. (2019). Researcher vulnerability: Implications for educational research and practice. *International Journal of Qualitative Studies in Education, 32*(4), 411–428.

Huckaby, M. F. (2011). Researcher/researched: Relations of vulnerability/relations of power. *International Journal of Qualitative Studies in Education, 24*(2), 165–183.

Johnson, B., & Clarke, J. (2003). Collecting sensitive data: The impact on researchers. *Qualitative Health Research, 13*(3), 421–434. DOI: 10.1177/1049732302250340.

Laar, A. (2014). Researcher vulnerability: An overlooked issue in vulnerability discourses. *Scientific Research and Essays, 9*(16), 737–743.

Lashuel, H. A. (2020). Mental health in academia: What about faculty?. *eLife, 9,* e54551.

Lee, R. M., & Renzetti, C. M. (1990). The problems of researching sensitive topics: An overview and introduction. *American Behavioral Scientist, 33*(5), 510–528.

Lovin, C. L. (2018). Feelings of change: Alternative feminist professional trajectories. In: Taylor, Y. & Lahad, K. (eds.) *Feeling Academic in the Neoliberal University: Feminist Flights, Fights and Failures.* Springer International Publishing AG, 137–161.

McKinney, F. (1976). Free writing as therapy. *Psychotherapy: Theory, Research & Practice, 13*(2), 183.

Mudrak, J., Zabrodska, K., Kveton, P., Jelinek, M., Blatny, M., Solcova, I., & Machovcova, K. (2018). Occupational well-being among university faculty: A job demands-resources model. *Research in Higher Education, 59*(3), 325–348.

Murphy, L. J., & Mitchell, D. L. (1998). When writing helps to heal: E-mail as therapy. *British Journal of Guidance and Counselling, 26*(1), 21–32.

Naidoo-Chetty, M., & du Plessis, M. (2021). Systematic review of the job demands and resources of academic staff within higher education institutions. *International Journal of Higher Education, 10*(3), 268–284.

Newell, J. M., & MacNeil, G. A. (2010). Professional burnout: Vicarious trauma, secondary traumatic stress, and compassion fatigue: A review of theoretical terms, risk factors, and preventive methods for clinicians and researchers. *Best Practices in Mental Health, 6*(2), 57–68.

Opstrup, N., & Pihl-Thingvad, S. (2016). Stressing academia? Stress-as-offence-to-self at Danish universities. *Journal of Higher Education Policy and Management, 38*(1), 39–52.

Ottenberg, S. (1990). Thirty years of fieldnotes: Changing relationships to the text. In: Sanjek, R. (Ed.) *Fieldnotes: The Makings of Anthropology.* Ithaca, London: De Gruyter.

Remsen Jr, J. V. (1977). On taking field notes. *American Birds, 31*, 946–953.

Richardson, L. (2000). New writing practices in qualitative research. *Sociology of Sport Journal, 17*(1), 5–20.

Richardson, L. (2001). Getting personal: Writing-stories. *International Journal of Qualitative Studies in Education, 14*(1), 33–38.

Richardson, L. (2002). Writing sociology. *Cultural Studies? Critical Methodologies, 2*(3), 414–422.

Richardson, L., & St Pierre, E. (2000). A method of inquiry. In: Denzin, N., & Lincoln, Y. S. (eds.) *Handbook of Qualitative Research.* London, Thousand Oaks, California, New Delhi, Singapore: Sage, 923–948.

Sieber, J. E., & Stanley, B. (1988). Ethical and professional dimensions of socially sensitive research. *American Psychologist, 43*(1), 49.

Tight, M. (2019). The neoliberal turn in higher education. *Higher Education Quarterly, 73*(3), 273–284.

Tolsgaard, M. G., Ellaway, R., Woods, N., & Norman, G. (2019). Salami-slicing and plagiarism: How should we respond?. *Advances in Health Sciences Education, 24*(1), 3–14.

Weil, M. (1989). Research on vulnerable populations. *The Journal of Applied Behavioral Science, 25*(4), 419–437.

Zempi, I. (2016). Negotiating constructions of insider and outsider status in research with veiled Muslim women victims of Islamophobic hate crime. *Sociological Research Online, 21*(4), 70–81.

Zempi, I. (2019, February 3). Testing Islamophobia: Researchers go undercover as Muslims for a month. Muslimvillage.com. https://muslimvillage.com/2019/02/03/131531/testing-islamophobia-researchers-go-undercover-muslims-month/. Last accessed 13 June 2022.

Zinn, M. B. (1979). Field research in minority communities: Ethical, methodological and political observations by an insider. *Social Problems, 27*(2), 209–219.

# 3

# QUALITATIVE ANALYSIS IN ONLINE RESEARCH

## Protecting against researcher vulnerabilities

*Olivia Brown, Julie Gore, and Adam Joinson*

### Research vulnerabilities in online research

Renewed attention has been paid to the importance of considering researcher vulnerabilities in qualitative research (Howard & Hammond, 2019; Bashir, 2020). Vulnerabilities refer to the possibility of experiencing risk or distress during the process of the research and have also been used to refer to feelings of burnout, fatigue, or vicarious trauma (Behar, 1996; Hendron, Irving, & Taylor, 2012). Experiencing vulnerabilities has traditionally been associated with sensitive research – research which poses a potential threat to those who are or who have been involved in it (Lee, 1993; Howard & Hammond, 2019). Example topics of sensitive research might include drug and alcohol addiction, domestic violence, terrorism, migration, and disability. Each of these topics is capable of evoking feelings of anxiety and distress, and as such, researchers are arguably more likely to experience vulnerabilities when investigating them.

How best to manage and respond to researcher vulnerabilities in sensitive qualitative research has been considered at length (Howard & Hammond, 2019; Liamputtong, 2007; Shaw, Howe, Beazer, & Carr, 2020; Sherry, 2013). For example, Liamputtong (2007) offers a detailed discussion of the potential harm of conducting sensitive research and provides a set of strategies aimed at protecting vulnerable researchers. To date, however, we suggest that there has been limited attention paid to the vulnerability that might be experienced by qualitative scholars engaged in new and emerging, often technologically dependent, methodologies. Here, we focus specifically on the vulnerabilities that might be experienced when conducting research online. We suggest that the online context has the potential to elicit vulnerabilities for two main reasons:

- The first reason pertains to the complexity of conducting online research with regard to legal, ethical, and privacy considerations.

DOI: 10.4324/9781003349266-5

Traversing this ethical and legal landscape is challenging, and mistakes can prove costly to researchers. For example, a researcher may unwittingly violate the privacy policies of a platform when obtaining the data for their analysis or may violate either the terms and conditions of a service or tort law[1] around scraping of content.

• The second reason relates to the fact that the online context presents new opportunities to research sensitive topics that might not have been possible using traditional qualitative methods.

For example, while qualitative studies on terrorism have been limited to a handful of interview studies in which scholars would have gone through a lengthy screening and ethical application process, it is now possible to acquire and analyse the social media posts of extremist groups with relative ease (see Scrivens, Davies, & Frank, 2020; Kleinberg, van der Vegt, & Gill, 2021).

In this chapter, we provide a framework for qualitative researchers wishing to utilize digital data in their research. First, we contextualize the importance and value of conducting qualitative research online, before identifying the many opportunities and benefits of adopting qualitative methods in this context. Next, we discuss why it is important to consider researcher vulnerabilities in the online context before introducing a step-by-step framework, considering each stage of the research process in turn – Design and Data Collection, Data Analysis, and Representing Findings. It is our intention that after reading this chapter, qualitative scholars will be encouraged to take advantage of the many opportunities afforded by digital data and that they will gain an understanding of how to protect themselves from vulnerabilities that may arise from working in this context.

## The online context – opportunities for qualitative researchers

Qualitative methods are often characterized by interviews, focus groups, and open-ended surveys. Through various iterations of these designs, qualitative researchers have provided a unique contribution to the academic literature, offering descriptions and interpretations of perceptions, cognitions, and social processes (Miles et al., 2014). However, with the accelerated adoption of networked technologies across society, there is an exciting opportunity for new avenues of qualitative research that move beyond existing methods (Andreotta et al., 2019). For instance, Meta platforms alone (e.g., WhatsApp, Facebook) are used by three and a half billion users each day for socializing and business and 76% of US adults reported using at least one social media site regularly (Auxier & Anderson, 2021; Richter, 2021). Such is the vast popularity of the Internet and social networking platforms, that they have now come to represent a medium in which individuals can express their views, connect with others, and engage in meaningful debate (Kietzmann et al., 2011; Das & Hodkinson, 2019). On the other hand, the online environment can also serve as a vector of harmful content, with individuals using it to propagate hate, commit crimes, and spread misinformation alongside a plethora of other harmful activities (Ferguson, 2017; Scrivens et al., 2020).

Given the increasing role of networked technologies across all sectors of society, it is not surprising that there has been a surge in research using digital data across a range of academic disciplines (Millington & Millington, 2015; Snelson, 2016). Social media platforms offer an unprecedented opportunity to access vast volumes of naturally occurring data, in a diversity of forms, at speeds not possible using conventional methods (Adjerid & Kelley, 2018). Currently, this research has been dominated by quantitative approaches, in which the focus has been on utilizing large datasets to examine causal links between variables of interest (Jowett, 2015). For example, Youyou, Kosinski, and Stillwell (2015) used data from 90,000 participants to build a predictive model of personality characteristics, based on Facebook "likes" while Popescu and Grefenstette (2010) predicted gender and location based on Flickr tags.

The advent of "big data" within social sciences has been celebrated for providing more statistical power, broader and more generalizable sample sizes, and for readily enabling analyses across time (Adjerid & Kelley, 2018). Coupled with the excitement surrounding the potential of "big data", there has been a rising concern about a lack of theory in some of this research, giving rise to a need for what has been termed "theoretically informed data science" (Yarkoni & Westfall, 2017; Hinds et al., 2022) and the development of hybrid "computational grounded theory" approaches that merge data-driven and qualitative methods (e.g., Nelson, 2020; Ophir, Walter, & Marchant, 2020). It is here where qualitative research might advance computational approaches, adding significant nuance to our understanding and interpretations of digital data, while also fuelling theory development in this context. Indeed, while quantitative studies remain suited to demonstrating causal and correlational relationships between variables, qualitative research is best placed to offer important insight into the context, purpose, and intent behind online posts (Ciesielska & Jemielniak, 2018). For example, sentiment analysis (a popular method of analysing large quantities of textual data) can quantitatively identify the sentiment of online posts by classifying it as positive, neutral, or negative (Kramer, Guillory, & Hancock, 2014). This is useful when measuring how events (e.g., an election) have been received across a population, notably; however, it cannot offer any understanding of how reactions might vary dependent on individual experiences and perspectives. We concur with the view that qualitative scholars are uniquely positioned to offer an alternative interpretation of big data and provide additional theorizing that may help alleviate some of the shortfalls of reductionist interpretations of big data (Strong, 2013). As argued by Mills, "we cannot understand human behavior and social action, without contextualizing the data and understanding the environment in which the data about social action occurs" (2018, p. 600). Thus, qualitative researchers can serve an essential role in furthering our understanding of big data and offer a fruitful opportunity to engage in meaningful mixed methods research (Ciechanowski, Jemielniak, & Gloor, 2020).

Aside from the opportunity to advance existing quantitative approaches to analysing big data, social media data also presents the opportunity for qualitative researchers to gain access to data that may previously have been impossible to acquire (Hesse et al., 2019). For instance, online forums and message boards present the opportunity to collect data on naturally occurring communication, without the presence of a researcher which can sometimes influence the type of interactions produced (Coulson, 2012; Jowett, 2015). This type of data collection is representative of what has been termed a "virtual focus group", in which participants are free to discuss topics without moderation and in a naturalistic setting (Holtz, Kronberger, & Wagner, 2012). Alternatively, online data can be captured to measure "real-time" responses to an unfolding event that would be not possible using conventional methods (Caliandro & Gandini, 2016). For example, in the immediate aftermath of emergency incidents, social media has become an arena in which individuals can share their opinions, gather information, and engage in joint sensemaking (Starbird et al., 2010; Neubaum et al., 2014). Data collected from this time period might offer insight into how people respond to uncertainty and advance theoretical understanding of how people behave during emergency events in a way that was previously only possible using a retrospective, temporality dependent analysis.

Further still, the online context provides qualitative scholars with access to data on stigmatized populations, as well as other sensitive topics that might not be accessible using traditional methods (Ray, Kimonis & Donoghue, 2010; Barratt & Maddox, 2016; Hesse et al., 2019). Despite attempts to widen participation and increase diversity in qualitative methods, there remain issues of access – for example, stigmatized, marginalized, or isolated communities may not be willing to take part in academic research (Palys & Atchison, 2012; Welles, 2014). When handled sensitively and ethically, social media data offers a window into perspectives that would otherwise remain unheard (Andreotta et al., 2019). For example, Ferguson (2017) utilized an ethnographic approach to gain a better understanding of why individuals might engage in buying or selling illicit drugs on the dark web, and Mirea, Wang, and Jung (2019) studied the motivations for accessing dark web marketplaces. Other scholars have used data from social media sites to study the content of posts on thinspiration (typically seen as pro-anorexia; Talbot, Gavin, van Steen, & Morey, 2017), and there have been numerous studies of extremists' use of online services, looking qualitatively at both Islamist (e.g., Krona, 2020), extreme right-wing groups (e.g., Brown, 2022; Lee and Knott, 2022) as well as the spread of conspiracy theories (e.g., Zeng & Schäfer, 2021).

## A framework for qualitative analysis of online research – protecting against research vulnerabilities

In light of the aforementioned opportunities and benefits of online research, we contend that the time is ripe for further use of qualitative methods in the study of digital data. We note, however, that inherent in this development is the potential for qualitative scholars to experience vulnerabilities when engaging in this type of research. Specifically, we anticipate that vulnerabilities are likely to be experienced in two over-arching ways: (i) ethical, legal, and privacy challenges, and (ii) through the increased likelihood of engaging with sensitive research topics.

In the following section, we first provide an overview of these two vulnerabilities, before introducing our step-by-step framework that aims to protect qualitative scholars from vulnerabilities when engaging in online research.

Online research presents a number of ethical, legal, and privacy challenges which pose a risk to qualitative researchers if not addressed appropriately. Acquiring, analysing, and publishing digital data present an ethical quagmire – scholars must continually grapple with questions around privacy, consent, data access, and the challenges surrounding publishing online posts (Tiidenberg, 2017). Established ethical guidelines designed for offline research may not offer the same certainty and utility when applied to the online context and this is further exacerbated by a lack of standardization and agreement across disciplines (Markham & Buchanan, 2012; Whiteman, 2012; Sugiura, Wiles & Pope, 2017). For instance, while acquiring informed consent is a vital and essential stage in traditional research designs to protect participant privacy and meet ethical standards (e.g., interviews, focus groups), it may not be necessary or feasible if data collection involves Tweets from thousands of users (British Psychological Society, 2017). These difficulties are further compounded by the evolving nature of technologies, with some scholars going as far as to refer to ethical guidance for online research as a "moving target" (Ackland, 2013). For qualitative scholars, especially those new to online research, navigating this ethical landscape is likely to be difficult and may increase the risk of experiencing vulnerabilities. While qualitative researchers might not face the ethical challenges that arise from computational approaches such as the manipulation of people's social media newsfeeds to study emotional contagion (Kramer, Guillory, & Hancock, 2014) or the automated identification of sexuality from faces (Wang & Kosinski, 2018), the risks posed to researchers by in-depth engagement with content and communities must be considered. When the ethical challenges of online research have been considered from a vulnerability perspective, they have tended to focus on protecting participants from vulnerabilities in the online context (see Tiidenberg, 2017 for an excellent guide here), as opposed to the researcher themselves (Conway, 2021).

Online research can also increase the likelihood of a researcher experiencing vulnerabilities through the potential it provides in studying sensitive topics. Traditionally, research on sensitive topics would require a lengthy period of planning – gaining access and trust to communities of interest, acquiring ethical approval, and arranging an appropriate time to conduct the research (see Gaudette, Scrivens, & Venkatesh, 2020). Indeed, while interview studies exploring topics such as terrorism, illegal drug use, and sexual exploitation exist, the time taken to acquire access and data can often preclude many scholars from researching such topics. In the online space, it is now possible to explore such topics with relative ease (Hanna, 2019; Sipes, Mullan, & Roberts, 2020). We argue that this ease presents a double-edged sword, as the speed with which data can be accessed may reduce the ability of scholars to prepare and limit the chances of experiencing distress of

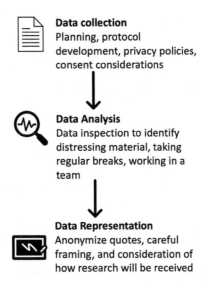

**Data collection**
Planning, protocol
development, privacy policies,
consent considerations

**Data Analysis**
Data inspection to identify
distressing material, taking
regular breaks, working in a
team

**Data Representation**
Anonymize quotes, careful
framing, and consideration of
how research will be received

**FIGURE 3.1**    Overview of the framework to protect against research vulnerabilities in online
research.

discomfort. Ferguson (2017) for example, suggests that this period of preparation is often underestimated by scholars embarking on sensitive research online and that an absence of preparation can increase the likelihood of experiencing distress of discomfort. While guidance exists for qualitative scholars engaging in sensitive research in an offline context (see Liamputtong, 2007), there is an absence of guidance for research online. Developing more detailed guidance for researching sensitive topics online will provide researchers with a safer and less vulnerable context in which to operate (Ferguson, 2017; Conway, 2021).

In the remainder of this chapter, we present a framework that addresses the risk of qualitative researchers experiencing vulnerabilities when conducting research online (see Figure 3.1 for an overview). Within this framework we focus on three key phases in the research process: (i) data collection; (ii) data analysis; and (iii) data representation. While we focus on sensitive research topics in particular to frame our discussion, it is our intention that many of these guidelines will be of use to scholars engaging in qualitative research online more broadly.

## Design and data collection

### How can I best prepare before beginning my data collection?

Online data collection, especially if it involves sensitive topics, ought to involve a great deal of preparation in order to limit the potential for a researcher to experience vulnerabilities (Fenge et al., 2019). While we offer further detail below on key ethical questions that must be asked when conducting online research, we also suggest that researchers first consult existing guidance and resources. For example, detailed guidance is provided by the Association of Internet Research (AoIR; Franzke, Bechmann, Zimmer, & Ess, 2020) and the British Psychological Society (BPS Guide for Internet Mediated Research, 2017) on the ethical considerations associated with online research. For sensitive research, it can also be useful to look for other relevant, context-specific resources that might offer some insight on the potential difficulties and vulnerabilities that may arise from the research. For example, in the study of terrorism and extremism, VOX-Pol provides a number of resources on how to protect your privacy and security when conducting research online (https://www.voxpol.eu/researcher-welfare-1-privacy/) and the Global Network on Extremism and Technology offer detailed ethical guidance on studying extremism on online platforms (https://gnet-research.org/wp-content/uploads/2021/01/GNET-Report-Researching-Extremist-Content-Social-Media-Ethics.pdf). From a methodological perspective, qualitative scholars new to online data collection might also consider accessing a range of tutorials or guides explaining how best to access digital data (see Caliandro & Gandini, 2016; Ciechanowski, Jemielniak, & Gloor, 2020).

In addition to consulting relevant existing guidance, it is important to set aside time to identify a relevant online platform with which to collect data from (Barratt & Maddox 2016; Ferguson, 2017). Most individuals use a variety of different online platforms, which will differ in their structural features and affordances (Brown, Smith, Davidson, & Ellis, 2022). As such, identifying an online platform that is relevant to the research question being asked is important, as we can expect behaviours to differ dependent on which platform an individual is using (Davidson & Joinson, 2021; Brown, et al., 2022). Once a relevant platform has been identified, it is important to consider how (or indeed whether or not) this data should be accessed (Barratt & Maddox, 2016). For example, if the research is concerned with an online extremist community, and this community exists on a dark-web forum, consideration must be given as to whether it is appropriate or safe for the researcher to access it. For legal protection, searches of dark-web forums should only be conducted using a virtual private network (VPN; either from your University or place of work) on a work-owned electronic device, and, if possible, on a specific device whose sole purpose is for collecting online data. Doing so will ensure that your personal data is protected (i.e., the IP address of a personal device), when downloading and accessing online materials. Relatedly, accessing this type of forum might require you to declare your research to relevant bodies within your institution, especially if the forum is likely to contain illegal or illicit activities. For example, in the UK, all education institutions must adhere to PREVENT guidance which is aimed at preventing radicalization and terrorism across society (Counter-Terrorism and Security Act, 2015). If accessing an extremist forum on the University or research organization's network, it is therefore important to notify the relevant staff members before doing so. This will ensure that you are protected from potential vulnerabilities that may be experienced if examining the data has potential legal implications. Likewise, if it is possible that accessing a specific online platform might involve viewing content which is indicative of a threat to life (either to the user or members of the public), it is essential that protocols are developed in advance that detail how this will be dealt with. Notifying relevant individuals within your institution/organization can add a further layer of protection in case the research that you are doing leads to unwelcome harassment or contact from the community that you are studying (Reyman & Sparby, 2019). This type of early consideration, particularly in sensitive and challenging online communities, can protect against vulnerabilities and ensure you are well-prepared prior to data collection (Conway, 2021; Gelms, 2021).

## What constitutes public and private data?

When conducting research online, it is important to consider the type of data that is being collected. Discerning whether online data can be identified as "public" or "private" is challenging (Kraut et al., 2004; Rooke, 2013; Jowett, 2015). Increasingly scholars acknowledge that it is no longer sufficient to classify all online data as public and separate it from the individual who posted it (Zimmer, 2010; Tiidenberg, 2017). Indeed, just because the data is accessible, it does not indicate that researchers can use it as they please (Boyd & Crawford, 2011). The aggregation of vast quantitative datasets has provided some scholars a platform with which they argue for privacy and anonymization. For qualitative research, in which there is likely to be a detailed examination of a smaller number of posts and/or users, this may prove more challenging. An important first step here is to examine the privacy policies of any given online platform. Different platforms will have distinctly different policies as to what data can be accessed and by whom, as well as users' expectations of privacy. For example, despite its recent launch of a researcher's API[2] (https://research.facebook.com/blog/2021/03/new-analytics-api-for-researchers-studying-facebook-page-data/), acquiring Facebook data (in particular Groups) remains challenging, both in terms of access permissions and in the limitations to the type of data that can be retrieved. Privacy policies are also subject to change, and it is important that researchers remain up to date with this. Take Twitter as an example – until recently, Twitter's privacy policy clearly stated that the majority of information hosted on its platform constituted "public data", including Tweet content, profile information, retweets, and the time a Tweet was sent. As such, this data was freely accessible via an API to academics who wished to use it for research purposes. However, in February 2023, Twitter implemented a new tiered payment system to their API, meaning that only those paying for access would be allowed to access and scrape Twitter data for research projects (see Barnes, 2023).

Second, and unrelated to formal policies, is to ask the question yourself as a researcher, what the implications might be of accessing data that, while not violating privacy policies, might be deemed to stray beyond "public" and into "private". The AoIR (Markham & Buchanan, 2012) guidance offers an important perspective here, outlining how the delineation between public and private domains in an online context may be harder to separate than those in an offline context. As such, questions of privacy ought to recognize that "privacy is a concept that must include a consideration of expectations and consensus" of those actively posting within the context of the study (Markham & Buchanan, 2012). In practice, this line of thought recognizes that those posting in online forums are often posting with the intention that the information only be shared within the community of active users that exist within that forum (Boyd, 2014). Accordingly, the decision as to whether data should be accessed will be highly related to the methods used and the type of data collected. For example, if the data is scraped from a large online platform (e.g., Twitter, YouTube), in which no password or sign-up is required to access it, then it is reasonable to assume that this data constitutes as "public" (see Ferguson, 2017). Although, if the data is collected utilizing ethnographic methods and involves direct interaction with users, not disclosing the means and purpose of the communication (i.e., for research) could be viewed as a violation of the users' privacy. These types of considerations also have relevance for questions of consent, which are discussed in the following section.

### Do I need to gain informed consent for the type of research I wish to conduct?

When it comes to questions of consent, researchers must not only comply with legal and ethical frameworks, but they must also consider a number of questions relating to their own interests, the interests of participants, the aims of the research, and the potential impact of their research on society (Wiles et al., 2007). Some sets of ethical guidance suggest that if consent is not obtained, then it is only permitted to report depersonalized data – for instance, removing names, identifying information, and demographic information (ESOMAR, 2016). A useful way to frame this in practice is to ask whether the research is "actor-centred" or "issue-centred" (Caliandro & Gandini, 2016). For example, if the research question was centred on examining public perceptions of a large-scale climate protest, then a qualitative examination of social media posts may not require informed consent from each author of the posts. In this research design, the focus would be on analysing and understanding a broad number of perspectives, without attaching the data to a small number of individuals (of course the presentation of the data would still require careful consideration, which we will come to later on in the chapter). Furthermore, the potentially large sample size that would come with this research would make it challenging, if not, entirely unfeasible to contact each participant in turn to request their consent (Norval & Henderson, 2020). Alternatively, if the research question aimed to understand perceptions of a handful of individuals, then informed consent would be important, as the analysis of the data would be closely related to the author behind the online post.

One exception here would be in instances where the research is centred on a sensitive topic aimed at contributing towards "public good". Individual users contributing towards illegal or illicit activities online would be unlikely to provide consent for their data to be examined. However requiring consent in this instance would prevent important research examining pertinent topics of societal signifi-cance (Jowett, 2015). In such instances, we would direct qualitative scholars to the British Psychological Society Ethical Guidelines for Internet Mediated Research which states that "undisclosed usage is justified on scientific value grounds" (BPS, 2017, p. 7).

## Data analysis

### *Examining the data – how can I reduce the likelihood of experiencing distress and discomfort?*

To reduce the likelihood of experiencing vulnerabilities during the analysis process, we recommended that researchers first take a detailed examination of the type of data that has been collected. When collecting data offline, the researcher has a level of control of the amount, type, and format of the data that is being collected. Depending on the method used, it is possible that when collecting data online, the researcher will not be entirely sure of everything that has been collected until after the event. Take an online web scraping tool as an example – scraping refers to the "automatic extraction of structured information such as entities, relation-ships between entities, and attributes describing entities from unstructured sources" (Sarawagi, 2008, p. 261). Breaking down this definition further, we can view an online platform like YouTube as an "unstructured source", containing a wide vari-ety of "structured information" (e.g., comments, meta-data like time, date, replies, comments, reactions). Since the source is unstructured, it is highly feasible during the scraping process, additional data might be collected that was not the intended target. For example, IP addresses might be obtained through the scraping process, which can then provide the location of a user (Sipes et al., 2020). It is therefore crucial that the data is examined to ensure that identifiable or personal informa-tion is removed or anonymized. If this is not possible in its entirety (especially so if informed consent was not obtained), then it is important to consider how this data can be safely and securely stored and how to ensure that the identity of the user is not compromised (Perez Vallejos et al., 2019).

Dependent on the format of digital data being analysed, it is also possible that alongside textual content, the dataset will include visual material (e.g., message board forums such as Reddit usually include images and memes, see Medvedev, Lambiotte, & Delvenne, 2017). Even if images are not the focus of the analysis, analysis of the text may be conducted in the context of the associated images. For sensitive research, this is especially important to consider as it is possible that harmful and distressing content may be viewed inadvertently. For example, memes (i.e., images or videos, usually accompanied by text) are an important element of far-right online subcultures and are used as a means to share ideology and propa-gate extremist beliefs (Hakoköngäs, Halmesvaara, & Sakki, 2020). Unfortunately, many of the memes used by the far-right are highly offensive, promote violence, and contain racist and upsetting imagery (Crawford, Keen, & Suarez-Tangil, 2021).

In these instances, in particular, it is necessary to consider the safety of your work environment in relation to yourself but also those around you. It is possible that colleagues may be inadvertently exposed to the content that you are viewing and experience vulnerabilities of their own.

Next, it is important that the researcher familiarize themselves with the data in detail. This is a conventional step of many methods of qualitative analysis (see Hsieh & Shannon, 2005; Braun & Clarke, 2006); however, it is especially important in online research because it may be the first time the researcher is reviewing the data in detail. During an interview or a focus group, it is possible to take notes and gain an understanding of the type of data to be analysed at the point of collection. This process of "active listening" can be exhausting for the researcher when conducting sensitive research offline, in contrast, for online research, it is the process of "active reading" that may lead to emotional exhaustion (Hanna, 2019). This early stage of active reading provides a vital point to make note of what portions or features of the data might be distressing and to help protect against vulnerabilities that might be experienced in the latter phases of analysis.

## How to gain perspective and remain focused on the analysis?

Analysing qualitative data requires a great deal of time and cognitive effort, and it can be easy to underestimate this and begin the analysis underprepared (Liamputtong, 2007). The difficulty in remaining focused can be exacerbated by sensitive topics and further still, this can increase the likelihood of experiencing distress or vulnerabilities from the analysis process. Evidence suggests that cumulative experience of examining sensitive data over time can lead to fatigue, a sense of isolation, and a feeling of being unprepared (Johnson & Clarke, 2003). Researchers may find it difficult to discuss their experiences, especially if they experience distress of discomfort (Dunbar et al., 2002). This distress has been referred to as "labour pains" and relates to the challenges of closely examining sensitive and potentially upsetting subject matters (Melrose, 2002). As noted by Conway (2021), it is the researcher's responsibility to continually remain mindful of their own positioning, identity, and experience to ensure that they are safe to continue with their online research. Taking regular breaks is important to ensure that focus is maintained throughout the analysis. We suggest researchers consider moving away from their workspace during their breaks (e.g., going for a short walk, moving to a different room) to provide some distance between themselves and the data. This is especially important when analysing sensitive data as it can provide the space to identify any areas of distress or discomfort and to gain some perspective on the aims of the research. Furthermore, we suggest that those engaging in sensitive online research do so in teams, to provide a space and support to discuss any ill effects of the analytic process and identify areas of distress or discomfort. It is especially important here to consider including additional colleagues on ethics applications to ensure that it is ethically appropriate to share and discuss the content of the data in its raw form.

## Representing findings

### *Can I use quotations to represent findings?*

The use of direct quotations when reporting qualitative research with online data is highly contested (Beninger, 2017; Webb et al., 2017; Thelwall & Thelwall, 2020). Unlike data using conventional methods, it is possible to reverse search quotations presented from online research and identify the author behind the post (Narayanan, Huey, & Felten, 2016). Furthermore, in conventional qualitative designs, informed consent is typically obtained, and during the process, the researcher can advise the participant of the use of data in academic reports. In online research, this might not always be the case, and the use of quotations must not only be appropriate when considering the individual behind the online content but also the policies of the online platform. Twitter, for example, explicitly states within its privacy policy that Tweets and usernames obtained from their API can be published (https://developer. twitter.com/en/docs/twitter-api). However, whether or not this is sufficient to permit publishing raw, non-paraphrased data is subject to much discussion, both in terms of whether it is appropriate to disclose the platform with which the data has come from and in terms of how quotes ought to be presented. For instance, the BPS Guide for Internet Mediated Research advises caution in disclosing the source of the data (for concerns of it being traced back to individuals), whereas Beninger (2017) argues that explicitly stating the source of the data can improve the reliability of online research. Similarly, the BPS (2017) suggests that paraphrasing quotes can be appropriate in order to protect the identity of users, whereas Webb et al. (2017) suggest that doing so can lead to concerns surrounding the integrity of the research.

For qualitative research especially this is of great importance and the decision of how best to proceed ought to link closely to the aims of the research. It is hoped that if the study is an examination of a handful of users, then (as outlined earlier) consent would be obtained and that this would include permission to use direct quotations in written reports. However, in instances where the research is examining wider perceptions and sentiment, we suggest a middle ground is likely to be most appropriate, where paraphrasing of quotes can be used to demonstrate the analytic process and give readers an understanding of the data, but the identity and anonymity of users are protected (see also Thelwall & Thelwall, 2020 for a detailed discussion). We would therefore urge qualitative scholars to exercise caution when presenting data from online research to avoid misrepresenting their findings, in addition to unwittingly identifying individuals from their online posts. This is especially important in instances in which informed consent has not been obtained and will ensure the privacy of participants is protected (Sipes et al., 2020).

### *What do I need to consider when framing my findings?*

Aside from considering how quotations might be represented in the publishing of research, the data ought to be analysed and presented in such a way that it does not harm the users to which the data belongs (especially if the users belong to a vulnerable population) (Caliandro & Gandini, 2016). In the offline context, qualitative researchers have the opportunity to develop empathy and rapport with their participants, which may offer crucial insight and understanding in the latter phases of analysis and the write-up of findings. This is not the case with online research and there is a risk that this can lead to psychological distance between researcher and participant(s), and potential for a misunderstanding or misinterpretation. For example, scholars must be wary that their findings might propagate existing stereotypes of vulnerable or stigmatized populations, and that this may, in turn, present vulnerabilities to the research themselves if they are misquoted or misrepresented in future academic discourse. Furthermore, in the offline context (e.g., interviews or focus groups), we can rely on cues and behaviours to inform our understanding of an interaction. This is not possible online and it is important to consider how the purpose and reasoning behind a post might be misinterpreted (or influenced by our own worldviews and experiences). Indeed, research shows that without face-to-face interaction, we can engage in "over-attribution" – meaning that we can sometimes inflate our perception of the person(s) posts that we are, and this can lead to increased stereotyping (Reicher, Spears, & Postmes, 1995). Other research has shown that individuals can engage in more extreme and offensive language online due to the effects of deindividuation (Lea & Spears, 1991; Williams et al., 2002). Considering these influences when presenting and discussing the findings of qualitative online research is important, and may influence the conclusions made from the data collected.

In addition to considering how findings might be presented with respect to the users themselves, there are also important questions surrounding how the data might be used, who might have access to it, and what might be the unintended consequences of publishing it (Reyman & Sparby, 2019). For instance, in the case of a forum centred on a topic closely tied to an illegal activity (e.g., illegal drug distribution, terrorism, child sexual assault), representations of the data must be considered in light of the potential risk that the findings might be used to advance illegal activities. Both UK Research & Innovation (UKRI, 2016) and The European Commission for Research and Innovation (2020) provide guidance for researchers to help identify any potential for research findings to be misused. Other relevant existing guidelines may also be relevant here in determining how to present findings – for example, Sage Research Methods guide (Salmons, 2016) offers suggestions for researchers conducting qualitative research online and the *Journal of Occupational and Organizational Psychology* provides guidance for evaluating qualitative research papers which may also provide a helpful checklist. Given the discussion and recommendations that we have provided here, the inclusion of statements concerning issues of researcher vulnerability is also warranted.

## Conclusion

Digital data has much to offer qualitative scholars, particularly in the study of sensitive topics that have typically proven difficult to access when utilizing conventional methodologies. We end in highlighting the importance of remaining recognizant of the potential vulnerabilities that might be experienced when working in this context – namely the complex legal and ethical landscape, in addition to the relative ease with which researchers can access sensitive and potentially distressing data. Here, we have provided a step-by-step framework for qualitative scholars wishing to embark on online research, offering guidance as to how to best protect against vulnerabilities when using digital data. It is our aim that after reading this chapter, researchers will be encouraged to take advantage of new and emerging data sources which continue to evolve and characterize many aspects of society.

## Notes

1 A tort occurs when a wrongdoing is committed, usually between two people. Tort law is a branch of private law that enables individuals to claim damages against the person who wronged them. See also https://plato.stanford.edu/entries/tort-theories/.
2 API is an acronym for Application Programming Interface. In simple terms, it can be understood as a software intermediary, allowing two applications to interact with one another. In the example of Twitter, the API allows researchers to read and write Twitter data.

## References

Ackland, R. (2013). *Web Social Science: Concepts, Data and Tools for Social Scientists in the Digital Age*. London, UK: Sage.

Adjerid, I., & Kelley, K. (2018). Big data in psychology: A framework for research advancement. *American Psychologist, 73*(7), 899. Retrieved from: https://doi.org/10.1037/amp0000190

Andreotta, M., Nugroho, R., Hurlstone, M. J., Boschetti, F., Farrell, S., Walker, I., & Paris, C. (2019). Analyzing social media data: A mixed-methods framework combining computational and qualitative text analysis. *Behavior Research Methods, 51*(4), 1766–1781. https://doi.org/10.3758/s13428-019-01202-8

Auxier, B., & Anderson, M. (2021). Social Media Use in 2021. *Pew Research Centre.* https://www.pewresearch.org/internet/2021/04/07/social-media-use-in-2021

Barratt, M. J., & Maddox, A. (2016). Active engagement with stigmatised communities through digital ethnography. *Qualitative Research, 16*(6), 701–719. https://doi.org/10.1177/1468794116648766

Barnes, J. (2023). Twitter Ends Its Free API: Here's Who Will Be Affected. *Forbes.* https://www.forbes.com/sites/jenaebarnes/2023/02/03/twitter-ends-its-free-api-heres-who-will-be-affected/?sh=4bf6d8fb6266

Bashir, N. (2020). The qualitative researcher: The flip side of the research encounter with vulnerable people. *Qualitative Research, 20*(5), 667–668. https://doi.org/10.1177/1468794119884

Behar, R. (1996). *The Vulnerable Observer: Anthropology That Breaks Your Heart*. Boston, MA: Beacon Press.

Beninger, K. (2017). Social media users' views on the ethics of social media research. In: Sloan, L., & Quan-Haase, A. (eds.), *The SAGE Handbook of Social Media Research Methods*. London: SAGE, pp. 57–73.

Boyd, D. (2014). *It's Complicated: The Social Lives of Networked Teens*. New Haven, CT: Yale University Press.

Boyd, D., & Crawford, K. (2011). Six provocations for big data. *A Decade in Internet Time: Symposium on the Dynamics of the Internet and Society (September, 2011)*. http://doi.org/10.2139/ssrn.1926431

BPS (2017). *Ethics Guidelines for Internet-mediated Research*. Leicester: British Psychological Society.

Braun, V., & Clarke, V. (2006). Using thematic analysis in psychology. *Qualitative Research in Psychology*, *3*(2), 77–101. https://doi.org/10.1191/1478088706qp063oa

Brown, O. (2022). Right wing extremism online. Can we use digital data to detect risk? https://crestresearch.ac.uk/comment/right-wing-extremism-online-can-we-use-digital-data-to-measure-risk/

Brown, O., Smith, L. G. E., Davidson, B., & Ellis, D. (2022). The problem with the internet: An affordance-based approach for psychological research on networked technologies. *Acta Psychologica*, *228*, 103650. https://doi.org/10.1016/j.actpsy.2022.103650

Caliandro, A., & Gandini, A. (2016). *Qualitative Research in Digital Environments: A Research Toolkit* (1st ed.). Routledge. https://doi.org/10.4324/9781315642161

Ciechanowski, L., Jemielniak, D., & Gloor, P. A. (2020). TUTORIAL: AI research without coding: The art of fighting without fighting: Data science for qualitative researchers. *Journal of Business Research*, *117*, 322–330. https://doi.org/10.1016/j.jbusres.2020.06.012

Ciesielska, M., & Jemielniak, D. (eds.). (2018). *Qualitative Methodologies in Organization Studies*. Cham, Switzerland: Palgrave Macmillan, p. 33.

Conway, M. (2021). Online extremism and terrorism research ethics: Researcher safety, informed consent, and the need for tailored guidelines. *Terrorism and Political Violence*, *33*(2), 367–380. https://doi.org/10.1080/09546553.2021.1880235

Coulson, N. S. (2012). Research using the internet: Methodological choices. In: Ramsey, N., & Hardcourt, D. (eds.), *The Handbook of the Psychology of Appearance*. Croydon: Oxford University Press, pp. 636–644.

Counter-Terrorism and Security Act (2015). https://www.legislation.gov.uk/ukpga/2015/6/contents

Crawford, B., Keen, F., & Suarez-Tangil, G. (2021). Memes, radicalisation, and the promotion of violence on Chan sites. In *The International AAAI Conference on Web and Social Media (ICWSM)*. https://doi.org/10.1609/icwsm.v15i1.18121

Das, R., & Hodkinson, P. (2019). Tapestries of intimacy: Networked intimacies and new fathers' emotional self-disclosure of mental health struggles. *Social Media+ Society*, *5*(2). https://doi.org/10.1177/2056305119846488

Davidson, B. I., & Joinson, A. N. (2021). Shape shifting across social media. *Social Media+ Society*, *7*(1). https://doi.org/10.1177/2056305121990632

Dunbar, C., Rodriguez, D., & Parker, L. (2002). Race, subjectivity, and the interview process. *Handbook of Interview Research: Context and Method*, 279–298. https://doi.org/10.4135/9781412973588.n18

ESOMAR (2016). ESOMAR guideline for online research. https://esomar.org/uploads/attachments/ckqtawvjq00uukdtrhst5sk9u-iccesomar-international-code-english.pdf

European Commission for Research and Innovation (2020). Guidance note – Potential misuse of research. https://ec.europa.eu/research/participants/data/ref/h2020/other/hi/guide_research-misuse_en.pdf

Fenge, L. A., Oakley, L., Taylor, B., & Beer, S. (2019). The impact of sensitive research on the researcher: Preparedness and positionality. *International Journal of Qualitative Methods*. https://doi.org/10.1177/1609406919893161

Ferguson, R.-H. (2017). Offline 'stranger' and online lurker: Methods for an ethnography of illicit transactions on the darknet. *Qualitative Research*, *17*(6), 683–698. https://doi.org/10.1177/1468794117718894

Franzke, A. S., Bechmann, A., Zimmer, M., & Ess, C. (2020). *The Association of Internet Researchers. Internet Research: Ethical Guidelines 3.0.* https://aoir.org/reports/ethics3.pdf

Gaudette, T., Scrivens, R., & Venkatesh, V. (2020). The role of the internet in facilitating violent extremism: Insights from former right-wing extremists. *Terrorism and Political Violence*, 1–18. https://doi.org/10.1080/09546553.2020.1784147

Gelms, B. (2021). Social media research and the methodological problem of harassment: Foregrounding researcher safety. *Computers and Composition, 59.* https://doi.org/10.1016/j.compcom.2021.102626

Hakoköngäs, E., Halmesvaara, O., & Sakki, I. (2020). Persuasion through bitter humor: Multimodal discourse analysis of rhetoric in internet memes of two far-right groups in Finland. *Social Media + Society.* https://doi.org/10.1177/2056305120921575

Hanna, E. (2019). The emotional labour of researching sensitive topics online: Considerations and implications. *Qualitative Research, 19*(5), 524–539. https://doi.org/10.1177%2F1468794118781735

Hendron, J. A., Irving, P., & Taylor, B. (2012). The unseen cost: A discussion of secondary traumatization experience of the clergy. *Pastoral Psychology, 61*(2), 221–231. https://doi.org/10.1007/s11089-011-0378-z

Hesse, A., Glenna, L., Hinrichs, C., Chiles, R., & Sachs, C. (2019). Qualitative research ethics in the big data era. *American Behavioral Scientist, 63*(5), 560–583. https://doi.org/10.1177/0002764218805806

Hinds, J., Brown, O., Smith, L. G. E., Piwek, L., Ellis, D. A., & Joinson, A. N. (2022). Integrating insights about human movement patterns from digital data into psychological science. *Current Directions in Psychological Science, 31*(1), 88–95. https://doi.org/10.1177/09637214211042324

Holtz, P., Kronberger, N., & Wagner, W. (2012). Analyzing internet forums: A practical guide. *Journal of Media Psychology: Theories, Methods, and Applications, 24*(2), 55. https://doi.org/10.1027/1864-1105/a000062

Howard, L. C., & Hammond, S. P. (2019). Researcher vulnerability: Implications for educational research and practice. *International Journal of Qualitative Studies in Education, 32*(4), 411–428. https://doi.org/10.1080/09518398.2019.1597205

Hsieh, H.-F., & Shannon, S. E. (2005). Three approaches to qualitative content analysis. *Qualitative Health Research, 15*(9), 1277–1288. https://doi.org/10.1177/1049732305276687

Johnson, B., & Clarke, J. M. (2003). Collecting sensitive data: The impact on researchers. *Qualitative Health Research, 13*(3), 421–434. https://doi.org/10.1177/1049732302250340

Jowett, A. (2015). A case for using online discussion forums in critical psychological research. *Qualitative Research in Psychology, 12*(3), 287–297. https://doi.org/10.1080/14780887.2015.1008906

Kietzmann, J. H., Hermkens, K., McCarthy, I. P., & Silvestre, B. S. (2011). Social media? Get serious! Understanding the functional building blocks of social media. *Business Horizons, 54*(3), 241–251. https://doi.org/10.1016/j.bushor.2011.01.005

Kleinberg, B., van der Vegt, I., & Gill, P. (2021). The temporal evolution of a far-right forum. *Journal of Computational Social Science, 4*(1), 1–23. https://doi.org/10.1007/s42001-020-00064-x

Kramer, A. D., Guillory, J. E., & Hancock, J. T. (2014). Experimental evidence of massive-scale emotional contagion through social networks. *Proceedings of the National Academy of Sciences, 111*(24), 8788–8790. https://doi.org/10.1073/pnas.1320040111

Kraut, R., Olson, J., Banaji, M., Bruckman, A., Cohen, J., & Couper, M. (2004). Psychological research online: Report of Board of Scientific Affairs' Advisory Group on the Conduct of Research on the Internet. *American Psychologist, 59*(2), 105. https://doi.org/10.1037/0003-066X.59.2.105

Krona, M. (2020). Collaborative media practices and interconnected digital strategies of Islamic State (IS) and Pro-IS supporter networks on Telegram. *International Journal of Communication, 14*, 1888–1910.

Lea, M., & Spears, R. (1991). Computer-mediated communication, de-individuation and group decision-making. *International Journal of Man-Machine Studies, 34*, 283–301. https://doi.org/10.1016/0020-7373(91)90045-9

Lee, B., & Knott, K. (2022). Fascist aspirants: Fascist Forge and ideological learning in the extreme-right online milieu. *Behavioral Sciences of Terrorism and Political Aggression, 14*(3), 216–240. https://doi.org/10.1080/19434472.2020.1850842

Lee, R. M. (1993). *Doing Research on Sensitive Topics*. London, UK: Sage.

Liamputtong, P. (2007). The sensitive and vulnerable researcher. In: *Researching the Vulnerable*. SAGE Publications, Ltd., pp. 71–94. https://doi.org/10.4135/978184920986

Markham, A., & Buchanan, E. (2012). Ethical decision-making and internet research. Retrieved from http://aoir.org/reports/ethics2.pdf

Medvedev, A. N., Lambiotte, R., & Delvenne, J. C. (2017). The anatomy of Reddit: An overview of academic research. *Dynamics on and of Complex Networks*, 183–204. https://doi.org/10.1007/978-3-030-14683-2_9

Melrose, M. (2002). Labour pains: Some considerations on the difficulties of researching juvenile prostitution. *International Journal of Social Research Methodology, 5*(4), 333–351. https://doi.org/10.1080/13645570110045963

Miles, M., Huberman, M., & Saldana, J. (2014). *Qualitative Data Analysis: A Methods Sourcebook* (3rd ed.). Thousand Oaks, CA: Sage.

Millington, B., & Millington, R. (2015). 'The datafication of everything': Toward a sociology of sport and big data. *Sociology of Sport Journal, 32*(2), 140–160. https://doi.org/10.1123/ssj.2014-0069

Mills, K. A. (2018). What are the threats and potentials of big data for qualitative research? *Qualitative Research, 18*(6), 591–603. https://doi.org/10.1177/1468794117743465

Mirea, M., Wang, V., & Jung, J. (2019). The not so dark side of the darknet: A qualitative study. *Security Journal, 32*(2), 102–118. https://doi.org/10.1057/s41284-018-0150-5

Narayanan, A., Huey, J., Felten, E. W. (2016). A precautionary approach to big data privacy. In: Gutwirth, S., Leenes, R., De Hert, P. (eds.), *Data Protection on the Move. Law, Governance and Technology Series*, vol. 24. Dordrecht: Springer. https://doi.org/10.1007/978-94-017-7376-8_13

Nelson, L. K. (2020). Computational grounded theory: A methodological framework. *Sociological Methods & Research, 49*(1), 3–42. https://doi.org/10.1177/0049124117729703

Neubaum, G., Rösner, L., Rosenthal-von der Pütten, A. M., & Krämer, N. C. (2014). Psychosocial functions of social media usage in a disaster situation: A multi-methodological approach. *Computers in Human Behavior, 34*, 28–38. https://doi.org/10.1016/j.chb.2014.01.021

Norval, C., & Henderson, T. (2020). Automating dynamic consent decisions for the processing of social media data in health research. *Journal of Empirical Research on Human Research Ethics, 15*(3), 187–201. https://doi.org/01.15157672/16545612694868139781835

Ophir, Y., Walter, D., & Marchant, E. R. (2020). A collaborative way of knowing: Bridging computational communication research and grounded theory ethnography. *Journal of Communication, 70*(3), 447–472. https://doi.org/10.1093/joc/jqaa013

Palys, T., & Atchison, C. (2012). Qualitative research in the digital era: Obstacles and opportunities. *International Journal of Qualitative Methods, 11*(4), 352–367. https://doi.org/10.1177/160940691201100404

Perez Vallejos, E., Koene, A., Carter, C. J., Hunt, D., Woodard, C., Urquhart, L., Bergin, A., & Statache, R. (2019). Accessing online data for youth mental health research: Meeting the ethical challenges. *Philosophy & Technology, 32*(1), 87–110. https://doi.org/10.1007/s13347-017-0286-y

Popescu, A., & Grefenstette, G. (2010). Mining user home location and gender from flickr tags. *Proceedings of the International AAAI Conference on Web and Social Media, 4*(1), 307–310. Retrieved from https://ojs.aaai.org/index.php/ICWSM/article/view/14046

Ray, J. V., Kimonis, E. R., & Donoghue, C. (2010). Legal, ethical, and methodological considerations in the internet-based study of child pornography offenders. *Behavioral Sciences & the Law, 28*(1), 84–105. https://doi.org/10.1002/bsl.906

Reicher, S. D., Spears, R., & Postmes, T. (1995). A social identity model of deindividuation phenomena. *European Review of Social Psychology, 6*, 161–198. https://doi.org/10.1080/14792779443000049

Reyman, J., & Sparby, E. M. (eds.). (2019). *Digital Ethics: Rhetoric and Responsibility in Online Aggression* (1st ed.). Routledge. https://doi.org/10.4324/9780429266140

Richter, F. (2021). Meta reaches 3.6 billion people each month. *Statista.* https://www.statista.com/chart/2183/facebooks-mobile-users/

Rooke, B. (2013). Four pillars of internet research ethics with Web 2.0. *Journal of Academic Ethics, 11*(4), 265–268. https://doi.org/10.1007/s10805-013-9191-x

Salmons, J. (2016). *Doing Qualitative Research Online.* SAGE Publications Ltd. https://doi.org/10.4135/9781473921955

Sarawagi, S. (2008). Information extraction. *Foundations and Trends in Databases, 1*(3), 261–377. http://doi.org/10.1561/1900000003

Scrivens, R., Davies, G., & Frank, R. (2020). Measuring the evolution of radical right-wing posting behaviors online. *Deviant Behavior, 41*(2), 216–232. https://doi.org/10.1080/01639625.2018.1556994

Shaw, R. M., Howe, J., Beazer, J., & Carr, T. (2020). Ethics and positionality in qualitative research with vulnerable and marginal groups. *Qualitative Research, 20*(3), 277–293. https://doi.org/10.1177/1468794119841839

Sherry, E. (2013). The vulnerable researcher: Facing the challenges of sensitive research. *Qualitative Research Journal, 13*(3), 278–288. https://doi.org/10.1108/QRJ-10-2012-0007

Sipes, J. B., Mullan, B., & Roberts, L. D. (2020). Ethical considerations when using online research methods to study sensitive topics. *Translational Issues in Psychological Science, 6*(3), 235–239. https://doi.org/10.1037/tps0000266

Snelson, C. L. (2016). Qualitative and mixed methods social media research: A review of the literature. *International Journal of Qualitative Methods, 15*(1). https://doi.org/10.1177/1609406915624574

Starbird, K., Palen, L., Hughes, A. L., & Vieweg, S. (2010, February). Chatter on the red: What hazards threat reveals about the social life of microblogged information. In *Proceedings of the 2010 ACM Conference on Computer Supported Cooperative Work*, New York, USA. (pp. 241–250). https://doi.org/10.1145/1718918.1718965

Strong, C. (2013). The challenge of big data: What does it mean for the qualitative research industry? *Qualitative Market Research: An International Journal, 14*(7), 336–343. https://doi.org/10.1108/QMR-10-2013-0076

Sugiura, L., Wiles, R., & Pope, C. (2017). Ethical challenges in online research: Public/private perceptions. *Research Ethics, 13*(3–4), 184–199. https://doi.org/10.1177/1747016116650720

Talbot, C. V., Gavin, J., Van Steen, T., & Morey, Y. (2017). A content analysis of thinspiration, fitspiration, and bonespiration imagery on social media. *Journal of Eating Disorders, 5*(1), 1–8. https://doi.org/10.1186/s40337-017-0170-2

Thelwall, M., & Thelwall, S. (2020). A thematic analysis of highly retweeted early COVID-19 tweets: Consensus, information, dissent and lockdown life. *Aslib Journal of Information Management, 72*(6), 945–962. https://doi.org/10.1108/AJIM-05-2020-0134

Tiidenberg, K. (2017). Ethics in digital research. In: Flick, U. (ed.), *The SAGE Handbook of Qualitative Data Collection*. London, UK: Sage, pp. 466–479.

UKRI (2016). Managing risks of research misuse: Joint policy statement https://www.ukri.org/publications/managing-risks-of-research-misuse-joint-policy-statement/

Wang, Y., & Kosinski, M. (2018). Deep neural networks are more accurate than humans at detecting sexual orientation from facial images. *Journal of Personality and Social Psychology*, *114*(2), 246. https://doi.org/10.1037/pspa0000098

Webb, H., Jirotka, M., Stahl, B. C., Housley, W., Edwards, A., Williams, M., ... & Burnap, P. (2017, June). The ethical challenges of publishing Twitter data for research dissemination. In *Proceedings of the 2017 ACM on Web Science Conference* (pp. 339–348). https://doi.org/10.1145/3091478.3091489

Welles, B. (2014). On minorities and outliers: The case for making big data small. *Big Data & Society*, *1*(1). https://doi.org/10.1177/2053951714540613

Whiteman, N. (2012). *Undoing Ethics: Rethinking Practice in Online Research*. New York: Springer.

Wiles, R., Crow, G., Charles, V., & Heath, S. (2007). Informed consent and the research process: Following rules or striking balances? *Sociological Research Online*, *12*(2), 99–110. https://doi.org/10.5153/sro.1208

Williams, K. D., Govan, C. L., Croker, V., Tynan, D., Cruickshank, M., & Lam, A. (2002). Investigations into differences between social-and cyberostracism. *Group Dynamics: Theory, Research, and Practice*, *6*, 65–77. https://doi.org/10.1037/1089-2699.6.1.65

Yarkoni, T., & Westfall, J. (2017). Choosing prediction over explanation in psychology: Lessons from machine learning. *Perspectives on Psychological Science*, *12*(6), 1100–1122. https://doi.org/10.1177/1745691617693393

Youyou, W., Kosinski, M., & Stillwell, D. (2015). Computer-based personality judgments are more accurate than those made by humans. *Proceedings of the National Academy of Sciences*, *112*(4), 1036–1040. https://doi.org/10.1073/pnas.1418680112

Zeng, J., & Schäfer, M. S. (2021). Conceptualizing "dark platforms". Covid-19-related conspiracy theories on 8kun and Gab. *Digital Journalism*, *9*(9), 1321–1343. https://doi.org/10.1080/21670811.2021.1938165

Zimmer, M. (2010). "But the data is already public": On the ethics of research in Facebook. *Ethics and Information Technologies*, *12*, 313–325. https://doi.org/10.1007/s10676-010-9227-5

# 4

# SUPPORTING EMOTIONALLY DEMANDING RESEARCH

## Developing Guidance for a University Research Centre

*Susie Smillie and Julie Riddell*

Throughout this chapter we will use the term 'emotionally demanding research' to describe research with participants, data or environments that has the potential to impact upon the wellbeing of the researcher. We use the term 'researcher' for brevity, but we encapsulate within this all those involved in the research process, staff members or students, including administrative and support staff as well as academic staff.

## Background

Secondary trauma, vicarious trauma, burnout, and compassion fatigue are all similar concepts that describe the impact that emotionally demanding work can have on an individual. Whilst there is substantial literature exploring the impact of emotionally demanding work, it has typically focused on those professions providing care, such as mental health workers, medical professionals, and support workers for marginalised or clinically vulnerable populations (Williamson et al., 2020).

Although research can often deal with emotionally demanding topics, the view of research as 'objective' or 'detached' from the subject can mean that the full impact of these topics on researchers is not fully acknowledged. The shift towards understanding the impact of emotionally demanding work on researchers, therefore, has been relatively slow (Dickson-Swift, James, Kippen, & Liamputtong, 2006; Nikischer, 2019) with researchers not seen as being 'at risk' in the same way as front line support staff (Williamson et al., 2020). Indeed historically, it has been seen as the mark of 'professional' research when one can remain objective and not become emotionally involved in the work (Williamson et al., 2020).

When the emotional impact of research is acknowledged within the literature the focus is most often on the emotional demand placed on participants that comes from discussing sensitive topics (Kumar & Cavallaro, 2018; Micanovic, Stelko, & Sakic, 2020) or on the positive effects that may result from taking part in research

DOI: 10.4324/9781003349266-6

(Gilbert, 2000). However, conducting research can expose researchers themselves to emotional demands in a variety of ways and increase the likelihood of negative effects on their physical and mental wellbeing (Bloor, Fincham, & Sampson, 2008).

While the focus of this book is on qualitative research, close and/or repeated interactions with participants or sensitive data can occur at many points during the research process irrespective of the discipline, subject matter, or methods of recruitment, data collection, or analysis. Collecting qualitative data directly from participants about their experiences of sensitive or emotive topics (e.g., in an interview about experiences of terminal illness) is perhaps the most obvious mechanism by which the researcher can be exposed to emotional demands, but it is not the only one. Other points in the research process that might provoke an emotional response include, but are not limited to, literature review, secondary analysis of data (including prevalence statistics), analysis of oral histories, photos, videos, case files, health records or other documents, survey data entry, transcription, paper writing, and reviewing (Arditti, 2015; Butler, Copnell, & Hall, 2019; Kumar & Cavallaro, 2018; Williamson et al., 2020).

Researchers are often drawn to, or become invested in, particular areas of research, employing empathy throughout the research process. The researcher's empathy can play a valuable role in building trust and rapport with participants, which can enable researchers to better conceptualise and analyse the data (Arditti, 2015; Davison, 2004). Emotional vulnerability is inherently linked to the process of being empathetic, but this emotional openness can be difficult to balance (Davison, 2004), and encouraging reflexivity and introspection in researchers needs to also take into consideration the potential negative effects that such individual responsibility might have (Borgstrom & Ellis, 2021). For participants, research can provide a space for those who want to share experiences, to talk to someone who actively wants to hear their experiences, which may feel empowering for the participant (Dickson-Swift et al., 2006; Williamson et al., 2020). However, this can result in challenges for the researcher in maintaining and communicating boundaries (Dickson-Swift et al., 2006; Fenge, Oakley, Taylor, & Beer, 2019). Whilst researchers can signpost participants to appropriate support, their role is not usually to provide a service which may actively help the participant. This can lead to feelings of guilt or discomfort when researchers feel that they are 'taking' the participants' experiences without providing anything in return (Nikischer, 2019). Blurring of boundaries between research and care-giving can occur during rapport building with participants, which plays an integral part of qualitative, and sometimes quantitative, participant recruitment and data collection (Dickson-Swift et al., 2006). These are particularly challenging to navigate when participants disclose experiences which resonate with those of the researcher themselves (Gill, 2021; Rowling, 1999). Furthermore, in circumstances where research is being carried out by those trained in a particular field (e.g., nurses, dieticians, counsellors, physiotherapists) or the intervention being evaluated is delivered by the researchers themselves, these boundaries can be even more challenging to maintain (O'Connor et al., 2022).

Exposure to emotionally demanding experiences, material, or processes can impact upon physical and mental health. Dickson-Swift et al. (2006) suggest that emotionally demanding research can have negative outcomes for the researcher, including but not limited to, sleep problems, headaches, exhaustion, stomach issues, depression, anxiety, feelings of being emotionally and physically drained, and threats to physical safety. These can not only have short-term direct effects on researchers' productivity and ability to engage with the material but can ultimately result in long-term burnout which may lead to researchers moving away from topic areas or research careers completely (Williamson et al., 2020). The impact of losing staff who are highly trained and have expertise within these fields can lead to significant costs to institutions in terms of both funding opportunities and institutional knowledge. Kumar and Cavallaro (2018) highlight the multiple ways in which research can be emotionally demanding and the potential long-term effects this can have on researchers and their work. The authors emphasise the need for embedding support at an institutional level in the systems and processes that already exist in research governance, as well as providing direct support through appropriate mentoring, supervision, and counselling.

In 2019, during a panel discussion on challenges in mental health research at an internal conference in the research unit where we were both based (Medical Research Council/Chief Scientist Office Social and Public Health Sciences Unit, University of Glasgow – MRC/CSO SPHSU), the subject of emotional impact on researchers was raised by a number of staff. In response to this, Susie was tasked with collating feedback from staff and postgraduate research students on their experiences of emotionally demanding research. This consultation with staff and students informed guidance that we then developed together, along with the input of a small group of colleagues, aimed at improving consistency in facilitating and supporting emotionally demanding research (EDR) being carried out within the research unit. During this process, we identified a gap that we felt able to attempt to fill by establishing a peer support network in Scotland, which we opened for membership in 2021 (Emotionally Demanding Research Network, Scotland).

The process and findings of this work form the basis of what is presented here, and in addition, we include reflections on both of our personal experiences with emotionally demanding research and on the input we have received from the wider research community as we have taken these conversations beyond our workplace. Personal experience with the impact of emotionally demanding research fuelled our initial interest in this area, but conversations with colleagues, both informally and in more formal settings, continue to drive our desire to contribute to change in the way researchers are supported with emotionally demanding research. We firmly believe that the integrity of the research we do is directly affected by the presence or absence of adequate support, so while institutions have a moral obligation to ensure the impact of emotionally demanding research on researchers is minimised, they also stand to benefit from the improved productivity of researchers and quality of research that can be produced when their staff and students are well supported.

## Our Personal Perspectives

We both have experience of emotionally demanding work both in and out of academia. For the last decade, that work has been in academic research environments but prior to that was in clinical, therapeutic, or educational settings. In some of these roles, we have been prepared for the work to be emotionally demanding, have seen appropriate structures in place to minimise the potential impact, have been supported throughout our work, and have felt able to draw on our personal knowledge of how to manage our own mental health in response to such challenges. However, we have also experienced an unexpected emotional demand, a lack of support and situations in which we have not felt personally prepared or equipped to cope with that. Since we began developing this guidance and peer network, we have been lucky to connect with many others who have experienced similar challenges and feel grateful to have been able to share with them and support each other.

## Researcher Consultation Process

In 2019, staff and students at the MRC/CSO SPHSU were invited to provide feedback on their experiences of emotionally demanding research in a group setting or individually. In response to this, some researchers shared relevant literature they had come across, some emailed their experiences and thoughts or met in person to share these. Those who were willing and available to take part in a larger group discussion met in May 2019.

A key piece of literature that was shared with us by a colleague was guidance that Emma Nagouse and Kay Guccione developed at the University of Sheffield in 2018–2019 (Guccione, 2019). The University of Sheffield guidance itself, and the accompanying explanation of the process through which Nagouse and Guccione had gone in developing this document and their local peer network (Guccione, 2018), informed our decision to structure our group discussion session into four main areas:

- **Our Experiences**: What types of experiences had been emotionally demanding for researchers.
- **Impact on us**: How researchers reported this kind of work had affected them.
- **Safeguarding and Coping**: Measures or strategies employed or experienced by researchers in the past, or currently, that were helpful.
- **What we need**: What researchers felt would be useful in addressing the need for support when dealing with emotionally demanding research.

This session involved 12 participants that included a mix of academic and support staff of varying levels of seniority, and postgraduate researchers (PGRs) at various stages of study. The session was audio recorded and we used flipcharts to record and reflect on contributions throughout the session. After the session we produced a summary of the main points, incorporating feedback from individual discussions we had with those who did not take part in the group session. This summary was then circulated to the researchers involved to check, comment on, and approve.

This summary document formed the basis for a guidance document written in conjunction with other members of the Research Support Group at the MRC/CSO SPHSU and drafts were circulated for comment to those researchers who had taken part in the feedback session and who were keen to contribute further.

## Key Elements of 'Guidance on Facilitating and Supporting Emotionally Demanding Research'

The guidance document that we produced reported on the feedback we had received in our consultation with staff and students, alongside recommendations for improving support from the planning stages onwards. This guidance was developed to encourage researchers, and research teams, to acknowledge their own vulnerability in doing research, whilst encouraging those involved to find strategies to manage emotional demands appropriately. In the guidance our aim was to highlight to those involved in planning, or conducting, research projects how their projects might become emotionally demanding for researchers, how those demands might then impact on the wellbeing of the researcher(s) involved, and how they might consider mitigating and managing such risks. Within these areas, we summarised, thematically, the feedback we had received from staff, and included hypothetical or anonymised examples for illustrative purposes based on the examples offered to us by researchers. In the following three sections that follow, we present these three areas in a similar way having elaborated on some elements based on the work we have done since then, establishing and managing a peer support network.

### Ways in Which Research Can Be Emotionally Demanding

In defining and categorising emotionally demanding research, Kumar and Cavallaro (2018) include Lee's (1993) definition of 'sensitive research' alongside three other types of emotionally demanding research:

> sensitive issues, personal trauma previously experienced, experience of traumatic life events during research, and unexpected events that arise during research in what was previously not identified as a sensitive issue.
>
> (2018)

They acknowledge that this categorisation is not exhaustive and is ever expanding. While we would agree with their conceptualisation, we propose an alternative categorisation which expands on this to include two areas that have been frequently raised by colleagues during the course of our work. Firstly, research conducted in environments, or with specific populations, that impacts on the emotional wellbeing of the research team member, regardless of the topic of the research. Secondly, the impact of the relationship with a research participant, and the sense of responsibility and duty towards participants that this can evoke in researchers. For the purposes of our guidance document and based on the feedback we received from researchers, we thematically categorise the ways in which research can be emotionally demanding as follows:

- Context:
  - The research topic itself being sensitive or distressing to the researcher, for example, researching experiences of bereavement;

  And/or

  - The level of exposure to the data, for example, repeated reading of transcripts of sensitive or distressing content;
  - The impact of the researcher's personal context, for example, if the researcher has had personal experience related to the topic area that causes them to be more susceptible to being emotionally affected by it than others;
- Setting of, usually, the fieldwork itself, including:
  - Concerns researchers have around personal safety or being in unsettling or upsetting environments, for example, in a prison environment;
  - Exposure to potential or actual harassment or discrimination, for example, experiencing verbal abuse as a fieldworker recruiting participants;
  - Witnessing emotionally distressing situations or events during fieldwork, perhaps unrelated to the research topic itself, for example, participants living in extreme poverty.
- Concern for participants:
  - The emotional response of researchers that comes from being concerned about the impact they, or the research process, have had on participants, especially when the research topic is particularly sensitive or distressing to the participants, for example, researchers being left ruminating on thoughts like 'did I cause harm' or 'did I do enough to safeguard'.

## Impact of Emotionally Demanding Research

Participants in the group discussion session were asked to reflect on how they felt that doing emotionally demanding research had impacted upon them. Researchers discussed specific examples of direct impact as well as general effects on wellbeing they experienced, in the short and longer term, that they attributed to periods of engaging in emotionally demanding research, often without adequate support. Grouped and anonymised examples of these were incorporated into the guidance document produced in order to offer both insight to those who have not had personal experience of the impact of emotionally demanding research, and reassurance and acknowledgement to those who have. A summary of the examples given by researchers is shown below but should not be considered an exhaustive list. We have categorised these effects to summarise for readers, but it is important to note that some of these may be experienced at any stage of emotionally demanding research and not necessarily in this order.

Short-term impact (during or soon after research task, 'in the moment')

- Challenging emotions as a result of empathising with participants' experiences, for example, sadness, anger, repulsion at what they have experienced;
- Negative emotions towards participants as a result of particular disclosures or opinions voiced by participants, for example, participants expressing bigoted views;
- Becoming distressed *during* research activities:
  - Impact on ability to continue with work in that moment;
  - Attempting to avoid being upset at work leading to 'taking it home';
  - If upset during participant contact:
    - Feeling unprofessional;
    - feeling worried about impact of this on participants;
    - feeling worried about impact of this on research data;
- Difficulties maintaining boundaries:
  - Balancing research commitments/workload/deadlines with duty towards participants' wellbeing;
  - Researchers who were responsible for delivering interventions, or researchers who are practitioners in, or have a background in, health and social care fields reported challenges with maintaining boundaries between their roles in collecting data, delivering interventions, or having a sense of professional duty or knowledge that went beyond the scope of their research role.

Medium-term impact (after research tasks, 'after the moment')

- Anxiety in relation to the research topic, for example, increased fear of experiencing the same as participants;
- 'Taking it home'/Feeling emotionally burdened;
- Feeling a strong sense of responsibility to participant(s):
  - Guilt around impact of research on participants;
  - Sense of inequitable exchange ('taking' data without offering sufficient compensation/support);
  - Concerns that not enough was done to safeguard or signpost participants, or that signposting may not be sufficient;
- Rumination, visualisation, and intrusive thoughts related to specific research data.

Longer-term impact (secondary, delayed, or 'knock on' effects)

- General mood changes outwith research environment and not directly related to thoughts about the research itself, for example, increased anxiety, lowered mood, and associated impact on behaviour, thoughts, physical feelings, and wellbeing;

- Vicarious trauma (McCann & Pearlman, 1990);
- Feelings and thoughts *as a result of feeling emotionally impacted* by the research, '*feeling bad about feeling bad*':
  - Guilt and feelings of letting others down:
    - Around impact on quality or volume of own work;
    - Around impact on supervisors or colleagues, for example, concern around 'offloading' or not 'pulling weight';
    - '*I should be able to cope with this*';

  - Isolation:
    - within the workplace, especially if the researcher is not working in a team or doing the same work as others;
    - outwith work where researchers are unable to talk to family/friends;

  - Feelings of inadequacy, self-criticism, low confidence in abilities;
  - Desensitisation towards a sensitive topic and the longer-term impact of this on researchers and how they approach their work, participants, and others in the team;

- Practical difficulties and behaviour changes:
  - Avoiding emotionally demanding tasks (including in those related to dissemination of the research and impact on career of this);
  - Taking longer to complete emotionally demanding tasks than the time allocated/expected;
  - Impact on other workload and productivity generally;
  - Concerns about implications of disclosing the emotional impact to managers/supervisors.

Challenges as a manager/supervisor of researchers engaged in emotionally demanding research
- Difficulties balancing demands of a project with ensuring team wellbeing;
- Vicarious trauma;
- Feeling unable to support appropriately or lacking signpost/referral options for staff;
- Concerns about impact on participants and research output.

## Mechanisms of Support

A list of considerations and strategies for mitigating and managing the risks of impact from conducting emotionally demanding research were incorporated into the guidance. These were based on the suggestions made by researchers during the discussion session but additionally drew on the broader literature and advice of researcher development staff. As we have developed the peer support network and continued to have conversations about what works, and does not, when it comes to supporting emotionally demanding research we have added to and amended this list, the expanded version of which we present below:

- Training: Improve awareness of emotionally demanding research and its potential impact by including information in training at the individual project level and broader departmental/institutional level. Researchers should be encouraged to participate in training that improves awareness of, and preparedness to plan or conduct, emotionally demanding research regardless of whether they are currently working in research of this nature.
- Study planning/design:
  - Risk Identification/Assessment: Potential emotional risks to researchers should be identified and assessed. If possible, this should be done in conjunction with the researchers who will be working on the study/project/task. This process should be given as much consideration as physical health and safety risks to researchers, and emotional risks to participants are given. Understanding where and when research can become emotionally demanding (see above) can help to identify risks. Whilst fieldwork and face-to-face participant contact may seem the most likely setting for research to be emotionally demanding, attention should also be given to other research and administrative tasks, and to varying research methodologies and study designs.
  - Appropriate mitigations should be included in study design in response to the identification of these risks, for example:

    - Timing and work allocation – Workload allocation and project timeframes should reflect consideration of the emotional risks to researchers that have been identified (see above). For example, allowing for slower pace of working, sharing of particular tasks amongst team members or adequate breaks to limit lengthy periods of exposure to emotionally demanding tasks.
    - Communicate role boundaries to participants – Participant information and scripting used with participants should emphasise the role of the researchers, especially where this is likely to be confusing, for example, where research is being conducted in healthcare settings alongside healthcare professionals, or where researchers are delivering interventions alongside data collection. Debriefing of participants, verbally or in materials given, can reiterate these roles and provide appropriate signposting to available support.
    - Physical boundary setting – Choices around physical settings of the research should reflect consideration of emotional wellbeing of researchers. Where possible researchers should be given information and guidance in preparation for entering emotionally challenging settings, as well as being appropriately supported during and after working in these settings. Home-working may require additional consideration of the impact

of sensitive or upsetting research materials being in researchers' homes, as well as how best to support researchers who are working remotely.
- Procedures for safeguarding participants – Researchers should be fully informed about escalation procedures for reporting safeguarding concerns and options for signposting participants in need of support. Ensuring researchers have confidence in such escalation procedures, understand their roles and responsibilities within them, and have options to signpost participants to can mitigate against feelings of 'not doing enough' to support or safeguard participants, or others.
- Plan and budget for specific support for researchers – see below.

- Providing Support to researchers:
  - Seek available resources in advance and signpost when appropriate. Having an awareness of available resources, training, workshops, and services within or through their institutions or research bodies will allow for quick responses to researchers in need of support. Having these available also sends an important message to researchers that their wellbeing is valued and fosters an openness that can encourage researchers to speak up about how they are feeling.
  - Debrief – Debriefing provides a space for researchers to express how they have been emotionally affected by particular tasks, in a timeframe that is as close to those tasks as possible (e.g., after an interview with a participant). Such conversations might include sharing or exploring possible coping strategies or might simply be focused on normalising and making sense of emotional reactions. The structure, length and frequency of these might alter throughout a project as different tasks are undertaken or different needs arise or dissipate.
  - Check-ins – If regular debriefing is not feasible, having a regular brief contact with researchers to both remind them of the need to protect their wellbeing during research and to allow an opportunity for them to raise any issues that cannot wait until the next supervision or line management meeting.
  - Peer support – While some researchers may rely on informal peer support from colleagues, providing space and time to do this in a more formal way can encourage researchers to take part and contributes to a culture that is supportive and understanding of the impact of emotionally demanding work. As with debriefing, peer support can create opportunities to share coping strategies but can help normalise emotional reactions to research and foster collegiality and solidarity among researchers involved in this kind of work.
  - Coping strategy identification – Allowing time for training, support, and self-reflection can encourage researchers to develop a sense of what works best for them in different contexts, identifying personal coping strategies. Having knowledge of these allows supervisors and line managers to have

better insight into both how to appropriately support individuals and how to plan similar studies in the future.

- Therapeutic support – providing access to formal counselling with trained professionals outwith the research team should be considered where appropriate. Models of clinical supervision from fields such as counselling and clinical psychology may also provide valuable insight for developing similar methods within research supervision.

- Ongoing study and line management/supervision:
  - Standing agenda items in line management or supervision meetings can allow regular review of emotional wellbeing and foster a sense of normalising discussions around impact of emotionally demanding work.
  - Discuss with researchers what support is helpful (or not) and what might need to change, encouraging reflection and adjustment of coping strategies and supports as an ongoing practice.
  - Consider the changing emotional demands as studies progress: analysis, writing, and dissemination may be emotionally demanding when taken in isolation, but even if this is not the case, if earlier stages of the study have been particularly emotionally demanding, then later stages may act as triggers.
  - Flagging data – Include content warnings on data to allow researchers working with this data in the future to be aware of, and assess, potential emotional risks. Field notes might also include details on settings for future waves of data collection or similar studies.

## Developing a Peer Support Network

Peer support was discussed at length during the feedback session we held with researchers and more informally between colleagues and during the writing of the guidance. Most researchers we spoke to had reached out to colleagues for support in informal ways, some had sought out a more formal mentor-based relationship, but it was almost universally agreed that having an organised peer support network would be particularly beneficial. In the beginning to develop ideas for how to prepare for, and set up, the network, we sought the advice of the Researcher Development team at University of Glasgow, and colleagues in other departments and institutions who had similar interests in this area. It was decided that we would set a geographical boundary (Scotland) in order to keep the administration of the network manageable and to increase the chances of in-person meetings when pandemic restrictions allowed, but that we would revisit this decision once the network was established.

We set up a small website[1] on a blogging site containing a brief explanation of emotionally demanding research and the aims of the network, and invited people interested in joining to provide contact details. We registered a Twitter account[2] for the network and in September 2021 began circulating the website link via social media, word of mouth, direct emails to colleagues, internal mailing lists, university news items, and through researcher development network contacts. As of November 2022, we have around 200 members based in, or researching in, Scotland. We have an additional 30 contacts from outwith Scotland who have requested to be kept updated with activities of the network, or who are interested in setting up similar networks where they are. Our members come from a range of sectors including academia, government, the National Health Service, voluntary and private sectors, as well as freelance researchers, and cover a wide range of research disciplines and methodologies.

We held our first meeting in November 2021 and asked attendees in advance to complete a series of questions around expectations and preferences for the network, including what researchers hoped to gain, how regularly they would prefer to meet, how they would like meetings to be structured, and what activities, beyond regular meetings, they felt would be beneficial. Themes from these responses were then presented at the first meeting and attendees were invited to discuss these further. When asked what members hoped to gain from being part of the network, the main areas were: sense of community/somewhere to turn; opportunity to learn from others; opportunity to talk about their own experiences; networking and collaboration (around impact of emotional research as well as own areas of research); support with raising awareness and encouraging change in organisations/institutions around emotionally demanding research.

Following member feedback, we formed a working group to manage the network and drive forward the various ideas that members had suggested and have begun to take action on some of these. Currently, we hold two types of meetings: (1) Monthly 'drop in' discussion sessions where people can share how they are feeling in an environment supported by others who have similar experiences. (2) Quarterly meetings where we update members or plan future activities and host a guest speaker or workshop facilitator to present to the group. We have an online private forum where members can introduce themselves, discuss particular issues, share resources, strategies, and literature. We have established a shared database so members can add their details and research experience if they are willing to be contacted by other members looking for someone with experience in a particular area.

## Reflections and Recommendations

Based on our personal experience, and the work we have done in developing guidance and managing the peer network, there are certain elements that appear to contribute to reducing the negative impact of emotionally demanding research on researcher wellbeing and that to some extent can be put in place or supported at an individual project/department level:

- **Planning** that takes this impact into consideration from the outset.
- **Reasonable support options** available to the researchers involved throughout the project should they need it.

- **Personal toolkits** developed by, and unique to, individual researchers in response to lived experience in and out of work, as well as opportunities for training and learning.

What we mean by 'personal toolkits' are the varying personal support and coping strategies that individuals mould throughout their lives and careers, as they learn about what impacts upon them emotionally, and what might help, or hinder, in different circumstances. Opportunities for training and skill development in the workplace can, of course, help and we use the term 'personal' to highlight the uniqueness of individual coping strategy 'toolkits' and not to place the responsibility fully on individuals to develop these alone. Developing these tailored and individually appropriate sets of strategies requires support and guidance from the literature, peers, line managers/supervisors, and institutions themselves. These toolkits might include self-care practices or a personalised 'tried and tested' understanding of helpful coping strategies (Butler et al., 2019; Rager, 2005). They might also include the less tangible, for example, a mindset that acknowledges and balances the risk of emotional impact with the value that emotional vulnerability can bring to the role (Hubbard, Backett-Milburn, & Kemmer, 2001). Opportunities to prepare oneself as much as possible for the upcoming research task, being given as much information as possible about potentially emotionally demanding elements, might also be seen as part of this toolkit (Fenge et al., 2019). The level of development of this 'personal toolkit' is often seen, mistakenly, as the only factor in determining whether someone is likely to be affected by emotionally demanding research and words like 'resilience' are often used to evaluate it, placing the onus on the individual researcher to be prepared. Considering *only* levels of preparedness or resilience focuses attention on the individual rather than the organisational structures and their responsibilities (Conolly et al., 2022). Likewise, considering these concepts as acquired skills assumes that senior or experienced researchers will not be affected by emotionally demanding research, which is not the case (Fenge et al., 2019). A problem that we have regularly encountered is the conceptualising of resilience as an end point: a skill to be acquired, a training box to be ticked. We propose that a more helpful view of resilience is as an ongoing practice involving elements of emotional vulnerability, reflexivity, and adjustment, often requiring concurrent support and guidance. However, we acknowledge that it can often be challenging as a researcher, particularly for those on short-term contracts (Leathwood & Read, 2022) or with budgets to manage, to balance project demands with the time and resources required to provide this support. There may be a view that this is 'wasted time' compared to time spent on tangible outputs such as publications or grant applications (Leathwood & Read, 2022), which is why support for change in practice must come from the institutional level. In our experience, the researchers most likely to be impacted by emotionally demanding research in a way that affects their wellbeing are not those without the personal toolkit, they are the ones without the adequate support available, working on studies where the emotional impact of the research has been overlooked. While developing our own coping strategies for doing emotionally demanding research should be as important as developing our other research skills it should not be considered the only aspect, or linked to seniority or level of experience.

The purpose, therefore, of these guidelines is to support researchers to move away from traditional ways of working where vulnerability and emotional responses are seen as negative individual responses which should be suppressed or resolved by training or 'upskilling'. Rather we support the view that vulnerability, or being open to emotion, can play a valuable role in qualitative research. As researchers, we are often drawn to the work we do, and driven to continue in it, because of empathy. This empathy can be an asset in steering us to do research with integrity and purpose, but it opens us to emotional impact (Davison, 2004). With emotional impact comes the risk that without good planning and support the wellbeing of researchers could be negatively affected and in turn the work that they do and their drive to continue doing it. We would suggest that by planning to minimise unnecessary risks, and embedding appropriate support from the outset of a project, the risk of negative impact on researchers will be reduced and that doing so will have a positive impact on the work they do. We feel strongly that this support should not simply be implemented at an individual level and that changes are needed even beyond those at a project or departmental level.

The supports and changes that we have been able to contribute to in writing guidance for researchers, developing a peer network, and indeed contributing to this book are small offerings in a landscape requiring more long-term adjustments at a more structural level. This work, for the most part, has been driven forward by early career researchers in their own time, those who are not only more likely to experience the impact of emotionally demanding research (Bloor et al., 2008; Hubbard et al., 2001) but are also more likely to be managing additional stressors such as lower pay and job precarity (McKenzie, 2021). The involvement of more senior colleagues in initiatives such as this is essential not only to help sustain measures and supports and raise awareness of their need, but also to encourage an attitudinal shift acknowledging the impact that emotionally demanding research can have at any career stage. Similarly, there is a need to raise awareness of the breadth of ways that research can be emotionally demanding, across different disciplines, employing different methods, and at multiple stages of a project. Acknowledging this within the research community can not only improve how studies are designed and carried out but might go some way to reducing the stigma around asking for support that prevents researchers from being more vocal about how this work is affecting them. The wider systems surrounding research have a role to play in shifting research culture by explicitly encouraging and recognising the importance of embedding researcher wellbeing throughout the research process (Bloor et al., 2008; Bloor, Fincham, & Sampson, 2010). Existing processes that are already in place to protect participant wellbeing and researcher physical safety could be adapted and expanded to require reflection on potential emotional risks to researchers. Funding bodies and ethics committees could explicitly request evidence that emotional demand has been considered in planning and budgeting, with suitable mitigations put in place. It is our view that if you have researchers who feel that you recognise the challenge that emotionally demanding research can pose, are willing to support them when they need it, and value the importance of providing that support, then you will have researchers who are more likely to do their best work. Appropriately and meaningfully supporting researchers doing emotionally demanding research can affect the participants they work with, the data collected, how it is analysed and interpreted, written up and disseminated, and ultimately the broader impact that research has.

## Acknowledgements

We would like to thank Elizabeth Adams, Jo Ferrie, Marcela Gavigan, Kay Guccione, Hazel Marzetti, Laurence Moore, Samantha Oakley, Raquel Bosó Pérez, and Sharon Simpson for their support and advice in developing the guidance and peer network. We would also like to thank all those who have supported and contributed to this work since 2019, from those who offered passing words of encouragement to us, to those who give their time and energy on a regular basis to facilitate the running of the peer network.

At the time of completing this work, SS and JR were funded by the UK Medical Research Council (MRC) and Scottish Government Chief Scientist Office (CSO) at the MRC/CSO Social & Public Health Sciences Unit, University of Glasgow (SPHSU16/MC_UU_00022/1, SPHSU18/MC_UU_00022/3).

## Notes

1  https://emotionalresearch.wordpress.com/.
2  https://twitter.com/EmotionalResrch.

## References

Arditti, J. A. (2015). Situating Vulnerability in Research: Implications for Researcher Transformation and Methodological Innovation. *Qualitative Report, 20*(10), 1568–1575. doi:10.46743/2160-3715/2015.2325.

Bloor, M., Fincham, B., & Sampson, H. (2008). Qualiti (NCRM) commissoned inquiry into the risk to well-being of researchers in Qualitative Research. Project Report. Cardiff University. https://eprints.ncrm.ac.uk/id/eprint/407/

Bloor, M., Fincham, B., & Sampson, H. (2010). Unprepared for the Worst: Risks of Harm for Qualitative Researchers. *Methodological innovations, 5*(1), 45–55. doi:10.4256/mio.2010.0009.

Borgstrom, E., & Ellis, J. (2021). Internalising 'Sensitivity': Vulnerability, Reflexivity and Death Research(ers). *International Journal of Social Research Methodology, 24*(5), 589–602. doi:10.1080/13645579.2020.1857972.

Butler, A. E., Copnell, B., & Hall, H. (2019). Researching People Who Are Bereaved: Managing Risks to Participants and Researchers. *Nursing Ethics, 26*(1), 224–234. doi:10.1177/0969733017695656.

Conolly, A., Abrams, R., Rowland, E., Harris, R., Couper, K., Kelly, D., ... Maben, J. (2022). "What Is the Matter with Me?" or a "Badge of Honor": Nurses' Constructions of Resilience During Covid-19. *Global Qualitative Nursing Research, 9*, 23333936221094862–23333936221094862. doi:10.1177/23333936221094862.

Davison, J. (2004). Dilemmas in Research: Issues of Vulnerability and Disempowerment for the Social Worker/Researcher. *Journal of Social Work Practice, 18*(3), 379–393. doi:10.1080/0265053042000314447.

Dickson-Swift, V., James, E. L., Kippen, S., & Liamputtong, P. (2006). Blurring Boundaries in Qualitative Health Research on Sensitive Topics. *Qualitative Health Research, 16*(6), 853–871. doi:10.1177/1049732306287526.

Fenge, L. A., Oakley, L., Taylor, B., & Beer, S. (2019). The Impact of Sensitive Research on the Researcher: Preparedness and Positionality. *International Journal of Qualitative Methods, 18*, 160940691989316. doi:10.1177/1609406919893161.

Gilbert, K. (Ed.) (2000). *The Emotional Nature of Qualitative Research* (1st edition). Boca Raton, FL: CRC Press. https://www.taylorfrancis.com/books/mono/10.1201/9781420039283/emotional-nature-qualitative-research-kathleen-gilbert

Gill, A. (2021). Reflexivity and Lived Experience of Out-of-Home Care: Positionality as an Early Parenthood Researcher. *Affilia*, 88610992110612. doi:10.1177/08861099211061210.

Guccione, K., & Nagouse, E. (2018). The Emotionally Demanding Research Network: Setting Up a Researcher-led Community. Retrieved from https://thinkaheadsheffield.wordpress.com/2018/03/01/the-emotionally-demanding-research-network-setting-up-a-researcher-led-community/

Guccione, K., & Nagouse, E. (2019). The Ethics of Emotionally Demanding Research. Retrieved from https://thinkaheadsheffield.wordpress.com/2019/03/12/the-ethics-of-emotionally-demanding-research/

Hubbard, G., Backett-Milburn, K., & Kemmer, D. (2001). Working with Emotion: Issues for the Researcher in Fieldwork and Teamwork. *International Journal of Social Research Methodology, 4*(2), 119–137. doi:10.1080/13645570116992.

Kumar, S., & Cavallaro, L. (2018). Researcher Self-Care in Emotionally Demanding Research: A Proposed Conceptual Framework. *Qualitative Health Research, 28*(4), 648–658. doi:10.1177/1049732317746377.

Leathwood, C., & Read, B. (2022). Short-Term, Short-Changed? A Temporal Perspective on the Implications of Academic Casualisation for Teaching in Higher Education. *Teaching in Higher Education, 27*(6), 756–771. doi:10.1080/13562517.2020.1742681.

Lee, R. M. (1993). *Doing Research on Sensitive Topics*. London and Thousand Oaks, CA: Sage.

McCann, I. L., & Pearlman, L. A. (1990). Vicarious Traumatization: A Framework for Understanding the Psychological Effects of Working with Victims. *Journal of Traumatic Stress, 3*(1), 131–149. doi:10.1007/BF00975140.

McKenzie, L. (2021). The Risks of Precarity: How Employment Insecurity Impacts on Early Career Researchers in Australia. In D. L. Mulligan, & P. A. Danaher (Eds.), *Researchers at Risk: Precarity, Jeopardy and Uncertainty in Academia* (pp. 115–129). Cham: Springer International Publishing.

Micanovic, L. S., Stelko, S., & Sakic, S. (2020). Who Else Needs Protection? Reflecting on Researcher Vulnerability in Sensitive Research. *Societies (Basel, Switzerland), 10*(1), 3. doi:10.3390/soc10010003.

Nikischer, A. (2019). Vicarious Trauma inside the Academe: Understanding the Impact of Teaching, Researching and Writing Violence. *Higher Education, 77*(5), 905–916. doi:10.1007/s10734-018-0308-4.

O'Connor, R. C., Smillie, S., McClelland, H., Lundy, J.-M., Stewart, C., Syrett, S., … Simpson, S. A. (2022). SAFETEL: A Pilot Randomised Controlled Trial to Assess the Feasibility and Acceptability of a Safety Planning and Telephone Follow-up Intervention to Reduce Suicidal Behaviour. *Pilot and Feasibility Studies*, *8*(1), 156. doi:10.1186/s40814-022-01081-5.

Rager, K. B. (2005). Compassion Stress and the Qualitative Researcher. *Qualitative Health Research*, *15*(3), 423–430. doi:10.1177/1049732304272038.

Rowling, L. (1999). Being In, Being Out, Being with: Affect and the Role of the Qualitative Researcher in Loss and Grief Research. *Mortality (Abingdon, England)*, *4*(2), 167–181. doi:10.1080/713685968.

Williamson, E., Gregory, A., Abrahams, H., Aghtaie, N., Walker, S.-J., & Hester, M. (2020). Secondary Trauma: Emotional Safety in Sensitive Research. *Journal of Academic Ethics*, *18*(1), 55–70. doi:10.1007/s10805-019-09348-y.

# 5

# ADDRESSING RESEARCHER VULNERABILITY WITH THE TRAUMA AND RESILIENCE INFORMED RESEARCH PRINCIPLES AND PRACTICES FRAMEWORK

*Natalie Edelman*

## Introduction

Writing this chapter has been a challenge for three reasons. First, my discomfort with my own vulnerability – and perhaps with the very concept itself. Second, my sense that the Trauma and Resilience Informed Research Principles and Practice (TRIRPP) framework I've developed to support both participants and researchers will be inadequate to the task, fuelled by Imposter Syndrome despite my lived experience as both a trauma survivor and an academic researcher. And third, my difficulty in writing as I had first intended, behind the safe curtain of the third person – a technique which I sometimes employ when I'm using a qualitative approach to support participants to safely recount experiences, but which proved impossible when I tried to use it to write this chapter.

And so I begin by stepping out from behind the safety of 'they' and 'them' and into the spotlight of 'I', noticing how this reveals not only my discomfort with my vulnerability but also my fear that perhaps I will have nothing to say, that the framework I have developed has too much unfilled space and will offer no scaffold for something as amorphous – as *leaky* – as vulnerability. But perhaps *leaky*, that uncomfortable word that calls to mind my days providing nursing care, is exactly the place to start. Human beings are leaky, not only in our physical selves, but in the way we affect each other, are constructed by each other, learn from and are moved by each other on conscious and other levels.

The slightly pejorative taint that the word 'vulnerable' carries speaks to this discomfort with the reality of how we affect one another, at least in the Western UK culture with which I'm familiar. Academic definitions of 'vulnerability' vary considerably and often speak to different population characteristics, but it is perhaps our shared non-academic understanding of the term which is the most important in thinking about the implicit ways in which vulnerability may be understood, felt

DOI: 10.4324/9781003349266-7

and responded to in our lives as researchers. The Cambridge dictionary definition of vulnerable is 'to be easily physically or mentally hurt, influenced, or attacked' (Cambridge, 2022) (para. 1) and it is perhaps this word 'easily' from which a stigma arises, particularly in Western social contexts where the internalised, psychological resilience of individuals (Hart et al., 2016) in withstanding adversity is so prized. It is interesting too that this definition encompasses being 'influenced' – sandwiched between 'hurt' and 'attacked', implying that to be easily affected in thought or action is itself a kind of harm that alludes to concerns around coercion and capacity to consent. And yet, as I've entered into discussions with colleagues and peers there emerges a fierce *defence* of our vulnerability as researchers, which perhaps pivots on this wider definition of being 'influenced' rather than overtly harmed. Certainly, a 'shared sense of humanity with participants, honouring emotional connectedness…' is seen as an important aspect of qualitative research, albeit one which can lead to secondary trauma (Williamson et al., 2020, p. 58).

Personally speaking, I came to this topic via a mixed-methods (survey and interview) study that I led, about the sexual and reproductive health needs of women with problematic drug use. In fact, my experiences in carrying out that study laid the foundations for the TRIRPP framework that I present in this chapter, specifically the ninth and tenth principles which speak to researcher well-being. As a mixed-methods sexual and reproductive health researcher, grounded more in quantitative than qualitative methods, I was disconcerted to find myself moved and upset by my interviewees' stories; in both trivial and significant ways my thinking was also changed. Does this reflect my vulnerability? I believe so. Was that problematic? For me, only in so far as the context around me indicated that I should not be 'easily' upset, I shouldn't need to share with another human being what the research interviews brought up for me, I should not question my practice as a researcher so drastically based on one study, I should not – in short – be 'easily influenced'. Beyond the self-doubt induced by others' concern about my vulnerability in doing the research, in myself I felt privileged and grateful for the experience, a feeling I retain 20 years later.

This sense of what one should not do, think or feel arises perhaps from traditional notions of scientific objectivity and neutrality in which we relate to the subject matter of our research in deliberately impersonal ways, even when employing qualitative methodologies (Williamson et al., 2020). Thus, acknowledging and engaging with our vulnerability as researchers becomes a political and perhaps even subversive act in which we resist an implicit but pervasive gold-standard of invulnerability to our participants' stories, sometimes even when employing qualitative methods (Williamson et al., 2020). And yet there is a need to reconcile this worthwhile resistance to dominant narratives about the perils of vulnerability with the reality that carrying out research *does* indeed have the potential to do us harm.

This desire amongst researchers to be both vulnerable and protected from harm, I argue, can be reconciled in the research context itself. The notion that the research context can effect change is the central premise upon which the TRIRPP framework is based, and which I have developed as a means of improving inclusivity and experience for both participants and researchers (and those who straddle both roles).

In the following sections, I give a brief overview of the literature that addresses researcher vulnerability in relation to the substantive nature of studies (their topics and populations) before exploring the different facets of research context surrounding those studies. I then set out the TRIRPP framework as a means of augmenting that context to support researchers in our vulnerability, focusing on the two principles that address researcher well-being in particular. Finally, I briefly compare these aspects of TRIRPP with recommendations from other literature and offer suggestions for further work.

## Researcher vulnerabilities and substantive research issues

In contrast to the focus on research context offered by TRIRPP, the majority of literature on researcher vulnerability focuses on how the *substantive* nature of different research topics impacts on the emotional and psychological well-being of the researcher. Specifically, most literature focuses on research into 'sensitive' topics, conceptualised using terms such as 'emotionally demanding research' (EDR) (Kumar & Cavallaro, 2018) and offering deconstruction and reflection on how sensitive topics can negatively impact researcher well-being. This literature, although ostensibly examining sensitive topics, focuses almost exclusively on how *qualitative* methods can negatively impact on researchers who are investigating those topics. First, empathy (the ability to feel *with* another through either use of imagination or shared experience) is highlighted as an important skill for research quality, which can leave the qualitative researcher vulnerable to receiving the transference of difficult emotions and to burnout (Gair, 2011). Second, the impact of participant disclosure has been identified as a mechanism which can cause 'secondary trauma' in the researcher (defined as the impact of indirect exposure to traumatic events) when a participant is recounting a traumatic memory for the first time in a 'raw and unprocessed' way (Williamson et al., 2020). Similarly, unanticipated disclosures have also been identified as an 'emotional risk' to researchers (Mallon & Elliott, 2019).

The World Health Organization (WHO), in discussing research on violence against women, identifies that secondary trauma among researchers can also occur where the research topic disrupts the researcher's general sense of safety in the world, and/or when the research topic triggers the researcher's own trauma memories (WHO, 2005). This intersection of the participant's and researcher's own stories is explored more fully in the literature on 'insider' research; shared experience may not only trigger researchers' trauma memories but also create tension and discomfort around being both insider and outsider in the qualitative research context (Dwyer & Buckle, 2009). The focus here remains on qualitative research, likely reflecting both the depth of involvement in research data, and the reflexivity and interrogation of researcher positionality that is common in many qualitative research approaches (Dwyer & Buckle, 2009).

Although given less attention in the literature, the possibility for sensitive topics to be traumatising through other forms of research activity other than qualitative interviewing has been acknowledged, such as the potential for secondary trauma to be experienced by those coding or transcribing qualitative interview data that pertains to sensitive topics (Loyle & Simoni, 2017). I would argue that literature reviewing too can prove difficult; in writing this chapter I have been too triggered by the research topics upon which some papers are predicated, to be able to read them fully, my admission of which feels almost heretical.

Overall then, the literature focuses on the impact of *sensitive topics* on researcher well-being. The literature sets out how this is made vulnerable, both through secondary trauma and the triggering of the researcher's own trauma, and enhanced by features of qualitative approaches such as data immersion and in-depth interviewing. Although there is little recognition of how other ways of encountering sensitive qualitative data (such as transcription and literature reviewing) might also affect researcher vulnerability, there is also little attention to the impact of the research context.

This focus on sensitive topics as the reason for researcher vulnerability is problematic because whilst certain subjects *may* be more 'sensitive' than others, trauma or secondary trauma in researchers can be triggered by issues other than the topic of interest. Understanding and attending to the ways in which these aspects of context can negatively impact researcher well-being provides opportunities to protect well-being whether the topic is of a sensitive nature or not. The following paragraphs set out a number of dimensions to the research context which can impact on researcher well-being and vulnerability: the researcher's personal experience, disciplinary culture, the physical context and structural and institutional issues.

## Looking beyond qualitative research on sensitive topics: the importance of context

The researcher's own trauma can be triggered not only by the research topic that a participant discusses, but by the context that the participant recounts, or by factors external to the participant's story such as the setting in which the data collection is taking place or the appearance of the participant or others in the research setting. In my own experience, I found recruiting in a homeless centre very difficult, not because of the interactions with the women I hoped to interview but because of the presence of inebriated men who were sometimes hostile to my presence. Thus, we can view the researcher's own trauma and/or their lived experience of conducting research (itself a feature of data collection and institutional settings and cultures) as part of the context that surrounds the substantive topic of interest.

Second, and equally troubling to me personally, has been my experience as a 'secret insider' – that is to say when I find myself working on a study for which I identify as a member of the population who are being studied (even if not the topic) but am not comfortable to share this within the research team. Non-disclosure may well be the most appropriate option in order to care for ourselves, particularly when working with colleagues across institutions with whom we have scant personal relationship.

Importantly, this 'secret insider' status can of course occur in both qualitative and quantitative methodologies if we choose not to disclose aspects of our personal lives. But quantitative research is more commonly a place where I find myself in this position, perhaps because it lacks a culture or methodology of reflexivity, but also because of assumptions made by and about the research team members' backgrounds, circumstances and experiences. On reflection, I feel this in part arises because the majority of female academic researchers are middle class or upper middle class. Although there is acknowledgement of how class, gender, age and ethnicity influence the research interview (Manderson, Bennett & Andajani-Sutjahjo, 2006), there is little if any academic discourse on how these factors impact on researchers' interactions with each other. This has placed me in the position of having to act as if I have shared experience of employing a nanny, having disposable income etc., and – just as difficult – speaking of myself as other (e.g. women who have experienced domestic violence). Alternatively, I am required to redress assumptions by initiating the disclosure of private information which I fear would create social awkwardness at the very least and at the worst would place myself 'under the microscope', despite the best intentions of everyone in the room. Noticing and laying down our assumptions about each other as researchers is a TRIRPP component that offers a subtle yet powerful way of changing the research context for the better.

This experience with working within quantitative paradigms speaks to not only methodological differences but to different cultural norms in conducting research. Working in a subject area (sexual and reproductive health) which employs mixed-methods approaches, I would argue that the presiding research culture – which again forms part of the *context* in which I conduct research – is quantitative in so far as it views: 'academic scientific endeavour as objective, detached and neutral, where researchers are not supposed to *feel* anything (other than perhaps satisfied or frustrated) about the work they undertake' (Williamson et al., 2020, p. 56).

Although I find my quantitative research colleagues to be no less warm or humane than those working in qualitative approaches, the very aim of 'objective' science is to, in that observation, be devoid of our own subjectivity such that there is a tendency to politely step over our own humanity at times. Arguably, the upper class, male exclusivity of early scientific endeavour has also dictated some of these norms around non-communication of emotion, vulnerability and an assumption of privilege and well-being between researchers.

These cultural norms do not only exist in relation to health sciences and there is a recognised need to examine researcher vulnerability more broadly across disciplines (Mallon & Elliott, 2019). For example, political science research has been identified as carrying a 'culture of self-neglect, rigorous work expectations, and denial of personal needs' (Loyle & Simoni, 2017, p. 144) that deepens 'research-related trauma', which they define as 'psychological harm that emerges from exposure to death or violence while engaging in'. Importantly, this definition of research-related trauma encompasses both environmental and topic-related exposure, highlighting the psychological harm that can arise from conducting research in environments which are physically dangerous. Although 'macro' settings such as conflict zones are the subject of this literature, 'micro' physical settings such as forensic psychiatric units for violent patients might also comprise physically dangerous environments that traumatise the researcher. Yet other settings, such as the homeless centre described above, may constitute environments where threat and violence are perhaps likely and where steps can be taken to ameliorate that. In the homeless centre in question, one researcher was spoken to in a very intimidating manner, following which we started working behind the counter of the on-site café – providing a physical sense of safety to the researchers while also encouraging dialogue and relationship building with attendees which further enhanced safety. Despite the obvious importance of physical safety and the potential for environments to become unsafe, little attention has been given to this issue in the literature beyond more generic considerations around lone-working (Mallon & Elliott, 2019), perhaps demonstrating again the afore-mentioned academic cultural norms.

The final aspect of context that is relevant to researcher vulnerability is the institutional and structural context. This creates working conditions that can compound secondary trauma or make the experience of researching sensitive topics more likely to result in trauma – for example where staff feel compelled to work long hours, with insufficient support and lack of control over their role, job security or requirements (Williamson et al., 2020). Precarity has also been highlighted as part of the broader 'hostile' environment afforded by neoliberalism in which academic research is now often undertaken (Pearce, 2020). Empirical work into researchers' experiences similarly found a lack of institutional responsibility for researchers' support needs, grounded in a lack of recognition of the emotional risks – in stark contrast to careful health and safety attention to the physical risks associated with lone-working etc. (Mallon & Elliott, 2019).

In summary then, there is a need to move away from understanding vulnerability in qualitative (or indeed any methodologies) as topic-based and instead to address it as a contextualised phenomenon encompassing personal experience, disciplinary culture, structural and institutional issues, and the physical environment in which research is conducted. The literature highlights how these various contexts in which research is conducted, can contribute greatly to the potential for researcher vulnerability to lead to harm, even where the substantive topic is not of a sensitive nature. The corollary of this is the notion that the research context itself can attenuate, exacerbate or present new adversities, or offer a site of resilience and well-being (Edelman, 2022). The TRIRPP framework is founded on this assumption. This focus on context rather than inherent vulnerability is in fact not new, the concept of 'susceptibility to harm' has been presented as an alternative to 'vulnerability' which explicitly recognises the context-specific nature of the latter (Levine et al., 2004).

## Describing the TRIRPP framework

The TRIRPP framework aims to encompass all methodologies and topics, taking a trauma and resilience informed approach to improve research inclusivity and experience for both participants and researchers by attending to the research context.

Specifically, as argued in the opening paragraphs of this chapter, the research context provides a space in which to 'support' researchers in our vulnerability, thus reconciling the need to attenuate potential harms with a conscious political resistance to the pathologising of our vulnerability.

The development of TRIRPP, including further detail on its conceptualisation, and existing research recommendations that were adopted into it, is set out elsewhere (Edelman, 2022), whilst the basic framework is given in the Appendix of this chapter. The ten principles are intended for application across research topics, populations and disciplines, while some of the associated *practices* suggested in the framework are necessarily specific to particular study designs. Importantly, the latter are not intended as an exhaustive list, but rather represent a starting point that will hopefully be added to by researchers across a range of health research over time. Principles One to Eight focus on improving experience for participants and those eligible to participate, while Principles Nine to Ten focus on improving experience for researchers, recognising that the researcher and the participant are largely still distinguishable roles, despite the growth of co-production and user-led approaches. The following section describes how trauma and resilience are understood and integrated in the framework as a whole. The chapter then focuses on the last two principles which attend particularly to researcher inclusivity, well-being and experience.

## Introducing the concepts of trauma and resilience

Trauma and resilience as concepts underpin, respectively, the principles of trauma-informed and resilience-informed care that are integrated within the TRIRPP framework and then applied to health and social care research. Both trauma and resilience are constructed as responses to contexts of adversity. Trauma can be understood as a failure of context; that is, the impact on neurology and sense of self of overwhelming adverse experiences not adequately contained by the individual, the environment or those around them (van der Kolk, 1994). The corollary of this is that social support provides the best protection against developing trauma responses, such as post-traumatic stress disorder (PTSD), to adverse events and contexts (van der Kolk, 1994). Resilience conversely, is a *positive* response to adverse contexts. Whilst some resilience informed approaches focus on 'internalised resilience' (psychological attributes and behaviours of individuals) (Hart et al., 2016), the Resilience for Social Justice informed (RSJI) approach which the TRIRPP framework uses, instead conceptualises resilience as: '…overcoming adversity, whilst also potentially subtly changing, or even dramatically transforming, (aspects of) that adversity' (Hart et al., 2016, p. 6).

The TRIRPP framework seeks to acknowledge the complexity and multiplicity of the topics of resilience and trauma, recognising in particular that trauma and resilience *co-exist* in contexts of adversity (Ungar, 2013) and taking the position that resilience emerges, and can be fostered, in the contexts of both trauma arising from Potentially Traumatic Events (which is how trauma is often conceptualised in contemporary resilience research) *and* the trauma that can arise from contexts of chronic adversity. Importantly, as trauma is considered a deficit, and resilience an asset, the trauma-informed aspects of TRIRPP address the need to protect researchers from harm, while the resilience-informed aspects notice and value researcher vulnerability as part of the human experience that can contribute to research quality.

## Principles Nine and Ten – attending to researcher well-being and inclusivity

Principles Nine and Ten, alongside associated practice recommendations and sources, are given in Table 5.1. The principle most directly relevant to researcher vulnerability is Principle Nine: *Support researcher well-being – recognising and supporting resilience and possible pre-existing trauma and traumatic impact from doing research.* Nonetheless, Principle Ten which addresses researcher inclusion, may also attenuate harm by attending to both the personal contexts which frame researchers' lives and the context in which they carry out research. In particular, noticing and attending to our assumptions about each other's lives has the power to ameliorate the discomforts I describe above – of 'othering' oneself, going along with others' inaccurate assumptions about our lives, or correcting those assumptions with the attendant vulnerability of self-disclosure.

Some of the other Principles and Practices set out in the remainder of the Framework set out in the Appendix may also indirectly support researcher well-being by addressing vulnerability. Relatedly, (Silverio et al., 2022) discuss how ensuring researchers have the skills to handle difficult qualitative interviews, will improve their own well-being as well as that of participants.

## Pre-existing work on supporting researcher vulnerability

Many of the practice recommendations associated with Principles Nine and Ten of the TRIRPP framework are augmented or directly adopted from existing publications. In particular, much of the pre-existing work that informs the practices associated with Principle Nine consists of publications on supporting researcher vulnerability – presented as recommendations to attenuate harm (arising from reviews, reflections or empirical qualitative research), rather than focusing on the building of resilience. Although these different publications may aim their recommendations for addressing researcher vulnerability at those researching particular topics or within particular disciplines, their suggestions are actually applicable more broadly, as they largely comprise adaptations to the context in which the research is happening.

Self-care is a recommendation running through many publications, which can be understood as a means of both attenuating harm and building resilience also. For example, Kumar and Cavallaro (2018) use reflexive accounts and literature review to present a conceptual framework for researcher self-care. Interestingly, they operationalise self-responsibility and self-care as facilitated by the institution (suggesting for example that research ethics committees mandate researcher self-care and that

**TABLE 5.1** Principles Nine and Ten of the Trauma and Resilience Informed Research Principles and Practices Framework

| Principle | Practice | Research stage | | | Origin of practice |
|---|---|---|---|---|---|
| | | Topic choice and study design | Recruitment and data collection | Analysis and dissemination | |
| 9. Support researcher well-being – recognising and supporting resilience and possible pre-existing trauma and traumatic impact from doing research | Regularly acknowledge that research can be emotionally demanding and that some or all research team members may have lived experience of trauma which can both negatively affect but also enhance our research practice and personal well-being | X | X | X | Edelman* |
| | Instigate and normalise scheduled debriefs with another researcher immediately after data collection and analysis sessions | | X | | Edelman* |
| | Create a clear pathway and regular opportunities for discussing concerns about the well-being of self or other research team members with the Principal Investigator/supervisor and/or institution | X | X | X | Edelman |
| | Instigate regular team well-being sessions and/or a community of practice which provide: 1. a safe space for sharing and reflecting; 2. embodied co-regulation practices such as deep breathing, meditation, journaling, colouring, drumming or walking which may also be undertaken individually | X | X | X | Edelman** |
| | Recognise emotional response and personal insights as a valuable contribution to research quality and knowledge creation, formalising these through research activity such as publication | X | X | X | Kumar and Cavallaro 2018 |
| | Identify external sources of emotional support such as university research mentoring and counselling services and normalise their use through modelling, anecdote and regular mention | X | X | X | Edelman*** |

| | | | | |
|---|---|---|---|---|
| | Seek funding for and provide/access training in managing the researcher–participant relationship (including transference of emotion, boundaries, recruitment and data collection in difficult environments, safeguarding and researcher safety) | | X | Edelman |
| | Alternate psychologically-demanding tasks with easy tasks that offer distance from research material encountered through transcription, qualitative or quantitative analysis etc. | X | X | Edelman* |
| 10. Remove barriers to conducting research arising from structural issues, disadvantage and stigma | Work on the assumption that researchers may be facing structural disadvantage, marginalised status or personal circumstances that may make research activity difficult to conduct | X | X | Edelman |
| | Invite honest conversation about practical barriers to conducting research and advocate to institutions where possible for these barriers to be removed (e.g. changing core working hours) | X | X | Edelman |
| | Invite honest conversation about stigma, othering and personal disadvantage and how research practice in the team might be changed to address this | X | X | Edelman |

* Adapted from Loyle and Simoni 2017
** Adapted from Loyle and Simoni 2017 and Mallon and Elliott 2019
*** Adapted from Kumar and Cavallaro 2018

self-care training is provided), with little mention of the research team or departmental level. In contrast, the research team (Loyle & Simoni, 2017) and wider department (Mallon & Elliott, 2019) are identified as key sites for acknowledging and responding to potential harms in research. Arguably it is these contexts that can offer an environment and culture of self-care, acting as sites of resistance to neoliberal agendas, as part of a RSJI congruent approach.

Recommendations to access training and otherwise equip oneself and one's colleagues with knowledge runs through much of the literature reviewed for this chapter. This includes not only learning about self-care as suggested above, but learning about trauma (Loyle & Simoni, 2017) and learning research skills (Silverio et al., 2022). This can include ethical dilemmas, such as how to manage the tensions that can arise during data collection between participant protection and empowerment, particularly the right to continue to participate while distressed (Isobel, 2021). Learning about, and employing, reflexivity is also mentioned in much of the literature as a tool to not only improve research quality but also personal coping abilities (Isobel, 2021; Mallon & Elliott, 2019). Similarly, identifying 'personal risk factors' for potential harm is a key recommendation for political science research (Loyle & Simoni, 2017), which perhaps reflects less disciplinary focus on reflexivity. A lack of attention to reflexivity within different disciplines and methodologies may also explain the lack of literature attending to researcher well-being in quantitative studies, echoing points made earlier in this chapter.

Self-care is largely referred to in very general terms in the literature with little description of specific self-care practices (Kumar & Cavallaro, 2018), although certain activities which are not badged as such, could well be considered self-care. For example, Loyle and Simoni (2017) recommend ensuring 'meaningful contact with others' and alternating psychologically-demanding tasks with easy tasks that offer distance from research material in order to balance work pressures with personal needs (Loyle & Simoni, 2017).

TRIRPP also offers a number of practices related to Principle Nine – that are suggested deliberately as on a group basis. This inclusion of group practice is intentional as a means of: 1. Building on the notions of resilience and trauma as context-bound such that group activity offers a meaningful support context; 2. Acknowledging how the concept of self-regulation of emotion is increasingly being challenged, with co-regulation recognised as more accurate and effective (Rosanbalm & Murray, 2017); 3. Challenging a neoliberal focus on individualism and self-responsibility.

### Critical reflections on addressing researcher vulnerability using the TRIRPP framework

It is important to note that TRIRPP has been developed by just one person. My own professional and personal experiences have shaped it, as has my perspective and privilege as a white, cis, UK-based principal research fellow. The TRIRPP framework as set out in this chapter is a nascent piece of work, designed to inspire further thought and development. In particular, there are currently clear limitations to its applicability and scope, both generally and with regard to researcher vulnerability. These and suggested future avenues of enquiry are acknowledged in these closing sections of the chapter.

## Limitations

The TRIRPP framework is founded on the central premise that the research context can effect change in order to improve inclusivity and experience for 'would be' and actual participants and researchers (as well as those who straddle both roles). Yet the *power* to affect that change will be limited according to macro and micro considerations including everything from the political and geographical setting through to the seniority and security of the researcher's position.

A number of practices recommended in TRIRPP and the broader literature directly require structural or institutional changes that cannot be enacted by individual researchers or teams – a fact which is under-acknowledged in the literature. For example, employing a psychologist (Loyle & Simoni, 2017) or accessing other external services (Mallon & Elliott, 2019) to support research team well-being will likely require funding which is outside the remit of what can be included in external or internal grant application costings. Similarly, empowering researchers by offering a greater role in study design and dissemination may be difficult in the context of short-term contracts, which bring their own vulnerability (Mallon & Elliott, 2019). Even changing practices within institutions such as greater ethics committee attention to researcher well-being (Mallon & Elliott, 2019) (Pearce, 2020) (Kumar & Cavallaro, 2018), or embedding emotional support at departmental level (Mallon & Elliott, 2019) can be difficult to instigate, except for those in senior management roles.

Cultural and intersectional issues pertaining to gender, sex and class may also present at institutional levels and within research team hierarchies, perpetuating and potentially compounding existing vulnerabilities. For example, Mallon and Elliott (2019) report the finding that female staff found it harder than male staff to discuss their emotional reactions to the research they were conducting – for fear of being seen as a 'hysterical' woman (Mallon & Elliott, 2019). Pearce reflects on how her precarity as a PhD researcher was attenuated by being white and middle class, whilst also reporting the struggles of being a marginalised researcher through her identity as a trans woman (Pearce, 2020). These cultural and intersectional issues are themselves context-specific; I was unaware of how Western-centric the TRIRPP framework is until it was implemented in a conflict zone (Gupta et al., 2021). Similarly, differences in culture and lived experience between Western researchers and local researchers and translators are highlighted by Loyle and Simoni (2017), pointing out how the latter are not able to leave and go 'home' in a way that gains them physical distance from the research site (Loyle & Simoni, 2017).

My awareness of such cultural and geographical limitations emerged only when the TRIRPP framework was first applied – to an educational-research study in a conflict zone in the Democratic Republic of Congo (Gupta et al., 2021) – when I realised that I had initially written TRIRPP on the assumption that the wider geographical setting was physically safe, and also that trauma and resilience would manifest in the same way, and require the same responses, regardless of culture and geography. In practice, the TRIRPP framework was actually being applied in a setting where *most* individuals were traumatised by the physical violence of war and where these traumatic events were ongoing and, alongside COVID-19, had huge deleterious effects on day-to-day life, health and well-being. In essence, the power of the TRIRPP framework to effect changes in the research context to address researcher vulnerability is limited by the very contexts in which the framework and researchers are located. This apparent impasse is important to recognise and address; in particular the involvement of senior figures and organisations can create movement and partial solution even where other aspects of context remain immutable.

## Recommendations for further work

This nascent framework and surrounding research require further work in a number of areas.

First, there is a clear need to develop TRIRPP in order to be applicable to a number of cultural settings – and also perhaps even more vitally – to work cross-culturally. This can be both on an inter-country level and also within single-domain studies. For example, current research by the author on the reproductive health needs of both citizen and asylum-seeking care leavers requires attention to different cultural understandings of trauma and resilience in the application of TRIRPP.

More work is also needed to better develop the tenth TRIRPP principle: *Remove barriers to conducting research arising from structural issues, disadvantage and stigma,* and to explore how barriers to conducting research intersect with cultural factors, well-being and vulnerability. In particular, these barriers may be very far-reaching and include everything from contractual requirements (short-duration fixed-term contracts may not be a viable employment choice for some) to concerns about working with the population of interest. This latter point may again intersect with Principle Nine. For example, the opportunity to study those who are perpetrators of sexual or other violent crimes may present concerns to potential research staff, and indeed it may be appropriate to position participants as part of the 'adverse context' to which TRIRPP might be applied to ameliorate researcher harm, no matter how uncomfortable such positioning may feel. These kinds of issues are important not only because of the potentially harmful effects on the researcher of doing research, but because these effects can negatively affect our ability to think clearly and the ways in which we interact with participants and others, negatively impacting the quality of the research itself and the participant experience (Loyle & Simoni, 2017).

It is also important to notice that currently the focus in the literature and TRIRPP Principle Nine is largely on reducing the risk of trauma and other harm – more work is needed to explore the positives of vulnerability and to better integrate that within conceptual understandings of resilience and the ways in which resilience might offer a site to resist the narrative of invulnerability as desirable in both personal and professional contexts.

As discussed in the opening sections, existing literature focuses understandably on qualitative research, predominantly in relation to sensitive topics. This likely reflects how researcher vulnerability may be more likely to increase susceptibility to harm in qualitative contexts but also that quantitative approaches do not traditionally consider and publish reflexive accounts of the research process and its impacts. Nonetheless, the potential for quantitative research to cause secondary trauma or be otherwise challenging has been acknowledged (Williamson et al., 2020) and the TRIRPP framework is intended to encompass quantitative and mixed-methods approaches as well as qualitative ones. Certainly, in my own experience as a mixed-methods researcher, I have found that quantitative data can itself be triggering, because of the personal context afforded by my own trauma, arousing at times feelings of shame, alienation or upset. Alongside the afore-mentioned difficulties with identifying as a member of the 'at risk' population under study, terminology in academic papers and discussions can be stigmatising and invalidating. For example, within my field of sexual and reproductive health research, there is widespread use of the phrase 'sexual behaviour' in relation to a range of variables that may cover both volitional and non-volitional sexual experiences. More work is thus needed to explore TRIRPP's application to quantitative research studies on sensitive topics, including how to support and harness criticality in order to challenge our own conventions in terminology, thought and process (Edelman, 2018).

Finally, all of the areas for development outlined above speak to the need to take an intersectional and reflexive approach that seeks to recognise and respond to our various positionalities – in order to take care of ourselves, our colleagues and our participants; to reduce barriers to participation; and to further conceptualise intersectionality in relation to researcher vulnerability, resilience and trauma. Reflexivity has the power to give voice to the researcher's own trauma and a number of the Principle Nine practice recommendations may act as spaces for reflexivity and processing, recognising and working with researcher vulnerability in a protective way. Nonetheless, any subsequent self-disclosure may be either beneficial or harmful, depending on the context of who is receiving and responding to that disclosure. Thus contexts of reflexivity, and perhaps a more explicit recognition of its place in the TRIRPP framework, offer another fruitful avenue to explore for further development.

## Conclusions

The TRIRPP framework is presented here as a context-situated response to researcher vulnerability that attempts to reconcile seemingly contradictory needs in relation to researcher vulnerability – protecting researchers from harm while defending that vulnerability as valuable and just. The TRIRPP framework offers a means of structuring our response to that vulnerability, attending to context in order to attenuate the risk of trauma and other harm and recognising the benefits of vulnerability for our research practice, ourselves as researchers and our participants, as part of a broader focus on researcher and participant resilience. Importantly, the TRIRPP framework places deliberate focus on group, team or departmental activity and support, rather than simply on individual self-responsibility and self-care – recognising the social aspect of context and seeking to resist neoliberal focus on the individual as the site of change.

Although this chapter has focused on the TRIRPP principles that concern researchers specifically, the other principles may also support researcher well-being and inclusivity through greater confidence and expertise to conduct research and deal with its messiness, and also as the lines between researcher and researched continue to dissolve. Importantly, the blurring of that distinction between 'researcher' and 'participant' is not only due to the growing popularity of co-production approaches, but due also to the willingness of 'professional' researchers such as myself to bring our own lived experience to our methodologies across a range of applied research domains. This chapter offers an attempt to do just that, to start a conversation, to try something new, to harness my own vulnerability in the pursuit of rigorous and ethical research practice for all involved in that enterprise.

## A. Appendix 1

Appendix: Trauma and Resilience Informed Research Principles and Practice

| Principle | Practice | Research stage | | | Origin of practice |
|---|---|---|---|---|---|
| | | Topic choice and study design | Recruitment and data collection | Analysis and dissemination | |
| 1. Take active steps to seek participation from disenfranchised groups and individuals<br>*Adapted from RSJI (Table 2, No.6)* | Develop and/or validate accessible and acceptable measurement tools with disenfranchised populations | X | X | | Hart |
| | Regardless of study population or type, question and recognise possible disenfranchisements to participation | X | X | X | Edelman |
| | Use transparent and clear language in Patient and Public Involvement work, study materials and study delivery with clear and honest expectations | X | X | X | Edelman* |
| | Employ sampling strategies designed specifically to ensure adequate representation from disenfranchised populations such as lower socio-economic groups, ethnic and gender minorities in quantitative as well as qualitative research | X | | | Edelman** |
| | Ensure PPI from disenfranchised individuals identified with a view to intersectionality – to inform data collection materials, and recruitment and dissemination plans and delivery | X | X | X | Edelman*** |

| Principle | Practice | Research stage | | | Origin of practice |
|---|---|---|---|---|---|
| | | Topic choice and study design | Recruitment and data collection | Analysis and dissemination | |
| 2. Unite with social justice; tackling deprivation and health inequalities *Adapted from RSJI (Table 2, No.1 & No.8)* | Ensure research questions take account of social inequalities, for example, by examining structural inequalities, socio-economic status | X | | | Hart |
| | Include socially-transformative elements into the research where possible – methods and intended impact | | X | X | Hart |
| | Advocate for research questions that focus on social practices rather than individuals as agents of change | X | | | Edelman** |
| | Develop impact plans that aim to improve understanding of the impact of inequalities and influence research and policy | X | | X | Edelman** |
| 3. Frame the researcher-participant relationship as relational *Adapted from TI (Table 1, No.5) & RSJI (Table 2, No.7)* | Emphasise right to refuse participation or to withdraw | | X | | Campbell |
| | As a researcher, aim to be warm, 'real' and not aloof. Give participants the choice to not only withdraw but also to continue to participate if distressed but wish to | X | X | X | Edelman |

| | | | | Source |
|---|---|---|---|---|
| | Provide alternative survey measures so that participants can opt out of triggering questions without alerting others to this | | X | | Campbell |
| 4. Empower individuals and communities through choice and agency *Adapted from TI (Table 1, No.3 & 4) & RSJI (Table 2, No.5)* | Where possible use co-production so that communities and individuals are researchers and agents of change | X | X | | Hart |
| | Where possible, give study participants control of recording devices – when to activate them and what is recorded | | X | | Edelman |
| | Give participants choices regarding where to sit and agreed signals for wanting to stop or take a break | | X | | Edelman* |
| | Give participants choices regarding data sharing | | X | X | Campbell |
| | Revisit informed consent at different stages of the research process according to participant preference and if practicable – actively remind participants of their right to withdraw or limit data sharing | | X | X | Edelman* |

| Principle | Practice | Research stage | | | Origin of practice |
|---|---|---|---|---|---|
| | | Topic choice and study design | Recruitment and data collection | Analysis and dissemination | |
| | Offer greater choice regarding withdrawal of data and communication of findings to participants – even in large-scale surveys and trials | X | | X | Edelman* |
| | Ensure participant information sheets are clear about what is meant by a research 'interview' – use of follow-up questions, enquiry about context and decisions, not counselling etc. | X | | | Edelman |
| 5. Emphasise strengths and resilience<br>*Adapted from TI (Table 1, No.7) & RSJI (Table 2, No.2, 3 & 5)* | Use active listening and validate experiences and feelings surrounding trauma if disclosed | | | | Edelman* |
| | Use the term 'survivor' rather than 'victim' if appropriate | | | | Campbell<br>Hart |
| | Validate expressions of resilience by participants | | X | | Edelman* |
| 6. Minimise re-traumatisation<br>*From TI (Table 1, No.8)* | Avoid intrusive procedures/questioning | | | | Campbell |
| | Use active listening and validate experiences and feelings if disclosure occurs | | X | | Edelman* |

| | | | |
|---|---|---|---|
| 7. Recognise potential impact of trauma and adversity in all participants *Adapted from T1 (Table 1, Nos. 1,. 6) & RSJI Table 2, Nos. 2, 3)* | Describe data protection strategies | | X | Campbell |
| | Don't ask about traumatic experiences unless relevant to study | | X | Edelman |
| | Don't assume agency – use neutral language (e.g. 'experience' rather than 'behaviour') and ask if decisions were freely made | X | X | Edelman |
| | Give information on mental health and social support resources in Participant Information Sheet regardless of the study topic | | X | Edelman |
| | Don't assume that studies of 'non-sensitive' topics or with general populations will not exclude or traumatise some individuals/groups – assume sensitivity possible and provide generic resources with Participant Information Sheets | X | X | Edelman |
| | 'In direct engagement data collection, understand and be prepared to hear a wide variety of traumatic experiences' p. 4769 | | X | Campbell |

| Principle | Practice | Research stage | | | Origin of practice |
|---|---|---|---|---|---|
| | | Topic choice and study design | Recruitment and data collection | Analysis and dissemination | |
| | Ensure both PPI and study consent and data collection happen in inclusive places that feel both emotionally and physically safe for everyone – clear unobstructed exits, opportunities to take a break or withdraw, clear expectations and instructions | X | X | X | Edelman* |
| | Ensure researchers receive adequate training to support distressed participants during and after interview and questionnaire participation | X | X | | Edelman |
| | Recognise and respect participants' coping mechanisms. For example, expressed desire to not become distressed, switching to third person description or completing a questionnaire in an alternative space | | X | | Edelman |
| 8. Strive to be culturally competent and promote safety *From TI (Table 1: No.9)* | Strive to ensure that cultural understandings and manifestations of the topic under study – for example, depression – are extant in the research questions, measurement tools and/or outcomes and impact plan | X | X | X | Edelman |

| | | | |
|---|---|---|---|
| Seek out and foster research environments that feel culturally safe, with careful attention to physical space, presence of different authority figures etc. Conversely, choosing to have a safe person present during a research interview may be appropriate | X | X | Edelman |
| Ensure culturally-relevant PPI to inform all study materials – avoid deceptive, vague or unintentionally offensive language | X | X | Campbell/ Hart |
| Ensure that PPI activities are directly concerned with identifying and redressing research questions, methods and outcomes which ignore cultural factors and which otherwise disempower individuals and/or populations | X | X | Campbell/ Hart |

| Principle | Practice | Research stage | | | Origin of practice |
|---|---|---|---|---|---|
| | | Topic choice and study design | Recruitment and data collection | Analysis and dissemination | |
| 9. Support researcher well-being – recognising and supporting resilience and possible pre-existing trauma and traumatic impact from doing research | Regularly acknowledge that research can be emotionally demanding and that some or all research team members may have lived experience of trauma which can both negatively affect but also enhance our research practice and personal well-being | X | X | X | Edelman**** |
| | Instigate and normalise scheduled debriefs with another researcher immediately after data collection and analysis sessions | X | X | | Edelman**** |
| | Create a clear pathway and regular opportunities for discussing concerns about the well-being of self or other research team members with the Principal Investigator/supervisor and/ or institution | X | X | X | Edelman |
| | Instigate regular team well-being sessions and/or a community of practice which provide: 1. a safe space for sharing and reflecting; 2. embodied co-regulation practices such as deep breathing, meditation, journaling, colouring, drumming or walking which may also be undertaken individually | X | X | X | Edelman***** |

| Recommendation | | | | Source |
|---|:---:|:---:|:---:|---|
| Recognise emotional response and personal insights as a valuable contribution to research quality and knowledge creation, formalising these through research activity such as publication if desired | X | X | X | Kumar and Cavallaro (2018) |
| Identify external sources of emotional support such as university research mentoring and counselling services and normalise their use through modelling, anecdote and regular mention | X | X | X | Edelman****** |
| Seek funding for and provide/access training in managing the researcher–participant relationship (including transference of emotion, boundaries, recruitment and data collection in difficult environments, safeguarding and researcher safety) | | X | | Edelman |
| Alternate psychologically-demanding tasks with easy tasks that offer distance from research material encountered through transcription, qualitative or quantitative analysis etc. | X | X | X | Edelman**** |

| Principle | Practice | Research stage | | | Origin of practice |
| --- | --- | --- | --- | --- | --- |
| | | Topic choice and study design | Recruitment and data collection | Analysis and dissemination | |
| 10. Remove barriers to conducting research arising from structural issues, disadvantage and stigma | Work on the assumption that researchers may be facing structural disadvantage, marginalised status or personal circumstances that may make research activity difficult to conduct | X | X | X | Edelman |
| | Invite honest conversation about practical barriers to conducting research and advocate to institutions where possible for these barriers to be removed (e.g. changing core working hours) | X | X | X | Edelman |
| | Invite honest conversation about stigma, othering and personal disadvantage and how research practice in the team might be changed to address this | X | X | X | Edelman |

\* Adapted from (Campbell, Goodman-Williams, & Javorka, 2019)
\*\* Adapted from (Hart, Gagnon, Eryigit-Madzwamuse, Cameron, Aranda, Rathbone, & Heaver, 2016)
\*\*\* Adapted from (Campbell et al., 2019) and (Shimmin, Wittmeier, Lavoie, Wicklund, & Sibley, 2017)
\*\*\*\* Adapted from (Loyle & Simoni, 2017)
\*\*\*\*\* Adapted from (Loyle & Simoni, 2017) and (Mallon & Elliott, 2019)
\*\*\*\*\*\* Adapted from (Kumar & Cavallaro, 2018)

# References

Cambridge. (Ed.). (2022). *Cambridge Dictionary Online*. Cambridge University Press.

Campbell, R., Goodman-Williams, R., & Javorka, M. (2019). A Trauma-Informed Approach to Sexual Violence Research Ethics and Open Science. *Journal of Interpersonal Violence, 34*, 4765–4793. doi:10.1177/0886260519871530.

Dwyer, S. C., & Buckle, J. L. (2009). The Space Between: On Being an Insider-Outsider in Qualitative Research. *International Journal of Qualitative Methods, 8*(1), 54–63. doi:10.1177/160940690900800105.

Edelman, N. L. (2018). Towards a Critical Epidemiology Approach for Applied Sexual Health Research. *Journal of Health Psychology, 23*(2), 161–174. doi:10.1177/1359105317743768.

Edelman, N. L. (2022). Trauma and Resilience Informed Research Principles and Practice: A Framework to Improve the Inclusion and Experience of Disadvantaged Populations in Health and Social Care Research. *Journal of Health Services Research & Policy, 28*(1), 66–75.

Gair, S. (2011). Feeling Their Stories: Contemplating Empathy, Insider/Outsider Positionings, and Enriching Qualitative Research. *Qualitative Health Research, 22*(1), 134–143. doi:10.1177/1049732311420580.

Gupta, S. M., G. Brandt, C. Falisse, J. Justino, P. Marion, P. Matabishi, S. Mze Somora, P. Nyabagaza, P. Kanyerhera, D. Kiemtoré, I. PolePole Bazuzi, & C. W. Ibrahim. (2021). *Funders Report BRiCE Project DRC and Niger: Midline Report Teacher Well-Being and Teaching Quality in Fragile and Conflict-Affected Contexts.* UK: Institute of Development Studies, University of Sussex.

Hart, A., Gagnon, E., Eryigit-Madzwamuse, S., Cameron, J., Aranda, K., Rathbone, A., & Heaver, B. (2016). Uniting Resilience Research and Practice with an Inequalities Approach. *SAGE Open, 6*(4), 1–13.

Isobel, S. (2021). Trauma-Informed Qualitative Research: Some Methodological and Practical Considerations. *International Journal of Mental Health Nursing, 30*(1), 1456–1469. doi:10.1111/inm.12914.

Kumar, S., & Cavallaro, L. (2018). Researcher Self-Care in Emotionally Demanding Research: A Proposed Conceptual Framework. *Qualitative Health Research, 28*(4), 648–658. doi:10.1177/1049732317746377.

Levine, C., Faden, R., Grady, C., Hammerschmidt, D., Eckenwiler, L., & Sugarman, J. (2004). The Limitations of "Vulnerability" as a Protection for Human Research Participants. *American Journal of Bioethics, 4*(3), 44–49. doi:10.1080/15265160490497083.

Loyle, C. E., & Simoni, A. (2017). Researching under Fire: Political Science and Researcher Trauma. *PS: Political Science & Politics, 50*(1), 141–145. doi:10.1017/S1049096516002328.

Mallon, S., & Elliott, I. (2019). The Emotional Risks of Turning Stories into Data: An Exploration of the Experiences of Qualitative Researchers Working on Sensitive Topics. *Societies, 9*(3), 62. https://doi.org/10.3390/soc9030062

Manderson, L., Bennett, E., & Andajani-Sutjahjo, S. (2006). The Social Dynamics of the Interview: Age, Class, and Gender. *Qualitative Health Research, 16*(10), 1317–1334. doi:10.1177/1049732306294512.

Pearce, R. (2020). A Methodology for the Marginalised: Surviving Oppression and Traumatic Fieldwork in the Neoliberal Academy. *Sociology, 54*(4), 806–824. doi:10.1177/0038038520904918.

Rosanbalm, K. D., & Murray, D. W. (2017). *Caregiver Co-regulation across Development: A Practice Brief.* Washington, DC: Office of Planning, Research, and Evaluation, Administration for Children and Families, U.S. Department of Health and Human Services.

Shimmin, C., Wittmeier, K. D. M., Lavoie, J. G., Wicklund, E. D., & Sibley, K. M. (2017). Moving Towards a More Inclusive Patient and Public Involvement in Health Research

Paradigm: The Incorporation of a Trauma-Informed Intersectional Analysis. *BMC Health Services Research*, 17(1), 539. doi:10.1186/s12913-017-2463-1.

Silverio, S. A., Sheen, K. S., Bramante, A., Knighting, K., Koops, T. U., Montgomery, E., ... Sandall, J. (2022). Sensitive, Challenging, and Difficult Topics: Experiences and Practical Considerations for Qualitative Researchers. *International Journal of Qualitative Methods*, 21, 16094069221124739. doi:10.1177/16094069221124739.

Ungar, M. (2013). Resilience, Trauma, Context, and Culture. *Trauma Violence Abuse*, 14(3), 255–266. doi:10.1177/1524838013487805.

van der Kolk, B. A. (1994). The Body Keeps the Score: Memory and the Evolving Psychobiology of Posttraumatic Stress. *Harvard Review of Psychiatry*, 1(5), 253–265. doi:10.3109/10673229409017088.

WHO. (2005). *Researching Violence against Women: Practical Guidelines for Researchers and Activists / Mery Ellsberg, Lori Heise*. Geneva: World Health Organization.

Williamson, E., Gregory, A., Abrahams, H., Aghtaie, N., Walker, S. J., & Hester, M. (2020). Secondary Trauma: Emotional Safety in Sensitive Research. *Journal of Academic Ethics*, 18(1), 55–70. doi:10.1007/s10805-019-09348-y.

# SECTION II

# Experiences of Researcher Vulnerability

# 6

# STICKING YOUR HEAD ABOVE THE PARAPET

## On the importance of researcher resilience in auto/biographical writing

*Kate Woodthorpe*

## Introduction

Writing about your own life and recognising the impact of the personal on the professional is not a new phenomenon within social sciences. Feminists have long debated the personal/professional interface, in part fuelling and fuelled by the development of auto/biography and autoethnography as social research methods (Ellis, 2004; Kara, 2020). Auto/biographic and autoethnographic work has recognised the (potential) impact of revealing details about one's life as an academic (Ronai, 1995; Letherby, 2022) and its use as a way to learn about oneself and your place in the world (Leather, 2019), and addressed questions as to whether or not writing about oneself is simply self-indulgent academic navel gazing (Sparkes, 2002).

But what if when writing auto/biographically or autoethnographically you are also including details about someone else's life? This is perhaps not so challenging when the other person is deceased (for example in Wilkinson & Wilkinson, 2020). But what if that person may one day read what you have written about them? And what if they are your own child?

This chapter shares my experience of writing auto/biographically about my medically complex young son, why I have done so, whether I have an obligation to do so, and how I have reached the point where I have decided to stop. After introducing myself and my son using the auto/biographical tradition, I recount how I have grappled with making visible aspects of our lives, and the implications of doing so. The chapter moves on to considering whether writing autobiographically about him/me constitutes an exploitation of his/our situation; whether I am acting as an academic, parent, or advocate; and whether choosing *not* to share information when I have an academic platform contributes to the ongoing socio-political concealment of him and children like him, before moving on to reflecting on the emotion work required to be an academic and to write auto/biographically; and

DOI: 10.4324/9781003349266-9

the importance of resilience in being able to be an academic that makes public very personal details. This is particularly pertinent when including your medically complex child in light of everyday cruelty, or 'trolling', online for people who are regarded as 'different' (Sherry, 2019).

## A brief auto/biography

I am a UK sociologist who specialises in death, dying, and bereavement. Over two decades I have conducted numerous empirical studies on end-of-life experiences and post-death choices, and spoken at length with hundreds of people who are bereaved or arranging funerals. I have also worked in close collaboration with the professional organisations and policymakers that support the end of life. I am therefore not unaccustomed to discussing the end of life, and I feel comfortable talking openly about topics that are often shunned by others.

In my academic work, I have always been driven by wanting to make a difference and the importance of recognising the humanity of the people involved in the research endeavour – be it the participants within research projects, colleagues, or even myself. To this end, at the outset of my career and long before my children arrived, I published on the emotional demands of conducting research on death and bereavement, and the extent to which a researcher's ontological perspective is shaped by first-hand, personal experience (see Woodthorpe, 2009, 2011). With a colleague, I have also written about the importance of social scientists demonstrating 'real world' insight and knowledge for stakeholders (Tilley & Woodthorpe, 2011), where we critiqued the pervasive assumption that anonymity is a moral and ethical 'good' within social science research. This was an issue that I did not foresee touching on my own life some ten years later when I wanted to write auto/biographically about my son.

Hence, I am not unfamiliar with the demands of conducting potential evocative and emotionally demanding research, nor writing about doing so, and arguably I was well equipped to write auto/biographically when my son arrived. My second child was born with a rare cranio-facial syndrome that results in his need for a tracheostomy to breathe safely. He has no cognitive difficulties that we are aware of and he is fun, cheeky, and gorgeous.

## *Why did I 'go public'?*

It was three years after his birth that I felt a strong compulsion to share what I had learned to date and my interaction with 'the system'. Those first 1000 days had been spent in a blur of hospitals and appointments: my son was in a high-level Neonatal Intensive Care Unit for three months after he was born, and in the first year of his life alone, he had five surgeries. He had been taken by emergency ambulance to hospital on numerous occasions, and up to his third birthday, we usually had around four to five medical appointments a week, some at a hospital a 45–60-minute drive away and some at home. At the time of writing, this has dropped to around one to two appointments a week, which I oversee and attend because (i) the organisational skills and quick thinking required to bring together a lot of complex information in appointments play to my skillset, and (ii) because in the first three years of his life, I significantly reduced my working hours to be able to accommodate the appointments and this trend has continued.

Alongside these numerous appointments, my son was repeatedly assessed for his needs and resulting care provision in the first few years of his life. This is because he requires specialist care: his airway means he can only be cared for by someone who is tracheostomy trained, as if it becomes blocked it is a life-threatening emergency. Because of his compromised airway, he is considered to have a life-threatening condition and is therefore eligible for Children's Palliative Care (see Postavaru, Swaby, & Swaby, 2021). Spending time at our local children's hospice, having carers in our house night and day, attending so many appointments (at last count we routinely deal with 20+ clinical and care specialisms), and navigating the bureaucracy of the care funding system had been overwhelming. And this overwhelm was for someone who is highly educated, has social and financial capital to draw on, and who has the confidence to self-advocate. It was on this basis, because of my background and academic platform, that after my son's third birthday I felt compelled to share my experiences and found an appropriate avenue to do so in a hybrid-academic opinion piece intended for a clinical paediatric audience (Woodthorpe, 2022). There, I wrote about being a Personal Health Budget holder and its associated bureaucratic demands. Around this time I also started to get involved in supporting national charities representing disabled and medically complex children, the result of which led me to be invited to meetings with senior governmental policymakers tasked with reviewing social care provision. During these interactions, I identified and positioned myself as 'Kate the mum' rather than 'Kate the academic'.

## The ambiguous position: advocate, parent, or academic?

The blurring of boundaries – whether I was writing auto/biographically as an academic in Woodthorpe (2022) or advocating as a parent to policymakers – quickly became difficult to manage, and I began to have a crisis of confidence as to whether I was exploiting my son to progress my career. I found myself in an ambiguous and uncertain position, simultaneously a professional academic, a parent carer, and an advocate:

> Social researchers concerned with domestic and intimate issues are involved in the social construction and material production of knowledge within the domain of public, and academic discourses. Ambiguity thus arises when we seek simultaneously to serve an academic audience while also remaining faithful to forms of knowledge gained in domestic, personal and intimate settings.
>
> *(Edwards and Ribbens, 1998, p. 2)*

The simultaneous multi-layering of roles has been noted in Jago's (2011) moving account of navigating her different roles and functions in the everyday with her partner and his children, and in my case led to much agonising and, in all honesty, regret. In many ways I had made some key decisions in my son's early life that set all this in motion: without (over) thinking, within several months of his birth I had consented to share his name and pictures with charities to help raise the profile of their work. His name and his condition were now 'out there' online and I could not get them back – something which I now question as I become aware of the perils of oversharing or 'sharenting' (Steinberg, 2017 cited in Saville, 2020). The risks of oversharing were further brought home when I learned that other parents gave their child a pseudonym or anonymised their condition to protect their privacy (for example Moxham, 2021). In those early days, I had, perhaps naively, wanted to be open about my son, his syndrome and its consequences, as he and I are *real* people, with *real* experiences and *real* feelings. I had not thought through the implications of making him public, of the potential for critique, nor of the consequences of him finding references to himself online or in my academic work later in life. Learning from this, in my auto/biographic academic work I have decided not to disclose his name or condition beyond reference to his tracheostomy.

In marrying my professional and personal life, my crisis of confidence was leading me to question what I was doing and why. Was I advocating for my son and all those children like him and their families? Or was I trying to exploit my experience as an academic who is used to writing for publication? Or was I seeking to counteract the often emotionless and dispassionate academic research on parenting a child with complex medical needs? It was these questions that led me to present on the ethics of writing auto/biographically at the British Sociological Association's Auto/Biography Annual Conference in the summer of 2021 and again at the University of Bath's Centre for Qualitative Research Symposium on Researcher Vulnerability in January 2022, on which the rest of this chapter is based.

## The personal and the professional

The remainder of this chapter is set against this auto/biographical backdrop: a melting-pot of ambiguity and uncertainty, while also recognising the responsibility of an academic platform. Certainly, I am not the first to grapple with these issues. Feminist writers in particular have long debated the intersection of 'public knowledge and private lives' (Edwards & Ribbens, 1998) and the location of the 'I' within social research (Letherby, 2003; Ellis, 2004). In terms of research ontology (broadly speaking, the influence of worldview on methods), this personal and professional interplay has been conceptualised in relation to the ontological positions of subjectivity and objectivity. Over 40 years ago Lakoff and Johnson (1980) recognised the limitations of such opposing ontological positions and identified 'intersubjectivity' as a way of conceptualising and recognising the researcher was an imperfect person producing robust insight and knowledge from a particular vantage point. In other words, Lakoff and Johnson argued, knowledge production was the outcome of an intermingled (and somewhat messy) personal and professional research process '… rather than the researcher being separate from the field of study' (Valentine, 2008, p. 6). In my specialist field of death studies, myself and colleagues have reflected at length on this intersubjective position given that the topic we study is one we have already experienced or will experience ourselves. As a result, we inevitably bring 'emotional baggage' and lived experience to our work (see Valentine, 2007; Visser, 2017; Woodthorpe, 2011; Mallon & Elliot, 2020). Within this literature is a recognition that the researcher's self shapes how research is conducted, data generated, and any subsequent analysis, not least because research participants will respond in particular ways according to the researcher's age, gender, ethnicity, communication skills, and so on (Woodthorpe, 2009). Moreover, elsewhere death studies academics have written auto/biographically about their own first-hand encounters with death and how their academic experience has shaped those intimate encounters (see for example Troyer, 2020), suggesting that the professional can also inform the personal.

This work within death studies has drawn on and contributed to a now well-established body of literature on auto/biographical and autoethnographic research methods, which principally involve writing about one's own life (Ellis, 2004; Kara, 2020). Within these literatures, there has been much discussion about the ethical implications of doing so, including questions about privacy, the risk of harm, the responsibilities that come with personal disclosure, and the value of identifying or anonymising others (see Parsons & Chappell, 2020). In her chapter on the Handbook of Auto/Biography, Saville (2020) has reflected on writing auto/biographically about her son, arguing that to mitigate the risk of being (or being seen to be) exploitative, auto/biographical work can be understood within a tradition of 'storytelling'. Saville's chapter has been critical to my reflections on the motive, purpose, and risks of writing about my son. As noted already, a central question for me in sharing information and writing auto/biographically was the extent to which I was exploiting my son for my career. After all, I got a publication out of my experience in an internationally reputable journal that led to new contacts and connections, and which I could put on my CV and contribute to my all-important citation metrics.

I realise this. But I also realise that as an academic with a voice and experience of writing, I may conversely have *a responsibility* to make public some of the experiences that are traditionally hidden behind closed doors, or to counteract the prevailing narrative of care burden and distress (see below). If I chose not to, I was painfully aware that I could be contributing to the marginalisation of disabled and medically complex children like my son and his peers (Rogers, 2020). By opting to *not* use my academic platform, I could therefore be complicit with the neglect of disabled and medically complex children in the public domain. After all, 'missing data, or the "silencing" of stories too traumatic to relieve, [means that] disabled communities may experience socio-political death' (Saville, 2020, p. 640).

I have dwelled at length on this question as there is no established social scientific literature on my son's syndrome, and a relatively small body of academic work on the lived experience of families of children with complex medical needs or in receipt of Children's Palliative Care. What does exist on the syndrome is mainly intended for clinical audiences, reduced to its genetic origins, cranio-facial symptoms, and subsequent surgical interventions (see Cobb, Green, Gill, Ayliffe, Lloyd, Bulstrode, & Dunaway, 2014); the everyday lived experience of the syndrome is entirely absent. At the same time, parenting a child with medical complexity, or a life-limiting or life-threatening condition, is chiefly discussed in academic literature in terms of 'care burden' and parental psychological distress (a good example of which is Boyden, Hill, Nye, Bona, Johnston, Hinds, Friebert, Kang, Hays, Hall, Wolfe & Feudtner, 2022). This prevailing narrative of burden and distress did not resonate with my experience, and I felt that in writing auto/biographically, I could, in some small way, rectify this perception (even misconception) of parental victimhood – and indeed, that I perhaps had an obligation to, as someone with a voice.

My ambiguous position, accompanied by concerns about potential exploitation and a contradictory sense of obligation, meant I reached an impasse relatively swiftly after writing Woodthorpe (2022). Similar to Saville (2020), I was acutely aware that sharing information about my son, who one day may read what I have said, was riddled with risk. Like Saville's son, mine is cognitively able and will one day – I hope – be an independent and fully functioning adult. And, like Saville, I have been (and am still) unsure as to whether – as he ages and becomes an adult – he would approve of my sharing information about his life during childhood:

> ... the telling of my own personal story and experiences implicate, not only myself, but the person I cherish most – my son. I am all too aware that, one day, my son may decide to read my work – and what then, *what would he make of it?*
>
> *(Saville, 2020, p. 636, original emphasis)*

Not only was I concerned about the ethics of sharing my son's information without his consent, but I was increasingly concerned about how exposed I would be in doing so and the bigger question of whether I would be resilient enough to deal with critique. In making the decision about whether to continue to write auto/biographically, I found myself returning to ideas about emotion work and resilience in academia. Originating from Hochschild (1979) and her conceptualisation of emotion management as a performative, affective, and embodied activity, emotion work has become one of the most enduring concepts in psychology, sociology, and allied disciplines over the last 40 years. Within the academy, it has been used to understand the practice of qualitative research (Dickson-Swift, James, Kippen, & Liamputtong, 2009) and the feelings of shame that can come from peer review (Horn, 2016). Within this context, putting one's ideas 'out there' and opening them to evaluation requires a consideration amount of resolve and resilience in being able to deal with rejection (ibid). Much has been written on the sources of personal resilience and why it matters in higher education (see for example Berg & Seeber, 2016; Jacobs, Cintrón & Canton, 2002), with working conditions producing an environment that requires an academic to have a 'thick skin' (Horn, 2016).

Certainly, the need for resilience in your *ideas* being subject to appraisal is well established in peer review, which is part and parcel of contemporary academic practice. But by 2022, as I write this chapter, academics do *much* more than peer review and sharing ideas in peer-reviewed publications. The twenty-first century academic is expected and required to be a self-promoter via 'public engagement' and 'knowledge exchange' activities (as they are called in the UK), actively disseminating work through social media, podcasts, media interviews, and working with others to generate research 'impact' (see Smith, Bandola-Gill, Meer, Stewart & Watermeyer, 2020). To do all of this is to expose one's ideas to non-academic audiences and be willing to be appraised *beyond* the academy. From my own experience, writing about 'evidence' and your analysis, even when openly recognising that this comes from an intersubjective ontological position, is a million times easier than when you are writing about the 'topic' of your own life and – most critically for me – about your own child. Whether one is publishing academically or sharing work with non-academics, the resilience that is required to be able to deal with potential criticism, scathing comments and reviews, and just downright rudeness necessitates enormous emotional energy and mental reserves (Boynton, 2021). The ability to do is a significant part of the job and requires capacity. This capacity, I have come to recognise over time, is something that I simply do not possess, as the vast majority of my energy is being channelled into keeping family life and my career afloat.

## When enough is enough

Understanding that I did not have the reserves to do the emotion work required to engage with critique, it was after I presented at the Centre for Qualitative Research annual symposium in early 2022 that I realised I was not in a position to write more auto/biographical work in this area. The academic 'topic' of complex medical needs in childhood and Children's Palliative Care is very close to my heart as a parent and advocate, and I am not able to deal with (or even contemplate) the emotion work that will be required to continue to put my son and myself 'out there'. The two presentations I have given to date have been a mechanism to test out ideas and learn from others, and this book chapter has been a cathartic way to reflect on this process and draw a line under it, for now. Beyond these, I do not have the resilience as an academic to deal with any fallout of sharing more detail of my son's or my personal life, and as an advocate, I will from hereon provide only limited and select support for charities that represent his syndrome. I simply feel too exposed in my ambiguous position as an academic, a parent, and an advocate. This decision was cemented when I read responses to a blog post by Rachel Wright, a nurse, trainer, and parent to a child with complex medical needs who has published accounts of her own experience. In response to the post, another parent commented 'You appear to be a narcissist who's only goal is to service your own ego, even if that is at the expense of your child's self-esteem' (used with permission from Born at the Right Time, 2016). Rachel dealt with this comment robustly but despite having 20 years of peer reviews under my belt, I felt a visceral reaction to seeing such an accusation and realised that I could not deal with such feedback from an anonymous source if I were to go any further with writing about my son and his/our experience, be that from an academic via peer review or a non-academic audience.

The susceptibilities of researchers, as real-life flawed human beings with fallibilities and feelings, are not often and openly acknowledged in the academy. Beyond debate about the practice of academic peer review – which is about reviewing and critiquing *ideas* not *authors* – there is scant recognition of the emotion work and resilience required for twenty-first century academics in putting themselves out there and their work into the public domain. I have found that this emotion work is amplified when sharing information within the auto/biographical tradition and when writing about your child (Saville, 2020). In terms of navigating the conflicting feelings I have outlined in this chapter, it is Saville's work that has reverberated with me the most, when she acknowledged the fear of making intimate information visible, while at the same time feeling a sense of obligation to publicise first-hand experience to help others. Saville's wisdom in pointing towards 'storytelling' as an ethos (or even mantra) in writing about her child has been heartening. This storytelling approach, she advocates, emphasises observation and interaction rather than first-hand embodied experiences, and reflects Birch's (1998) warning to be mindful of the *why* and *what* you produce, and how it could be consumed. A philosophy of storytelling has contributed to this chapter and fed into Woodthorpe (2022), which involved recounting my son's care needs and the multifaceted roles I have been required to undertake since his arrival: as his translator, educator, facilitator, nurse, personal assistant, and project manager. In Woodthorpe (2022) I felt I was sharing my story up to that point, and that that story could be helpful to the clinical paediatric readership. In writing this chapter I feel I have shared our story in terms of *the process* of writing autobiographically and revealing what I have been through to get to the point where I bow out. By telling this story I am acknowledging my privileged academic platform, accounting for sharing some of his information to date, and making visible some of the intellectual and ethical grappling I have gone through in deciding whether to continue. I have told a story about how I have reached a threshold that I cannot breach, even if – for now – it means I am contributing to the marginalisation or concealment of my son and people like him.

In coming to this conclusion, I have drawn on what I call my 'my inner barometer'. A gut instinct, this barometer has helped me to determine whether or not I am being ethically exploitative or, conversely, neglecting my obligation as an academic to give voice to a hidden world. My barometer tells me to stop for now and that if I chose to return to writing auto/biographically in the future, it will be as an academic storyteller. If I become that storyteller, I will rely heavily on those who have trodden the path before me in sharing their personal experiences, most notably Saville (2020), and I will trust my husband and, in time, my son himself, to determine what to reveal and what should remain private.

## Conclusion

This chapter has considered the ethical implications of writing about your own child and the emotion work required when working within the auto/biographical tradition. It has considered issues of exploitation versus obligation, the blurring of identity when it comes to being an academic/parent/advocate, and revealed how I have reached the point where I have decided to stop writing auto/biographically. It has shown how resilience – the mental and emotional energy to share insight and deal with the consequences – is absolutely critical for the twenty-first-century academic who is expected to continually make public their work, not only to their peers, but to the general public and stakeholders. For me, writing autobiographically about my son and thus making him/me public includes risks to him and *future* him, and my inner barometer is telling me to stop. If I return to writing about him in the future, it will be within the tradition of academic storytelling advocated by Saville (2020). I urge anyone interested in this area to read her work.

## Acknowledgements

One day my son might read this chapter, or be told about it by someone else. I may not be around to discuss with him why I wrote it and what I felt I could contribute through doing so. To him, know that in writing this chapter I have sought to make sense of the challenges of sharing and not sharing yours and our experience, and where I have now drawn the line. I am incredibly proud of you and the person you are becoming. You are incredible and I love you very much.

## References

Berg, M., & Seeber, M.K. (2016). *The Slow Professor: Challenging the Culture of Speed in the Academy*. Toronto: University of Toronto Press.

Birch, M. (1998). Re/constructing research narratives: Self and sociological identity in alternative settings. In J. Ribbens, & R. Edwards (Eds.), *Feminist Dilemmas in Qualitative Research: Public Knowledge and Private Lives* (pp. 171–185). London: Sage.

Born at the Right Time (2016). Four reasons my son won't accept his 100% attendance award. Blog post, date accessed 12/05/22, available online at: https://www.bornatther ighttime.com/2017/07/01/son-wont-accepting-100-attendance-award/

Boyden, J.Y., Hill, D.L., Nye, R.T., Bona, K., Johnston, E.E., Hinds, P., Friebert, S., Kang, T.I., Hays, R., Hall, M., Wolfe, J., & Feudtner, C. (2022). Pediatric palliative care parents' distress, financial difficulty, and child symptoms. *Journal of Pain and Symptom Management*, 63, 271–282.

Boynton, P. (2021). *Being Well in Academia: Ways to Feel Stronger, Safer and More Connected*. London: Routledge.

Cobb, A.R.M., Green, B., Gill, D., Ayliffe, P., Lloyd, T.W., Bulstrode, N., & Dunaway, D. (2014). The surgical management of Treacher Collins syndrome. *British Journal of Oral and Maxillofacial Surgery*, 52, 581–589.

Dickson-Swift, V., James, E.L., Kippen, S., & Liamputtong, P. (2009). Researching sensitive topics: Qualitative research as emotion work. *Qualitative Research*, 9, 61–79.

Edwards, R., & Ribbens, J. (1998). Living on the edges: Public knowledge, private lives, personal experience. In J. Ribbens, & R. Edwards (Eds.), *Feminist Dilemmas in Qualitative Research: Public Knowledge and Private Lives* (pp. 1–23). London: Sage.

Ellis, C. (2004). *The Ethnographic I: A Methodological Novel about Autoethnography*. Oxford: Altamira Press.

Hochschild, A.R. (1979). Emotion work, feeling rules, and social structure. *The American Journal of Sociology*, 85, 551–575.

Horn, S.A. (2016). The social and psychological costs of peer review: Stress and coping with manuscript rejection. *Journal of Management Inquiry*, 25, 11–26.

Jacobs, L., Cintrón, J., & Canton, C.E. (Eds.) (2002). *The Politics of Survival in Academia: Narratives of Inequity, Resilience, and Success*. Lanham, MD: Rowman & Littlefield Publishers.

Jago, B.J. (2011). Shacking up: An autoethnographic tale of cohabitation. *Qualitative Inquiry*, 17, 204–219.

Kara, H. (2020). *Creative Research Methods: A Practical Guide*, 2nd ed. Bristol: Policy Press.

Lakoff, G., & Johnson, M. (1980). *Metaphors We Live By*. Chicago, IL: Chicago University Press.

Leather, M. (2019). Finding my professional voice. In B. Humberstone, & H. Prince (Eds.), *Research Methods in Outdoor Studies*. London: Routledge, 130–140.

Letherby, G. (2003). *Feminist Research in Theory and Practice*. Buckingham: Open University Press.

Letherby, G. (2022). Thirty years and counting: An-other auto/biographical story. *Auto/Biography Review*, 3, 13–31.

Mallon, S., & Elliot, I. (2020). What is 'sensitive' about sensitive research? The sensitive researchers' perspective. *International Journal of Social Research Methodology*, 24, 523–535.

Moxham, J. (2021). *The Cracks That Let the Light In: What I Learned from My Disabled Son*. London: Endeavour.

Parsons, J.M., & Chappell, A. (Eds.) (2020). *The Palgrave Handbook of Auto/Biography*. Basingstoke: Palgrave Macmillan.

Postavaru, G.-I., Swaby, H., & Swaby, R. (2021). A meta-ethnographic study of father's experiences of caring for a child with a life-limiting illness. *Palliative Medicine*, 35, 261–279.

Ronai, C.R. (1995). Multiple reflections of child abuse: An argument for a layered account. *Journal of Contemporary Ethnography*, 23, 395–426.

Rogers, C. (2020). Social justice and disability: Voices from the inside. In J.M. Parsons, & A. Chappell (Eds.), *The Palgrave Handbook of Auto/Biography* (pp. 599–607). Basingstoke: Palgrave Macmillan.

Saville, K.-M. (2020). Co-constructed auto/biographies in dwarfism mothering research: Imagining opportunities for social justice. In J.M. Parsons, & A. Chappell (Eds.), *The Palgrave Handbook of Auto/Biography* (pp. 633–656). Basingstoke: Palgrave Macmillan.

Sherry, M. (2019). Disablist hate speech online. In M. Sherry, T. Olsen, J. Solstad Vedeler, & J. Eriksen (Eds.), *Disability Hate Speech: Social, Cultural and Political Contexts* (pp. 40–66). London: Routledge.

Smith, K., Bandola-Gill, J., Meer, N., Stewart, E., & Watermeyer, R. (Eds.) (2020). *The Impact Agenda: Controversies, Consequences and Challenges*. Bristol: Policy Press.

Sparkes, A.C. (2002). Autoethnography: Self-indulgence or something more. *Ethnographically Speaking: Autoethnography, Literature, and Aesthetics*, 9, 209–232.

Tilley, E., & Woodthorpe, K. (2011). Is it the end for anonymity as we know it? A critical examination of the ethical principle of autonomy in the context of 21st century demands on the qualitative researcher. *Qualitative Research*, 11, 197–212.

Troyer, J. (2020). *Technologies of the Human Corpse*. Cambridge: MIT Press.

Valentine, C. (2007). Methodological reflections: Attending and tending the role of the researcher in the construction of bereavement narratives. *Qualitative Social Work*, 6, 159–176.

Valentine, C. (2008). *Bereavement Narratives: Continuing Bonds in the Twenty-First Century*. London: Routledge.

Visser, R. (2017). 'Doing death': Reflecting on the researcher's subjectivity and emotions. *Death Studies*, 41, 6–13.

Wilkinson, S., & Wilkinson, C. (2020). Performing care: Emotion work and 'dignity work' – A joint autoethnography of caring for our mum at the end of life. *Sociology of Health and Illness*, 42, 1888–1901.

Woodthorpe, K. (2009). Reflecting on death: The emotionality of the research encounter. *Mortality*, 41, 70–86.

Woodthorpe, K. (2011). Researching death: Methodological reflections on the management of critical distance. *International Journal of Social Research Methodology*, 14, 99–109.

Woodthorpe, K. (2022). Being a personal health budget holder: Becoming a 'professional parent'. *Archives of Disease in Childhood*, 107, 100–101.

# 7

# AFFECTING ACCOUNTS

## Autobiographical memoirs and the vulnerable researcher

*Cassie Lowe*

## Introduction

The methodology of textual analysis has hitherto seen little attention concerning notions of vulnerability in the researcher. However, this vulnerability is a particularly prevalent consideration regarding the researcher of autobiographical writing, where an author will take time to detail their life experiences in their texts in much the same capacity as many interview participants. The point at which a researcher undertaking this approach can become vulnerable is arguably dependent on the topic of focus for the text. Many of the texts within this genre focus on traumatic and sometimes horrific experiences in the author's life, and many scholars of these texts can, therefore, be adversely affected by undertaking the lengthy qualitative analysis of them. A researcher utilising a textual analysis approach of such memoirs will spend many hours reading and re-reading passages, exploring the language used, and applying methodological frameworks to work towards a better understanding of the author's experience as represented in the text. Researching through these means offers a first-hand account of the author's experience of events they have witnessed or been part of and offers an in–depth and rich picture of this experience. This can, however, also cause some vicarious distress in the researcher who, whilst committed to sharing and understanding these narratives, can feel affected by the accounts they are reading. It is this impact on the researcher that requires greater attention in relation to their own vulnerability.

The concept of researcher vulnerability has been explored in relation to the individual experience (Komaromy, 2020), but not yet in the context of individual text-based research specifically. Despite this gap in the literature, researcher vulnerability has many connections with the experience of undertaking textual analysis of autobiographies of a sensitive nature. Researcher vulnerability more broadly has been aligned with research that explores sensitive topic areas or activities that

DOI: 10.4324/9781003349266-10

can put the researcher at risk of harm, which could be emotional, physical, or psychological (Lee, 1993; Lee & Renzetti, 1993; Downey, Hamilton & Catterall, 2007). Jafari et al. (2013, p. 1193) provide a useful representation of these risks in their conceptual model of researcher vulnerability. They describe several catalysts for researcher vulnerability, such as sensitive contexts, physical contexts, emotional exposure, interpretivist and/or qualitative research methods, working within lone researcher paradigm, closeness/immersion in the field, and empathetic responses. These catalysts can create experiences of researcher vulnerability, such as emotional distress, threat to physical safety, guilt, fear, frustration, uncertainty, isolation, and heightened levels of stress. Finally, the potential outcomes of this are described as being burn-out, with the project's completion being put in jeopardy, de-sensitisation, personal reflection, and researcher disempowerment.

This chapter offers an opportunity to expand understanding on the different ways a researcher can be made vulnerable. For the purposes of this chapter, the focus is on the emotional and psychological impact on the researcher undertaking textual analysis, whose field of study can greatly affect their overall sense of emotional and mental wellbeing. The impact of this can inspire feelings of guilt, anger, fear, anxiety, and states of hopelessness in the researcher (Dickson-Swift, James, Kippen & Liamputtong, 2009; Jafari, Dunnett, Hamilton & Downey, 2013; Mallon & Elliott, 2021). Jafari et al. corroborate this and highlight that the level and intensity of vulnerability in the researcher is centred on the emotional impact of the experience (2013, p. 1189). With this focus of vulnerability in mind, the discussion in this chapter will be supported by my own experiences researching life-writing texts, which have led me to recognise and appreciate the vulnerabilities of researching traumatic autobiographical memoirs. A discussion of this is pertinent for researchers in this field more broadly, as exposure to emotionally demanding research can lead to stress, isolation, exhaustion, and further increase the risk of vulnerability (Woodby, Williams, Wittich & Burgio, 2011). I have chosen to shed my perceived 'cloak of invulnerability' as a researcher (Mallon & Elliott, 2019, p. 11) to offer a starting point for further exploration and discussion. This is in the hope that this discussion will lead to better support for researchers both in qualitative methods more broadly and specifically for those undertaking textual analysis of trauma-focused autobiographies.

To start to understand researcher vulnerability in the context of textual analysis, this chapter will first outline the research method of textual analysis, to draw out its comparisons to wider qualitative methods and pose some considerations for the approach. It will thereafter consider the practice of what is commonly referred to as 'trigger warnings' (content notes that are deployed in an attempt to prepare viewers and readers for difficult texts or discussions to which they may be vulnerable) in this context, which is an approach gaining popularity in the educational setting, particularly in the arts, humanities and social sciences research fields. This is an important point for this chapter to discuss as the increasing practice of providing trigger warnings offers a key consideration for this form of qualitative research in relation to notions of vulnerability. It will explore to what extent this approach can be positioned as a potential ally to researcher vulnerability to support the textual analysis researcher. This chapter will then turn to explore autoethnographically the vulnerabilities of undertaking this form of research further. I will discuss two memoirs from the French author Annie Ernaux, whose works are more recently gaining critical attention, to draw out and discuss to what extent the vulnerable researcher paradigm can be extended to the researcher of autobiographies, but also to highlight where the limitations, or differences, might be. These texts have been chosen as they are examples of two texts that have had a significant impact on the author of this chapter and thus offer an opportunity to explore the concept of researcher vulnerability in the context of textual analysis autoethnographically. I will turn to each text separately to explore researcher vulnerability in light of my own experiences, so that it might encourage further exploration into the vulnerabilities faced by the scholar of traumatic, or emotionally sensitive, autobiographical writing, which could be extended to include wider textual analysis more broadly. Following this, I will consider the notion of researcher vulnerability as described in the literature, to ground my experiences in light of those described by other qualitative researchers in contexts dissimilar to my own, to explore the usefulness of the term in relation to textual analysis. This chapter aims not to dissuade such valuable research, but to offer a greater application to the term of researcher vulnerability and to conclude that there is an ethical imperative that research institutions must consider more meaningfully the impact of vulnerable research on the textual analysis researcher at the point of project creation and approval.

## Textual analysis qualitative research

The textual analysis research methodology is at its foundation comparable to the thematic analysis of transcripts undertaken in qualitative research more broadly. In the process of textual analysis, one reads with a mind to the theory or phenomena they are exploring, and themes within the text are established through the process of active reading (see McKee, 2003, for an outline of textual analysis methodology). For example, for the two primary texts considered in this chapter, I was guided by the Freudian and Kristevan psychoanalytical framework, which enabled me to draw out key themes within Annie Ernaux's memoirs, *Happening* and *I Remain in Darkness*, through exposing the commonalities in language, behaviours, and descriptions of her experiences. This is not unlike the active reading of qualitative analysis more broadly, which Braun and Clarke describe as being one in which the researcher plays an active role in identifying patterns/themes and selecting those that are of interest to the research (Braun & Clarke, 2006). As it is in thematic analysis of transcripts in other qualitative methods, so too it is in textual analysis that '[a] theme captures something important about the data in relation to the research question, and represents some level of patterned response or meaning within the data set' (Braun & Clarke, 2006, p. 82). So, in many ways, the methodological approach can be understood as mirroring that of broader thematic analysis of qualitative data. The distinction, then, lies in the form. I have not, nor has anyone else, collected this data through an interview or focus group, nor has the task been set in a research capacity for an autobiographical author to be a 'research participant' who has been asked to keep notes of their experiences. Annie Ernaux is an avid writer of diaries and constructs her memoirs from these notes, but not with a mind solely to having them read and qualitatively analysed in this capacity, unlike the informed consent of research participants in other qualitative approaches.

Nevertheless, autobiographical memoirs provide an account of an experience directly from the subject; one that has been crafted to convey the exacting specifications of an event in the author's eyes. Ernaux writes in the opening to her memoir, '[a]bove all I shall endeavour to revisit every single image until I feel that I have physically bonded with it, until a few words spring forth, of which I can say, "yes, that's it."' (2019b, p. 19). The autobiography situates the author as the main subject of focus for their narrative and requires them to engage with their experiences deeply over a length of time to convey them as accurately as possible within the confines of language. It can be positioned, therefore, to be more considered in its form than that of an interview research participant, who verbally communicates their story, with limited ability to revise or edit their choice of words post hoc. However, both approaches to narrative telling provide valuable data for the researcher. In the interview setting, a participant will express their experience in the language that best captures their understanding of and relationship with their experience. In this setting, they use language that is selected in the moment, which arguably often makes the response emotionally rawer and also enables non-verbal communication channels, such as tone and body expression, though, this is often left out of the final transcription analysis (Warr, 2004). Written qualitative data, for example in the form of open-text boxes on surveys, might also be written with haste and thus fall into this category, though this is certainly not the rule and therefore might have more autobiographical tendencies in its considered linguistic selection. In the writing of an autobiography, the author crafts their narrative with a highly considered approach; time is taken to ensure the words chosen pin down the experience with more precision and with this it is potentially purposefully trying to be more emotionally affecting to the reader. Whether the language used to describe the person's experience is verbally selected in the moment of data collection, or time is taken by the person to consider and redraft their descriptions, both narrative forms can be seen to be equally emotive through different means, and therefore affective for the researcher.

With the autobiographical writing of experiences in mind, the ability authors have to redraft and edit their writing might give rise to questions concerning the potentially fictitious nature of this genre. One might ask the following questions of this form: what about biographical selectivity? What of the writer's ability to embellish and exaggerate facts? What of their subjectivity in relation to the events experienced? And so, how can a considered, carefully crafted account be used for qualitative analysis to understand 'real' and 'raw' experiences like those, you might say, of participants describing events in an interview? These are valuable questions to ask of this form of narrative and they might at first appear to set a distinguishing quality between life-speaking in a research interview context and life-writing as a genre for qualitative research. To counter this argument, a quote from R. Victoria Arana could offer some insight, excusing the masculine pronoun, she states,

> it is a rare autobiographer who himself believes he is truly undressing. Most autobiographers think they are performing in full and elaborate costume [...] most psychoanalysts would agree with them. A person hardly ever stands psychologically naked before another, for where self-protection is not neurotic it is a mature art.
>
> *(1983, p. 64)*

To respond to the questions posed above, then, one must ask another, when are we not standing before another in a full and elaborate costume? And the above questions could, therefore, be asked in turn of the interview participant. One might argue that the research participant in an interview is responding in conditions that require integrity to their responses, which do not confine the writing of an autobiographer on an ethical ground. However, it can be reasonably suggested to counter this, that we all proceed with some form of protective layer of an elaborate costume, whether crafting a literary text or telling our story verbally to another. It is very rare that we stand entirely psychologically naked, no matter the context. Selection, misremembering, and exaggeration can impact all forms of narrative responses in qualitative methods.

The multiple iterations to an autobiography, crafted in the most part by the author, but also often at the disposal of an editor who may play a minor or major part in the final published document, provide room for creative manipulation of their experiences – some aspects brightened or shaded depending on their view or the impression they wish to make. However, in other qualitative analyses this is present in the participant but also in another guise through the researcher's role in transcribing and analysing the data in their reports and publication. The positionality of the researcher and their role in co-constructing the narratives of the participants in writing up the research plays an influential role in the final presentation of the data (Scotland, 2012; Rowe, 2014). In much the same way an author will shape their text based on highlighting key moments or details, the researcher, too, will shape their publication based on what they determine to be key phrases or descriptions of the participant's experiences. Complicating these matters further in qualitative research is the role the question set has in the data collected. The construction of the questions, with minor semantic changes, can alter the shape of the answers given and direct the responses from the participants. The researcher of both autobiography and transcribed interview accounts are then further bound by interpretation of the words written. This interpretation may be inaccurate in terms of the meaning intended by the author or participant, but no less valid as the role of the researcher must also be foregrounded in the co-construction of meaning.

This all raises epistemological questions to consider for both approaches. Is the goal of qualitative research to pursue absolute truths? Or, rather, as I would argue, is it to uncover subjective understandings of reality that we can then draw links, infer, and build theory through this co-construction of knowledge? This is not the wider focus of this chapter, but it is important to set the groundwork to highlight the qualitative approach of textual analysis and to consider to what extent researcher vulnerability in this field can be explored alongside other qualitative methods. So, whilst the delivery of the person's narrative differs in form, there are also similarities where one might have initially thought there to be irreconcilable differences. What is key to both qualitative approaches to research is that the narrative, the experience, and the subject are at the centre of the research approach. What is key for this chapter, however, in discussing the qualitative approach of textual analysis, is that the vulnerabilities being increasingly recognised for other researchers in this field should be further extended to include textual analysis researchers alongside them.

### Blurbs, synopses, trigger warnings: are they an ally to vulnerable research in textual analysis?

While the subject is, and should remain, at the centre of the research approach, greater attention should start to be considered for the researcher and the impact the narratives shared can have on them. This chapter will now turn to consider further the form of narrative in an autobiography in relation to the researcher's 'readiness' to be exposed to potentially triggering narratives. The impact a text can have on a researcher will differ between individuals due to their wider experiences and personal history, however, there are some topics that are more widely accepted as sensitive either emotionally or ethically. It is worthwhile considering to what extent a potential ally to the vulnerable researcher in a textual analysis context might be found in the use of trigger warnings, as an increasingly common educational practice used in higher education (Charles, Hare-Duke, Nudds, Franklin, Llewellyn-Beardsley, Rennick-Egglestone, Gust, Ng, Evans, Knox, Townsend, Yeo, & Slade, 2022). Trigger warnings are a method used to provide students with a forewarning that the content of a text or lesson might be distressing for them, so they can avoid this if it may cause them harm. This might be due to past traumas or experiences that can be upsetting for students to read about, view, explore, and discuss. Lockhart asserts that 'the purpose of a trigger warning is not to facilitate individuals' avoidance of traumatizing stimuli, but to prepare them to encounter such stimuli' (Lockhart, 2016, p. 64), emphasising that they are necessary tools for educators to have in order to assign the difficult and traumatic material that may expose students' vulnerabilities. Supporting this, Karasek argues that the use of trigger warnings allows disadvantaged groups to participate in upsetting topics and provides a more inclusive environment (2016).

However, the use of trigger warnings within higher education is not without its controversies. Vatz highlights that the use of trigger warnings is 'academically destructive' as they cease free speech at universities, where open-minded inquiry should be at the centre of learning rather than 'coddling' and 'infantilising' students (2016, pp. 53, 57). Jones et al. support this view that trigger warnings should come with their own warning and conclude that the use of trigger warnings in higher education classrooms had little impact on those who had experienced trauma (Jones, Bellet, & McNally, 2020). On the contrary, further research suggests that such warnings increased the anticipatory anxiety of students with no history of trauma and that, in a manner that is countertherapeutic, they caused trauma survivors to view their experiences as more central to their life narrative (Jones et al., 2020, p. 941). This leads us to consider that perhaps trigger warnings are not quite such an ally of the vulnerable researcher of texts, after all. More recently, educationalists propose a reframing of the phrase from 'trigger warnings' to 'content notes' (e.g., content note: the following text includes issues such as x and y), which might alleviate some of the issues raised by Jones et al., as it shifts the focus to information provision in a more value-neutral approach. Whether effective as a means to create a more inclusive environment, or, whether they work only to increase anxiety over a text being studied, it is important that we continue to consider the impact a text can have on the researcher and recognise that texts of this nature can be deeply affecting to individuals.

It is at this point that one might draw attention to the fact that for most texts, literary and film in particular, there is usually a forewarning to a certain extent on the blurb or synopsis of the text, irrespective of whether the 'trigger warning' label is applied. However, blurbs and synopses do not cover all events contained within a text purposefully, as these are often part of the narrative's development or twist. The two texts that will provide a focus for this chapter clearly state the subject matter in the blurb, Annie Ernaux's autobiographical memoir *Happening* highlights to the potential reader that this text is about her experience of receiving a clandestine abortion. The same is true of her memoir *I Remain in Darkness*, which focuses on her experiences of her mother's cognitive decline due to dementia. One might argue, therefore that this should have prepared me, and, by extension, other researchers in this field, for the experience of reading the traumatic and emotionally sensitive material contained within the text. Though, to counter this argument, one might also therefore argue that knowingly collecting data on a sensitive topic is enough to prepare a researcher for the topics at hand, however, as will be discussed later, this is not the case for other areas of sensitive qualitative research. A researcher cannot ever fully predict the impact a research topic will have on them, and what connections their subjects' experiences might have with their own, even if, and especially when, these connections and sensitivities are perhaps unconscious to and unexpected for the researcher (Howard & Hammond, 2019). Simply knowing that a topic of discussion in an interview or the events described in a memoir are of a sensitive nature does not automatically provide a protective and unbreakable barrier between the researcher and the subject of the narrative as will be discussed below. Trigger warnings or content forewarnings might not be the direct answer to this field of research, but there is still a need to consider the researcher's experience, and ensure care for them individually, to bring this vulnerability to the discussion more centrally and to consider frameworks or support packages that might be more appropriate to the task.

## Affecting accounts: autoethnography

I will now turn to the two texts which led me to consider the role of researcher vulnerability in textual analysis. At first, I thought the concept disconnected from the qualitative research I undertook in my capacity as a doctoral student of literature, however, in discussing the experiences described in researcher vulnerability with a colleague, I began to see distinct connections with what I had felt, which illuminated my experiences of researching literary texts of a sensitive and ethical nature. As researcher vulnerability seeks to centre the voice of the researcher and their experiences of research, I will now turn to these experiences of vulnerability in my own research autoethnographically, to provide some insight into the ways in which a text can affect a researcher during and beyond the analysis of an autobiography. It is my hope that this section, whilst focusing on my own subjective experience, will offer an opportunity to understand how and in what ways the concept of researcher vulnerability can apply to this context.

I will begin with my reflections on the first of two primary texts for this discussion, Annie Ernaux's autobiographical memoir, *Happening*. Part of the strength and prowess of Ernaux's writing style is its uniqueness. In place of the crushing and weighty blows of sentimentality in her writing style, she favours precise, crisp, and clean-cut descriptions. It is a text that is both emotionally exhausting and psychologically gripping. It is this text, *Happening*, that I have spent long hours poring over, deeply familiarising myself with Ernaux's account, memorising quotations, understanding it thematically, guided by psychoanalytic theory, and in many ways fulfilling the Freudian 'repetition compulsion' about which I was writing.[1] I first read Annie Ernaux's text *Happening* for my doctoral studies, and the affective nature of this text was staggering for me. Like many of her memoirs, *Happening* is short and uncompromising. As Ernaux describes her experiences, so we, too, follow each assault, each moment of despondency, and the final climactic and explosive scenes of the abortion. As I have indicated, the language is unforgiving to those who endeavour to hear her story. For example, in her description of the crescendo of her efforts to abort, she writes,

> I was seized with a violent urge to shit. I rushed across the corridor into the bathroom and squatted by the porcelain bowl, facing the door. I could see the tiles between my thighs. I pushed with all my strength. It burst forth like a grenade, in a spray of water that splashed the door. I saw a baby doll dangling from my loins at the end of a reddish cord.
>
> *(Ernaux, 2019b, p. 61)*

It is a powerful account, one that deservedly takes its toll to mirror the anguish and horrors of women who are trapped in these desperate circumstances, or worse.

It is a text that has stayed with me, and I believe it always will. The emotional weight experienced in reading and connecting with both the autobiographies present in this study remains with me. Such narratives need to be heard and deserve to be told as it speaks volumes to the stories of women across the globe today who face unsafe and illegal abortions. The statistics report from the World Health Organization shows that between 2010 and 2014, on average 56 million induced abortions occurred each year and, among the 56 million, 25 million of those were classified as unsafe abortions and eight million were deemed to be carried out in least-safe and dangerous conditions (World Health Organization, 2019). Perhaps it is with this context, that such practices and experiences are still so staggeringly common for so many women, that this text grips you so tightly and stays with you thereafter. Ernaux's talents lie in the pared-back nature of her writing; it is not laboursome nor self-pitying, but rather assertive, clear-cut, and direct. In reading this text, I felt the strength of its affect; my subjectivity as a fleshly living body felt attacked and felt in many ways exposed to the trauma of her experiences. In reading the descriptions of her life at this pivotal junction, I felt marked by the encounter, brandished by the scenes that unwaveringly deliver the reality of her despair and loneliness. It is a heavy subject matter, one that demands greater attention and research, but also one that stays with you. This text exposes you to the weight of the necessity of sharing and amplifying Ernaux's voice and others like hers who have experienced this.

The second text of focus for this section that deeply affected me also necessitates consideration in light of the notion of researcher vulnerability albeit in a different capacity. Ernaux's 1997 text *I Remain in Darkness* is a powerful reflection of familial love and the shifting role of her mother from protector to protected. In this text, we follow Ernaux's desperate attempts to help save her mother from dementia, followed by the inevitable decline and loss of her parent. This second text affected me in a different way to *Happening*. I felt angry for the women who have no options but to face an illicit abortion and horrified by Ernaux's personal account; it spoke to me as a human being and as a woman. However, *I Remain in Darkness* strongly affected me in a way that I had not been expecting. I was undertaking broader research into Ernaux's other memoirs, to support some of the conclusions for my thesis and read this text alongside others. *I Remain in Darkness* is a text that significantly affected me, and there were multiple points in my reading of the memoir where I had to stop and take considerable time in between sessions to get through the text. At the time, in 2018, I was beginning to suspect my own mother, who was 56 at the time, was starting to have problems with her memory and cognitive abilities. She has now been diagnosed with dementia, but at the time it was only a suspicion, and I was plagued by the ever-multiplying 'what ifs' and 'whens'. My response to this text was a stark realisation of my own vulnerability in relation to this topic and it was one of the strongest personally felt reactions I have ever experienced reading a literary text. The emotive and sensory imagery conjured up by Ernaux in this text still stays with me. Passages still come to mind when I am at a particularly low point in thinking about my mother's condition and I am unable to escape them. Ernaux describes early scenes in her mother's decline such as,

[i]nvariably, she mistakes my study for her bedroom. She opens the study door just a crack, realizes it's the wrong room and gently closes the door [...] Mounting panic. In one hour, the same thing will happen again. She has no idea where she is.

*(Ernaux, 2019a, p. 18)*

Examples such as this depict a not-too-distant future for my mother, which will unavoidably tumble quickly into the more emotionally hurtful and degrading episodes Ernaux describes later in her memoir, which still feel too raw to admit. The blurb did not provide enough forewarning for me to truly appreciate how much these suspicions about my mother were affecting me, how emotionally vulnerable and sensitive I was due to my initial suspicions, and it was not until I read this text that I felt the future being brought to me in a painful and stark realisation. I feel this sensitivity even more strongly now as the diagnosis is still fresh, which leads me to think; what if I had to read this text now? Perhaps having some knowledge of the concept of researcher vulnerability would allow myself to grant some grace to my experience, but perhaps I might, nevertheless, still feel the deeply affecting nature of this account.

## Affecting accounts and researcher vulnerability

Prior to my conversations with a colleague about the different ways a researcher can be made vulnerable, I had never considered textual analysis as being a methodology connected with this concept. For the most part, it takes place in safe locations, the subjects of study (authors) are not present during the research and unpredictable physically, unlike the participants and contexts associated with other qualitative methods (Jafari et al., 2013), and the accounts being read have not been recorded and transcribed by the researcher. The researcher undertaking textual analysis does not need to build rapport with the subject, unlike the live participant in other qualitative methods, and so there is no need to form a meaningful connection necessarily, where rapport is otherwise imperative for data collection (Dickson-Swift et al., 2009; Jafari et al., 2013). These differences are worth highlighting because they do distinguish the vulnerabilities of a researcher with live participants in a way that puts them at physical risk in addition to other vulnerabilities. However, the more I have considered the concept in relation to my own experiences, the more I have begun to realise the similarities in what I had experienced with those of vulnerable qualitative researchers more broadly, and consider that perhaps other researchers who undertake textual analysis of autobiographies of a sensitive nature have felt the same way. Perhaps at times they, too, have felt vulnerable.

Exploring the notion of a vulnerable researcher in the context of the qualitative research of textual analysis has led to a greater understanding of my experience. The research undertaken for these texts was draining of emotional and mental energy; spending five years reading these texts multiple times and writing and rewriting and analysing passages like the examples quoted above has burnt these narrative images into my mind. Micanovic et al. describe researcher vulnerability as '"emotionally demanding research," […] research that demands a tremendous amount of mental, emotional, or physical energy, and potentially affects or depletes the researcher's health or well-being.' (2020, p. 3). My mental and emotional state felt wounded by these texts, perhaps in different ways but certainly they are affectively charged texts for me. This does not also account for the peripheral research required to confidently discuss topics such as abortion, which informs one's understanding and engagement with the horrors of the text anew. Dickson-Swift et al. discuss the research of Alexander et al. (1989) who describe researchers who were greatly impacted by reading and analysing transcriptions of rape and sexual assault victims (Dickson-Swift, James, Kippen, & Liamputtong, 2007, p. 328). To draw some comparisons, the narrative account of *Happening* is an account of the author's experiences of sexual assault and the trauma of undertaking a back-room abortion – the memoir is a self-transcribed account of this traumatic experience. Other autobiographies may well cover topics of a similar nature to those in Alexander et al.'s study. These are true stories, an autobiography is just the literary form of this experience.

These traumatic stories are affecting the researcher regardless of the form of delivery. Of the vulnerable researchers, Dickson-Swift et al. assert that '[u]ndertaking qualitative research can be life-changing experience for some researchers, providing them with opportunities to assess certain aspects of their lives.' (2007, p. 342). Both texts described above affected me deeply. They spoke to me in my emotional and mental weak spot, one that I had not been aware of being such a vulnerable area of my psyche and forced me to assess my concerns in a new light. In *I Remain in Darkness* Ernaux painted a clear picture of the 'what ifs' and 'whens' and *Happening* gripped, infuriated, and left me feeling bruised by what I read. The impact of the exposure to these texts, and the emotional connections I have had with them have had profound consequences in my personal and professional life. Both experiences have led to action, the former forced me to take an active role in pursuing my suspicions about my mother with numerous doctors to get a diagnosis and support. The words of Ernaux echoing in my mind as I sought a diagnosis for her cognitive impairment. The latter has inspired a sense of necessity to act, which has shaped my future research on social inequalities and ignited a desire for my research hereafter to amplify the voices of those experiencing injustice. Whilst both have had some positive outcomes in the long term, as they provided opportunities to reassess and redirect my own efforts personally and professionally, the exposure has undeniably been emotionally draining and mentally affecting in many ways. This leads me to consider that if I had been a different person, in different circumstances, whether the outcomes would have been different. Perhaps those life-changing experiences that Dickson-Swift et al. (2007) describe above might not always lead to positive action, where for me it was a drive towards 'doing something about it' – 'it' being the emotional connection the texts had with my own vulnerabilities that caused my distress. This might be a common experience for other researchers, and it is both the affect and the effect that the text can have on a researcher that needs greater attention, with regard to both the positive and negative consequences of emotionally demanding research.

## Conclusion and recommendations

Whilst emotional responses in the qualitative researcher paradigm are seen to be a valuable part of the process, there lies in this the potential for a vulnerability that has hitherto been under-researched in relation to textual analysis of autobiographical memoirs. In my own experience, I have found that I corroborate with Davison's (2004) findings, that vulnerable research forces you to confront your own current or past traumas and I am interested to see to what extent other researchers of autobiographies have found this to be true of their experiences. Whilst the debate over the use and value of 'trigger warnings' continues, perhaps the essence of a discussion around greater support for researchers undertaking exploration of sensitive subjects is not too far removed from this debate. This is not to suggest that the precautions taken to consider the effects of these vulnerabilities for researchers need be, to use my earlier quotation from Vatz, 'infantilising' (2016, p. 57), but rather that this might open up a greater understanding to the research process for textual analysis and of researcher vulnerability in this field. The connection a researcher has to their subject, their participant or their topic of study is highly influential and can often have a positive relationship with the research process as one of reflexivity, but there is perhaps more to be considered alongside this for the vulnerabilities of this research that has yet to be explored in greater depth. Too often is the researcher positioned to be hidden or considered an unfeeling jar of objective containment. The process of socialisation in academic research culture places value on the objectivity of scientific research above all else, which leads to a sense of discomfort for the researcher in speaking about or recognising their own emotions (Dickson-Swift et al., 2009, p. 66). However, the experience of vulnerability can influence the researcher's engagement with and ultimately their analysis of the phenomena (Jafari et al., 2013; Komaromy, 2020). In recognising and appreciating that the researcher's emotions can give rise to vulnerability, we can not only better support researchers but also open the conversation more meaningfully around what effect this can have on the data and respect that this is a communicative process between research and researcher.

This chapter seeks not to suggest that the researcher's experience of vulnerability mirrors that of the people describing their stories and experiences. Nor should it be viewed as an attempt to dissuade researchers from undertaking this vulnerable research, as it is also often the topics that have an associated trauma or ethical sensitivity that require further research and understanding, to highlight the issues, work towards breaking down barriers, create opportunities, and expose inequality and injustice. These areas of focus are of paramount important to qualitative research, as the methodological approach enables an in-depth and rich data set, based on narratives of experience that give a window into lives often very different to the researcher's own (Warr, 2004). What this chapter aims to stress is that such research can have implications on researcher vulnerability, and this must include those researchers of traumatic autobiographies, which must have greater attention given to it. Ethics procedures are often aligned with a focus on the bureaucratic elements, rather than the impact on the researcher to protect them from harm or the shifting contexts of conducting research with participants (Robinson, 2020; Mallon & Elliott, 2021). This is a particularly pertinent and yet under-researched area in relation to text-based areas of sensitive research. The question of whose responsibility it is to provide support and what that support should look like still remains (Mallon & Elliott, 2019). However, this is an aspect of researcher experience that can have far-reaching consequences for those involved and so more practical steps need to be taken to work towards providing support, such as appropriate training in self-care and introducing researcher journals as a tool to enable emotional awareness and expression (Howard & Hammond, 2019). Considerations for researcher vulnerability could potentially be given at the research design and proposal stages to ensure that the individual's own vulnerabilities have been considered, and/or that, where necessary, the appropriate provision is in place to support all qualitative researchers of affecting accounts, including those undertaking textual analysis of traumatic or emotionally sensitive autobiographies.

## Acknowledgements

I would like to take this opportunity to thank my friend and colleague Dr. Jo Batey for introducing me to the concept of researcher vulnerability and being an excellent sounding board for this research. I would also like to thank Dr. Stuart Sims, who has remained a steadfast mentor for my professional development over the years and whose insightful feedback helped to shape my ideas for this chapter.

## Note

1 'Repetition compulsion' is a psychoanalytic theory first developed by Sigmund Freud in his essay 'Repeating, Remembering, and Working Through'. In this essay, he discusses his observation that subjects in his studies found themselves repeating events, or circumstances akin to the event, which have caused them trauma in their past. This manifests in their present experiences until, Freud proposes, they can be 'worked through' through psychoanalytic exploration.

## References

Alexander, J. G., de Chesnay, M., Marshall, E., Campbell, A. R., Johnson, S. & Wright, R. (1989). Parallel reactions in rape victims and rape researchers. *Violence and Victims, 4*, 57–62.

Arana, V. R. (1983). The psychoaesthetics of autobiography. *Biography, 6*, 53–67.

Braun, V. & Clarke, V. (2006). Using thematic analysis in psychology. *Qualitative Research in Psychology, 3*, 77–101.

Charles, A., Hare-Duke, L., Nudds, H., Franklin, D., Llewellyn-Beardsley, S., Rennick-Egglestone, S., Gust, O., Ng, F., Evans, E., Knox, E., Townsend, E., Yeo, C. & Slade,

M. (2022). Typology of content warnings and trigger warnings: Systematic review. *PLoS ONE*, *17*, 1–14.

Davison, J. (2004). Dilemmas in research: Issues of vulnerability and disempowerment for the social worker/researcher. *Journal of Social Work Practice*, *18*, 379–393.

Dickson-Swift, V., James, E. L., Kippen, S. & Liamputtong, P. (2007). Doing sensitive research: What challenges do qualitative researchers face? *Qualitative Research*, *7*, 327–353.

Dickson-Swift, V., James, E. L., Kippen, S. & Liamputtong, P. (2009). Researching sensitive topics: Qualitative research as emotion work. *Qualitative Research*, *9*, 61–79.

Downey, H., Hamilton, K., & Catterall, M. (2007) Researching vulnerability: What about the researcher? *European Journal of Marketing*, *41*, 734–739.

Ernaux, A. (2019a) (Originally published, 1997). *I Remain in Darkness*, trans. Tanya Leslie. London: Fitzcarraldo Editions.

Ernaux, A. (2019b). (Originally published, 2001). *Happening*, trans. Tanya Leslie. London: Fitzcarraldo Editions.

Howard, L. C. & Hammond, S. P. (2019). Researcher vulnerability: Implications for educational research and practice. *International Journal of Qualitative Studies in Education*, *32*, 411–428.

Jafari, A., Dunnett, S., Hamilton, K. & Downey, H. (2013). Exploring researcher vulnerability: Contexts, complications, and conceptualisation. *Journal of Marketing Management*, *29*, 1182–1200.

Jones, P. J., Bellet, B. W. & McNally, R. J. (2020). Helping or harming? The effect of trigger warnings on individuals with trauma histories. *Clinical Psychological Science*, *8*, 905–917.

Karasek, S. (2016, September 13). Trust me, trigger warnings are helpful. *The New York Times*. Retrieved from: https://www.nytimes.com/roomfordebate/2016/09/13/do-trigger-warnings-work/trust-me-trigger-warnings-are-helpful

Komaromy, C. (2020). The performance of researching sensitive issues. *Mortality*, *25*, 364–377.

Lee, R. M. (1993). *Doing Research on Sensitive Topics*. London: Sage Publications.

Lee, R. M., & Renzetti, C. M. (1993). The Problems of Researching Sensitive Topics. *Researching Sensitive Topics*, ed. by Renzetti, C. M. & Lee, R. M. London: Sage Publications, 3–13.

Lockhart, E. A. (2016). Why trigger warnings are beneficial, perhaps even necessary. *First Amendment Studies*, *50*, 59–69.

Mallon, S. & Elliott, I. (2019). The emotional risks of turning stories into data: An exploration of the experiences of qualitative researchers working on sensitive topics. *Societies*, *9*, 1–17.

Mallon, S. & Elliott, I. (2021). What is 'sensitive' about sensitive research? The sensitive researchers' perspective. *International Journal of Social Research Methodology*, *24*, 523–535.

McKee, A. (2003). *Textual Analysis: A Beginners Guide*. London: SAGE Publications.

Micanovic, L. S., Stelko, S. & Sakic, S. (2020). Who else needs protection? Reflecting on the researcher vulnerability in sensitive research. *Societies*, *10*, 1–12.

Robinson, C. (2020). Ethically important moments as data: Reflections from ethnographic fieldwork in prisons. *Research Ethics*, *16*, 1–15.

Rowe, W. E. (2014). Positionality in Action Research. *The Sage Encyclopedia of Action Research*, ed. by Coghlan, D. & Brydon-Miller, M. London: SAGE Publications, 627–628.

Scotland, J. (2012). Exploring the philosophical underpinnings of research: Relating ontology and epistemology to the methodology and methods of the scientific, interpretive, and critical research paradigms. *English Language Teaching*, *5*, 9–16.

Vatz, R. E. (2016). The academically destructive nature of trigger warnings. *First Amendment Studies*, *50*, 51–58.

Warr, D. (2004). Stories in the flesh and voices in the head: Reflections on the context and impact of research with disadvantaged populations. *Qualitative Health Research, 4,* 578–587.

Woodby, L., Williams, B. R., Wittich, A. R. & Burgio, K. L. (2011). Expanding the notion of researcher distress: The cumulative effects of coding. *Qualitative Health Research, 21,* 830–838.

World Health Organization. (2019). Preventing unsafe abortion evidence brief. Retrieved from: https://apps.who.int/iris/bitstream/handle/10665/329887/WHO-RHR-19.21-eng.pdf?ua=1

# 8

# RESEARCHER, FIGHTER, CUNT

## Vulnerability and violence in the MMA field

*Zoe John*

## Situating vulnerability and MMA

There are varied debates on whether a formal definition of vulnerability would do justice to the concept, given the variability and situatedness of how vulnerability could be perceived (e.g., Green 2007; Fineman 2008; Wrigley 2015). For instance, within these debates, I am not vulnerable in the physical sense, given that I am educated, able-bodied, and independent. Perhaps this is partly *why* I experienced the problems that I did – with ignorance to a vulnerability based on these aforementioned categories. In actuality, I experienced a social vulnerability in my research on gender, violence, and embodiment in mixed martial arts (MMA), stemming from the power dynamics of coach-athlete relationships, and the gendered norms within the MMA sporting space.

MMA is a competitive fight sport in which two fighters use a range of martial art techniques in order to knock out or submit their opponent. Techniques draw from various stand-up and ground-based martial arts and combat sports, such as Muay Thai (Thai kickboxing), Grecko Roman wrestling, Brazilian jiu-jitsu (BJJ), and Judo. Over the last ten years, various research has drawn upon ideas of violence, embodiment, and gender in MMA (e.g., Abramson & Modzelewski 2010; Channon 2020; Channon, Quinney, Khomutova & Matthews 2018; Mierzwinski, Velija & Malcolm 2014), a sport often tied to discussions of hyper-violence and hyper-masculinity (e.g., Bowman 2020; Downey 2014; Vaccaro & Swauger 2016; Van Bottenburg & Heilbron 2006). In my early research experiences, the ethnographic work of MMA fascinated me (Spencer 2012, 2014) – given that I was practising MMA myself between 2012 and 2016. However, those studies were mostly about men and often researched by men, inspiring my entry point into the academic study of MMA (John 2016).

DOI: 10.4324/9781003349266-11

My experience in the sport fostered an embodied skill and capability that enabled me to participate in a flexible researcher role, including my participation in MMA classes. This role provided insight limited by previous research on these topics: a woman as an ethnographic researcher and as a participant in MMA. Some research documented the tensions among women in combat sports, including mixed-gender training (e.g., Paradis 2012; Lafferty & McKay 2004). However, with different embodied skills and the mixing of traditionally hyper-masculine stand-up sports with those more ground-based, there were significant contributions to make academically. I continued this flexible role through to my ethnographic research in 2018 (John 2022), which furthered my interest in embodiment and violence and how gender mediated interaction. The research was primarily focused upon one MMA club, given the pseudonym Fight or Flight MMA.

Fight or Flight MMA was a popular MMA club located in the UK in a developing industrial estate, and the fame of the club certainly preceded my intention to research it. In previous years, I had heard of the club, and I had even previously watched Fight or Flight fighters in organised MMA events. The club was particularly known for its "rough around the edges" aesthetic, as commented by the opponents of Fight or Flight MMA fighters before their bout. I had also heard of some women fighting out of Fight or Flight MMA, which was a particular interest. The methods I used were typical for ethnographic study: participant observation and interviews. I collected data over a five-month period (May–September 2018). However, the research was also highly embodied and reflexive, given my flexible researcher role, in which my body *produced* "the very cultural physicalities" observed and experienced within the ethnographic space (see Giardina and Newman 2011, p. 530).

The research focused on the situated understandings of action and how "frames" (Goffman 1974) of action are observed and managed. Included in this management was the interest of gendered bodies and how those bodies might alternate the meaning of action and framework. The research consequently drew from a feminist perspective (e.g., Butler 2004, 2011; Young 2005), particularly given the interest in mixed-gender sparring. A critical and gendered account of violence and embodiment emerged, where women's bodies experienced differential treatment in training and fighting; ignored, avoided, and sexualised. Equally, what came to light and what is the central feature of this book chapter were the gendering possibilities of violence in that ethnographic space, where the embodying of skills (and my treatment as a researcher) was reiterated through toxic and heteronormative gendered norms operating as "just" humour (Kelly 1987, 1988). I experienced this "humour" as a researcher, as a woman, and as a member of the club. The three poems presented in the chapter mirror these experiences, although (as the reader will discover) the roles and moments are not so easily separated.

Most participants in the research were men with only two other women in Fight or Flight MMA, which is not unusual in research on martial arts and combat sports.

In fact, I was the only woman in other MMA clubs previously (John 2016). Given the low number of women, and my interest in women's experiences, my flexible researcher role was therefore important to not only observe but *feel* the experience of women; like how many men would fake injury to avoid training with me, the differences in touch when hitting me, or in their inattention to my gaze when needing to pick partners (John 2022, pp. 131–137).

My relationships with the coaches in previous research, all men, were very different from the coach in Fight or Flight MMA, however. While some would tell men to hit and touch my body to "show her a little respect" (John 2016, pp. 53), during the first few sessions upon entering Fight or Flight MMA, I felt a sense of separation from my initial love of fieldwork and the expectations of coaching I had previously. I didn't look forward to picking up my boxing gloves or my notebook for training or observing, and I didn't look forward to seeing what the coach thought of my sparring. I didn't want to return to Fight or Flight MMA at all really, where a sense of unease was felt in the pit of my stomach when I had to travel there. These feelings were primarily due to the "humour", which was targeted and directed at me each session.

## Humour in the field

The vignettes below, which are derived from field notes, interviews, and my reflection, correspond to the different roles taken within the club, all of which triggered "humorous" responses from Fight or Flight MMA's coach Steve (pseudonym). My initial shock, and what remains etched in my mind, occurred during my second time observing the club:

> I sat down on one of the benches at the side of the dojo with my notebook, preparing to write. The coach comes over to me: "You jumping in"? I reply quickly, "No, got a big game on Saturday". "Got any baddies?" he asked. "Nah, just knackered". I sat there with little expression on my face. I was so tired at this point. Not in the mood. Coach ends with, "Nobody cares". A few seconds pass while he continues to stare at me. I don't really react. He then pretends to suck a penis before turning away to carry on with the class. Field notes, 14/05/2018.

I remember being dumbfounded. In previous research, humour was part of the everyday action of the club but was never directed towards me. Perhaps I was becoming '"one of the lads"? Several instances were similar repeated throughout attending Fight or Flight MMA: there was a call to my role to participate when I wanted only to observe, and on my decline, there would be sexualising consequences (such as simulated penis sucking). There were also completely unrelated calls, moments that I have found difficult to analyse purely due to the unprovoked nature of the response. For example:

I waved to encourage Lilly while training, writing at the end of the dojo floor. The coach walks over to me. I look at him, confused. "Fuck you", he says. He walks away. Field notes, 29/08/2018.

Fuck you?

There was something so interesting about me writing which exacerbated these situations, and Gurney (1985, p. 49) experienced similar issues when writing her notes. Maybe this sexualised humour was a form of punishment for not participating in the class, a very selective and personal degradation to try and sway my participation. There were also many instances while training in which I received "humour" unrelated to writing:

Sarah, Lilly, and I were on the dojo mat with coach, and I readjust my sports bra before we started. At that moment, Steve is standing beside me and mimics adjusting breasts on himself and laughs. I look around to the other women in confusion. I shout to him, "Hey! They get sweaty and out of place, okay? Let me have my moment to sort it out".

Sarah joins the conversation: "I can confirm: is annoying".

Coach then continues to rub his legs in a creepy manner, licking his lips while doing so. It was, just bizarre. Field notes, 04/07/2018.

Today I was taking part in the beginner class. Before the class started, I decided to go on the punching bag. I suddenly heard Steve's voice: "Zoe is a cunt, Zoe is a cunt" sung in a very melodic tune. I tried to think of something funny to say in response: "Ha! Yeah, that's not the first time it's been sung to me this week either. I should get a t-shirt". Coach looks at me for another moment with a blank expression, then turns away. I carry on punching the bag, confused. Field notes, 30/07/2018.

Unprovoked and training by myself, I seemed to be an easy target. I wonder what the actual purpose was in singing that I was a cunt. Does Steve know how to talk to women performing in martial arts without these strange and insulting narratives? I felt a need to retaliate ("I tried to think of something funny to say"), which Steve did not necessarily appreciate or expect, given the "blank expression" and dismissal in turning away. I was fed up. On reflection, perhaps interviewing Steve would have been helpful (and no doubt an interesting discussion), but there were too many feelings of discomfort. My rebuttal was potentially doing repair work, also trying to be the "funny" person and to one-up him. At moments in my initial analysis, I seemed to underestimate my own strategies of saving face or sticking up for myself (and seem less vulnerable?), this example being one of them – trying to join in at least or show that someone beat him to it.

I kept these moments to myself, hiding them away in my field notes and research journal – some moments I could not even comprehend. In fact, it was only when talking over the data with supervisors that the realisation of my vulnerability was realised. For some time, I brushed off these moments and defended the circumstances because "He's like that with everyone" – to which one of my supervisors simply replied, "Is he?". It made me think of the forms of action taking place and, if he did "make jokes" with others, and what possible role did this all have.

It seemed that toxic and abusive humour was the atmosphere of Fight or Flight MMA which was recipient designed, with men as feminised and women sexualised. It was a humour that demonstrated the power between Steve and club members too, given that humour was one-dimensional: from Steve to the club and not the other way around. The comments made to others (and me) were also normalised and justified through the interactive work of club members, framing action as "just" humour by joining with laughs or awkwardly starting laughter to define and "make matters regarding perspective clear" (Goffman 1974, p. 255). Putting up with this humour and leaving it unchallenged is also arguably linked to protecting against the possibility of being excluded – to not be singled out further within the social dynamics of the club (and the consequent vulnerability of being alone).

Given the gender disparity within the MMA club and the fact that rarely all three women would be there, it was often me receiving humour from Steve in an exacerbated way. There was also a distinction in Steve's humour towards the club (usually public and demonstrating to others in the club as an "audience") to humour directed to me, which often felt secretive and selective: for me and my ears alone. The displays of "humour", such as penis sucking, were also usually while I was sitting down, with Steve standing over me in-between coaching. There was an embodied display of the coach-athlete power dynamic in that sense, and perhaps even an attempt to realign the power dynamic between researcher-participant that Steve himself may have felt vulnerable too.

Members of the club also referred to their personal status with Steve as a coach or friend ("He's a great guy, really"), including Sarah who mentioned that "It [humour] makes you feel like one of the lads". The falsehood of belonging of being "a lad" is arguably what I believed going into my supervision – that receiving all this humour is something to be exchanged within that space to belong there. Still, I did not know how to begin tracing the issues encountered or even contemplate analyses for some time on realising this strange and secret interactional routine. I equally needed to become more vulnerable to progress these thoughts; being open and honest about feeling exposed, susceptible, and alone.

The first issue bringing difficulty was that I didn't realise I was vulnerable until I left the field, coming to see that I experienced sexist hustling (Gurney 1985) and harassment while researching and participating. Sexual hustling can include putting up with derogatory behaviour in exchange for access to the space and participants, but also potential rapport and acceptance within the research encounter (Gurney 1985, pp. 43–44; Richards 2015, p. 393). Forms of sexual hustling can equally come in the form of various jokes, flirting, innuendoes, or sexual references, "which place a female researcher in an inferior and devalued position" (Gurney 1985, p. 12). No doubt, I often felt inferior and devalued, being "the target of sexist slurs and comments" (Richards 2015, p. 401) in most sessions.

I felt almost voiceless in a way, realising the effect of these feelings in the field and how they were producing other moments: stopping me from standing up for myself, asking questions, and saying the things I really wanted to say. Coming to realise that this was more than "just" humour and figuring out how to represent these vulnerable moments in the field in my analysis, was a key turning point.

## Realising vulnerability and representation

Admittedly, my initial thoughts around vulnerability were too specific, very much in relation to the risks of being physically vulnerable from being robbed or attacked (from strangers), and traditional understandings of power relations in the research encounter. For instance, I planned my routes meticulously should any potential injury occur in training. I had emergency phone numbers (and emergency snacks), taxi numbers, and painkillers. For my observations of MMA fighting events, I contemplated robbery, train accidents, and (perhaps ironically) harassment as a lone female researcher as a highly situational risk (Sampson & Thomas 2003). These more physical risks were something that I was aware of before going into the field, something that I could actually look out for. In contrast, while I planned for the physical side of training – which for other researchers could be defined as a physical vulnerability – I did not plan so much for the relational, social, or even psychological forms of vulnerability in my personal relationships in the field, or how these may develop in such a processual and complex way.

Still, I had my ethical approval "ticked"; there were consent forms filled in and information sheets in the pockets and bags of the club members. I thought, therefore, that the research process in the field would be relatively straightforward – as had my previous research. Perhaps my sense of ease should have been the first warning or early premonition – an ignorance of vulnerability (Gilson 2011) with my initial perception of vulnerable status also relative to participants rather than the researcher. As many of us come to realise in research and everyday life, however, hindsight is often 20/20.

Overtime and coming full circle, these feelings made more sense, with sexual harassment and bullying not uncommon in research (e.g., Arendell 1997; Gailey & Prohaska 2011; Gurney 1985; Lumsden 2009; Sharp & Kremer 2006) or for women in sport (Fasting et al. 2014; Krauchek & Ranson 1999). These experiences played a large part in the difficulties during analysis when translating embodied feeling into writing and analytic prose, particularly when the boundaries between experiences, emotions, and language are blurred (Maclure 2013, p. 172). How should you feel when participants lick their lips at you? Or tell you to suck a penis? Or call you a cunt? How objective can you be when you are *forced* to be the data in such an extreme way? Realising my inner and abject feelings required a re-viewing of my initial interest in violence in the research, with the poem "Fighting Phallusy" (Figure 8.1) a starting point to these realisations:

> "Fighting Phallusy" represents the normalising of the gendered violence/s which took place in training through humour, where (hetero)normative

### *Fighting Phallusy*

Masculinity?
What is it to be?
Typecasting bodies,
categories – not free?
Is it just observed? Felt?
Discursive? Is it belonging or
"Other" perspective? Masculinity?
Is it invisibility? Or has it
a sense of its own
fragility? *"Keep that for
the bedroom, get on
with the drills"*. Can
gendered bodies be
separate from skills?
Masculinity? Brings
my body to the fore,
front of the class he
approached when bored.
*"Zoe is a cunt"*: coach says
melodically, while mention
of dicks quoted periodically.
Even when writing, banter's
straight from the belt. "*I was
gonna say gobble, gobble
but that could seem like something else"*.
Masculinity? It's even in the pens. Coach
mentioned Sherlock then *"Normally a cock"*. Leaning on the cage was
another funny case, where hetero-masculinity was forced upon the face, of fighters in
training or learners on the cusp – *"Watch your baby factories"*, or *"Very nice, how much?"*.
Masculinity? Can you escape it? *"You jumping in?" coach asks (then pretends to suck a
penis)*. Learning skills, feeling weak, stopping if hot – so many reasons for penis: "*You need
to toss 'im off"*. Masculinity? Why is it there? *"Says another thing about 'dick' which I can't
quite hear"*. The definitions aren't sparing, the sense of bodies aren't loose. *"Hop into my
guard. Any excuse"*. Masculinity? It revolves around junk, junk between legs *"Oh I get top
bunk"*. The closeness of their bodies presents a fine line. *"The ol' bollocks in the armpit but
I'm sure we'll get on fine"*. Was there even a session without dicks, balls, or cunts?
Harassment was evident. Heteronormativity takes front.

FIGURE 8.1  Fighting Phallusy.

ideals had to be continually upheld and reiterated (Butler 2004, 2011) through
words and points of address (hence the phallus). This humour was an inescap-
able part of the training and research experience where women *were* the joke,
femininity *was* the joke, and sexual violence *was* the joke. Steve's behaviours
are producing an intelligible, normative gendered body of "MMA fighter"
in this way (Butler 1990), where the performativity of MMA masculinity is
dualistic and dichotomous.

To be a "member" of Fight or Flight MMA club centred upon a language and treatment through humour that was sexualising, homophobic, and degrading. We are seeing in the poem "Fighting Phallusy" a short yet intense representation of issues surrounding coach-athlete relationships too – of a "culturally accepted violence" (Stirling & Kerr 2008, p. 126) that often fills sporting spaces (see, e.g., Fasting, Chroni & Knorre 2014; Krauchek & Ranson 1999). The imagery of the phallic stanza also helps to visualise the issues around "embodying" skills, where humour penetrated throughout the gym and interrupted the process of intersubjective and reflexive moments necessary for skill embodiment (Crossley 2004, 2005).

Writing poetry through creative analytical practice (CAP) was useful to illustrate the contradictions and rawness of the data, being a presentation and untangling of the intangible experiences of being there and across ethnographic spaces and moments (see also Lapum 2008). CAP also expressed the emotions and displacement in the field, helping to construct "the feeling" that I could not quite place while in the field initially, managing my realisations of vulnerability and revitalising the analysis through this new method of knowing (Richardson 2000; Richardson & St Pierre 2005, p. 962). Perhaps "affect" in the Deleuzian sense, the data are in part the "sense-event" (MacLure 2013, p. 643) of being a researcher and the heavily emotive moments that were not always realised "in" the field.

Made from various field notes, interview extracts, and my own thoughts, the poems (or poem-ish writing [Lahman, Richard & Teman 2019; Sparkes 2021]) are highly reflexive, especially around lines that blur outsider/insider relationships and between the varying dynamics of power and authority. These dynamics are also represented across the next poem in the chapter, a written progression in "figuring out" not just the data but realising the social and interpersonal moments of vulnerability across my roles in the field. It is challenging, for instance, to separate the roles of researcher and participant throughout observing Fight or Flight MMA, and how my body contributed to the framing of action or potential intentions of involvement. "Zoe is a Cunt" demonstrates these problems well, illustrating the difficulties of being called upon by the coach to use my flexible role. As below, the boundaries of practice and vulnerability are blurred, and the poem brings together the awkward moments as a researcher, woman, and MMA practitioner which are interlinked and inseparable:

### Zoe is a Cunt

"What kind of things can you be learning from sitting on your bum scribbling notes?"
The coach always wondering, asking questions, making jokes.
I've almost lost count on his questions to my call,
As a researcher; fighter; woman; when doing nothing at all.

"Hey, Anne Frank!" he yelled over to me.
"Getting your diary out again?" he quoted regularly.
But also asks a favour of "Zo, you jumping in?"
And on declines of invite, there's mimics of penis sucking.

"Nobody cares," – he confirms with delight,
As I sit to write my notes rather than fight.
"We're one short if you wanna join in?"
A fighter smirks next to me. "You're missing out. That could be you
vomiting".

Even when standing awaiting instruction,
"Zoe is a cunt" often filled introduction.
Whether he mentioned "Dear diary" or "You havin' a roll?"
Coach always watching, asking, laughing: in control.

A significant amount of "humour" was incited by my writing on the side of the dojo. It is interesting that so many debates and discussions of subjectivity involve themes of "going native", and yet, it was precisely when I was not participating in the class that this harassment was experienced. Perhaps, given that I could, in theory, participate, Steve perceived me as lacking in MMA masculinity, thus challenging me. Alternatively, there could be a threatening sense of my presence. If I was training, I could not be writing or researching (or at least it could be perceived that way). It is difficult to separate what positionality of mine Steve was calling upon given that I see myself in various ways: Zoe the researcher, the MMA practitioner, and an athlete in other sports. It may be that Steve is *refusing* to see me in these different ways and trying to deny them in his humour – it is far easier for him to reduce me to *something* rather than acknowledge the multiple positions I take.

Given that constructions and dualisms of masculinity/femininity often rely on simplicity, and the humour emphasises this twofold, my body and relations must also be simplified to reproduce that gendered dualism. I am a woman first and foremost who therefore must be sexualised. I am also Zoe who is researching and writing notes on Steve and his club that could potentially be threatening (from his perspective). Maybe Steve even feels vulnerable at moments, given that I might be the "phallus" through the power of my pen observing him. Either way, the focus I received from Steve was exacerbated so I know my place – often with consequences of suggested penis sucking or harassment. I wonder if I could have done anything to even make a difference in the treatment, but even if I were to train more, for longer, or even have a fight, I would still never truly be "one of the guys" (Green 2016, p. 425) or part of the "family" (Spencer 2012, p. 150). If I was going to be in that space as a woman or as a researcher, something was going to be said by Steve.

The crafting of these poems illuminated a stark contrast to previous analytical notes that I thought were so concise, enabling a different perspective or "look" to the ethnographic experience – a "different lens through which to view the same scenery" (Sparkes & Smith 2012, p. 162). I started to learn more about myself by piecing different words together, with the alternative configurations of the data and the different lens allowing re-viewing of "humour" that erected the space, and to come to terms with the fact that these words and gestures were not actually "just" humour.

On occasions when writing these poems, there was an embodied sense of my hand simply pouring out words and writing before I knew what the text was leaving behind, like an unconscious decision or an "unbeknown knowledge" (Uotinen 2011), which seeped through my pen onto paper. One such poem is "No", a poem previously hidden in the appendix of my thesis that felt too raw at the time to incorporate into the main text; moments where I felt small and silent without an ability to *do* something (or perhaps even angry that I let it happen in the first place). The poems gave space to verbally "do", and to express my anxious reflections over thoughts of what my vulnerability could have extended to:

**No.**

No.
I don't want you to call me a cunt,
or lick your lips,
or rub your thighs,
asking how much I cost,
with your eyes on me,
legs around me,
or pretending to suck a dick.

No.
I don't want you to shout, "Fuck you",
or talk about my mouth,
like it's a service,
always open,
usually filled with cock.

No.
I don't want to feel this way
but you make me feel -
silent,
alone,
polite.
I wait for the clock,
to free me,
and my notes –
to run away.

No.
I don't understand you.
It's almost on purpose,
you want me –
to feel small.

Like something for you –
to walk on
at one point,
to admire the next –
yours to tease.

No.
I just want to be away,
counting down the weeks,
hoping it will change,
or get better –
to stop feeling confused,
or like a failure,
because I don't want to be there
as researcher,
or member.

No.
I want to go home,
and put this away –
take down my posters,
to hide,
to smile,
to take a breath,
and start over.

"No" was written shortly after one of my counselling sessions taken during the writing of my thesis. There were several interlinking reasons for applying for this counselling, arguably linking to forms of vulnerability too: the stress of balancing jobs and paying rent, grieving an anniversary of a friend's death, and wondering if I would ever in fact finish my research. However, Steve's "humour" was a primary cause, so much so that I was having panic attacks around potentially bumping into Steve again (highly unlikely as that was), or what might happen upon publication. There were also many things I felt when writing this poem. I felt like a shit feminist and a shit researcher, wanting to print my thesis off so I could feel the satisfaction of ripping it all up into pieces. I still feel lingering feelings of confusion and admission too that, despite counselling and conversation with colleagues, supervisors, and attendees at conferences, I still felt like I was a bad researcher for taking so long to write about it, and for not standing up for myself or interviewing Steve.

The effects of vulnerability were overwhelming and evident in these counselling sessions, but also through my supervision for many months. Having to talk over the feelings I had of returning to Fight or Flight MMA each week, remembering those nervous tingles in my stomach, how my eyes looked at the floor upon my arrival, my rush to get back on the train in case someone offered me a lift home: it was difficult and indeed made me feel more vulnerable for some time. I see these moments more clearly now and the irony that in a space of what could have been physical empowerment and liberation was a vulnerable space – leaving me feeling breakable and takeable instead (see McCaughey 1997, p. 37).

I know that bullying, harassment, and abuse are all possibilities of what these interactions across the vignettes and poems could be. It is also difficult to know how the analysis of "humour" would change in other research on MMA and sport if women were included as participants or involved in the analysis. Other instances of abuse, bullying, or violence have arguably been analysed or passed aside as examples of other "risqué jokes" (Dunning 1996, p. 192), for example. Equally, the examples in this chapter are another contribution to growing awareness of researcher positionality, and to the realisation that vulnerability not only applies to research participants but to researchers (and that we are often vulnerable even when we do not perceive ourselves to be). This brings me to the final section of this chapter: a note on looking forward, the "what now?", and the implications of these encounters.

## Conclusion

I do not know how long I would have stayed if I wanted to learn MMA or fight, or if I had further research requirements to spend in the field. The exchanges we make as researchers to belong or have access to spaces, or indeed the exchanges we make as athletes to train and compete, are prevalent in the sexual hustling noted in this chapter. Such exchanges also carry very real consequences on our performance, and our work, but importantly our vulnerability where the perceptions of relationships in the field are often thoughts of reciprocity and trust. It is unfortunate that growth (and arguably resilience [see Walklate 2011]) can come out of vulnerability, and for me, to be vulnerable meant being open to new things through feeling out of place. Still, I have been able to progress the understanding of what vulnerability can mean, and better the skills and awareness as a researcher to manage those vulnerabilities – including developing an analysis that I could not previously and may never have had if not for being vulnerable.

To be vulnerable enabled this chapter to be crafted, and there are practical points to bring forward that can be put into practice as researchers, staff members, and mentors. We can look forward in excitement and reflection on what we can do to challenge the dynamics and understandings of not only vulnerability but humour as an interactive tool or form for managing gendered violence. Included in these challenges are paying more attention and respecting abject feelings in the field and to encourage CAP to unpack some of the loads and clarify data analysis and representation as researchers. I would also strongly advise any researcher to reach for help, even if you cannot necessarily put into words what it is that is wrong. Talking through a situation, such as awkward "humour", could make a difference, whether that is talking with a research lead, supervisors, or counsellors. You may find the helplines below as a useful starting point to find out more information and start a conversation:

https://www.mind.org.uk/
https://www.acas.org.uk/sexual-harassment/if-youve-been-sexually-harassed-at-work

At various points in my writing (more so when I experienced a rare rush of confidence and adrenaline), I considered returning to the club to show Steve some of the poems. I feel confident, then I feel scared. At the point of writing this, I do not think I will. I do not think I would ever be ready to be in front of Steve or the club again. "Checking" with participants has long been an important practice when discussing matters of validity and credibility, and arguably of vulnerability in the traditional researcher-participant relationship and power dynamic (e.g., Lincoln & Guba 1985; see also Birt, Scott, Cavers, Campbell & Walter 2016). However, the particularities of power and the social and psychological vulnerabilities for myself are what I am putting forward first and foremost.

Furthermore, although it may be easier for researchers with more embodied privilege (and some researchers have acknowledged this [e.g., Spencer 2012, p. 168; Green 2011, p. 383; Green 2016, pp. 7, 425]), dualisms of objectivity/subjectivity cannot be so neatly divided from the data and research presented in this chapter. Those divides are equally a fallacy (or phallusy) for what makes a piece of research useful or of quality and what is a worthy contribution. The data and poems presented in this chapter are an important example of the relevance and requirement of subjective inclusions in publication, and the alertness of our vulnerability that warrants fuller explication. Those of a more traditional or realist stance may question the integrity of the analysis when doing so. In fact, readers may find that "poetry" and "data analysis" mentioned together may be oxymoronic "or perhaps even just moronic" (Shapiro 2004, p. 172). These poems, however, are part of a critique around some of the ways we assume to know what we know and how we might express emotions and vulnerability tied and inseparable to the research.

The poems are based on moments that were unexpected because there is little to no mention of hustling, harassment, or indeed the reality of being vulnerable as a researcher elsewhere: where women are not included as participants because of low numbers or not concerned in discussions of masculinity (e.g., Green 2016; Vaccaro & Swauger 2016); where research has not focused on mixed-gender sparring (e.g., Spencer 2012); or where the researcher is both inside and out, both welcomed and harassed. These unexpected and undesired moments of fear and confusion were so central to my research experiences and are *the* data. Paying attention to these moments, taking them seriously, and weaving them throughout our notes, analysis, and prose develop the stories we tell – whether of our participants or of our own vulnerable ventures that we (un)willingly or are forced to experience.

## Acknowledgements

Thank you to my PhD supervisors EJ Renold and Robin Smith for the support and guidance across the journey, who often saw the brunt of my vulnerabilities. My thanks also to Leah Hibbs, who inspired me to take on the "phallus" in different ways.

# References

Abramson, C. M. & Modzelewski, D. (2010). Caged morality: Moral worlds, subculture, and stratification among middle-class cage-fighters. *Qualitative Sociology, 34*, 143–175.

Arendell, T. (1997). Reflections on the researcher-researched relationship: A woman interviewing men. *Qualitative Sociology, 29*, 341–368.

Birt, L., Scott, S., Cavers, D., Campbell, C. & Walter, F. (2016). Member checking: A tool to enhance trustworthiness or merely a nod to validation? *Qualitative Health Research, 26*, 1802–1811.

Bowman, P. (2020). In toxic hating masculinity: MMA hard men and media representation. *Sport in History, 40*, 395–410.

Butler, J. (1990). *Gender trouble: Feminism and the subversion of identity*. New York: Routledge.

Butler, J. (2004). *Undoing gender*. New York: Routledge.

Butler, J. (2011). *Bodies that matter: On the discursive limits of "sex"*. 2nd ed. London: Routledge.

Channon, A. (2020). Edgework and mixed martial arts: Risk, reflexivity and collaboration in an ostensibly 'violent' sport. *Martial Arts Studies, 9*, 6–19.

Channon, A., Quinney, A., Khomutova, A. & Matthews, C. (2018). Sexualisation of the fighter's body: Some reflections on women's mixed martial arts. *Corps, 1*, 383–391.

Crossley, N. (2004). Ritual, body technique and (inter) subjectivity. In: K. Schilbrak (Ed.), *Thinking through ritual: Philosophical perspectives* (pp. 31–51). London: Routledge.

Crossley, N. (2005). Mapping reflexive body techniques: On body modification and maintenance. *Body and Society, 11*, 1–35.

Downey, G. (2014). 'As real as it gets!' Producing hyperviolence in mixed martial arts. *JOMEC Journal, 5*. doi: 10.18573/j.2014.10268.

Dunning, E. (1996). On problems of the emotions in sport and leisure: Critical and counter-critical comments on the conventional and figurational sociologies of sport and leisure. *Leisure Studies, 15*, 185–207.

Fasting, K., Chroni, S. & Knorre, N. (2014). The experience of sexual harassment in sport and education among European female sports science students. *Sport, Education and Society, 19*, 115–130.

Fineman, M. (2008). The vulnerable subject: Anchoring equality in the human condition. *Yale Journal of Law and Feminism, 20*, 1–23.

Gailey, J. A. & Prohaska, A. (2011). Power and gender negotiations during interviews with men about sex and sexually degrading practices. *Qualitative Research, 11*, 365–380.

Gilson, E. (2011). Vulnerability, ignorance, and oppression. *Hypatia, 26*, 308–332.

Giardina, M. D. & Newman, J. I. (2011). Physical cultural studies and embodied research acts. *Cultural Studies ↔ Critical Methodologies, 11*, 523–534.

Goffman, E. (1974). *Frame analysis: An essay on the organization of experience*. New York: Harper & Row.

Green, S. (2007). Crime, victimisation and vulnerability. In: S. Walklate (Ed.), *Handbook of victims and victimology* (pp. 91–118). Cullompton: Willan.

Green, J. (2011). It hurts so it is real: Sensing the seduction of mixed martial arts. *Social & Cultural Geography, 12*, 377–396.

Green, K. (2016). Tales from the mat: Narrating men and meaning making in the mixed martial arts gym. *Journal of Contemporary Ethnography, 45*, 419–450.

Gurney, J. (1985). Not one of the guys: The female researcher in a male-dominated setting. *Qualitative Sociology, 8*, 42–62.

John, Z. (2016). "Take your tampon out and let's get moving!": Gender, character and skill in mixed martial arts. Master's thesis, Cardiff University.

John, Z. (2022). "Normally a cock": Embodiment, gender and violence in mixed martial arts. Doctoral dissertation, ORCA. https://orca.cardiff.ac.uk/id/eprint/151256/

Kelly, L. (1987). The continuum of sexual violence. In: J. Hanmer & M. Maynard (Eds.), *Women, violence and social control: Explorations in sociology. British Sociological Association conference volume series* (pp. 46–60). London: Palgrave Macmillan.

Kelly, L. (1988). 'It's happened to so many women': Sexual violence as a continuum. In: L. Kelly (Ed.), *Surviving sexual violence* (pp. 74–137). Cambridge: Polity.

Krauchek, V. & Ranson, G. (1999). Playing by the rules of the game: Women's experiences and perceptions of sexual harassment in sport. *Canadian Review of Sociology, 36*, 585–600.

Lafferty, Y. & McKay, J. (2004). "Suffragettes in satin shorts"? Gender and competitive boxing. *Qualitative Sociology, 27*, 249–276.

Lahman, M. K. E., Richard, V. M. & Teman, E. D. (2019). ish: How to write poemish (research) poetry. *Qualitative Inquiry, 25*, 215–227.

Lapum, J. L. (2008). The performative manifestation of a research identity: Storying the journey through poetry. *Forum: Qualitative Social Research, 9*, Article 39. doi: 10.17169/fqs-9.2.397.

Lincoln, Y. S. & Guba, E. G. (1985). *Naturalistic inquiry*. Newbury Park, CA: Sage.

Lumsden, K. (2009). 'Don't ask a woman to do another woman's job': Gendered interactions and the emotional ethnographer. *Sociology, 43*, 497–513.

MacLure, M. (2013). Promiscuous feminists postscript. *International Journal of Qualitative Studies in Education, 26*, 625–628.

McCaughey, M. (1997). *Real knockouts: The physical feminism of women's self defense*. New York: NYU Press.

Mierzwinski, M., Velija, P. & Malcolm, D. (2014). Women's experiences in the mixed martial arts: A quest for excitement? *Sociology of Sport Journal, 31*, 66–84.

Paradis, E. (2012). Boxers, briefs or bras? Bodies, gender and change in the boxing gym. *Body & Society, 18*, 82–109.

Richards, J. (2015). 'Which player do you fancy then?' Locating the female ethnographer in the field of the sociology of sport. *Soccer & Society, 16*, 393–404.

Richardson, L. (2000). Writing: A method of inquiry. In: N. K. Denzin & Y. S. Lincoln (Eds.), *Handbook of qualitative research* (pp. 923–948). 2nd ed. Thousand Oaks, CA: Sage.

Richardson, L. & St Pierre, E. (2005). Writing, a method of inquiry. In: Y. Lincoln & N. K. Denzin (Eds.), *Handbook of qualitative research (959-978)*. 3rd ed. Thousand Oaks, CA: Sage.

Sampson, H. & Thomas, M. (2003). Risk and responsibility. *Qualitative Research, 3*, 165–189.

Shapiro, J. (2004). Can poetry be data? Potential relationships between poetry and research. *Families, Systems & Health, 22*, 171–177.

Sharp, G. & Kremer, E. (2006). The safety dance: Confronting harassment, intimidation, and violence in the field. *Sociological Methodology, 36*, 317–327.

Spencer, D. (2012). *Ultimate fighting and embodiment: Violence, gender, and mixed martial arts*. London: Routledge.

Spencer, D. (2014). Sensing violence: An ethnography of mixed martial arts. *Ethnography, 15*, 232–254.

Sparkes, A. C. (2021). Poetic representations, not-quite poetry and poemish: Some methodological reflections. In: E. Fitzpatrick & K. Fitzpatrick (Eds.), *Poetry, method and education research: Doing critical, decolonising and political inquiry* (pp. 41–50). London: Routledge.

Sparkes, A. & Smith, B. (2012). Embodied research methodologies and seeking the senses in sport and physical culture: A fleshing out of problems and possibilities. *Research in the Sociology of Sport, 6*, 167–190.

Stirling, A. & Kerr, G. (2008). Defining and categorizing emotional abuse in sport. *European Journal of Sports Science, 8,* 173–181.

Uotinen, J. (2011). Senses, bodily knowledge, and autoethnography: Unbeknown knowledge from an IVU experience. *Qualitative Health Research, 21,* 1307–1315.

Vaccaro, C. A. & Swauger, M. L. (2016). *Unleashing manhood in the cage: Masculinity and mixed martial arts.* Lanham: Lexington Books.

Van Bottenburg, M. & Heilbron, J. (2006). De-Sportization of fighting contests: The origins and dynamics of no holds barred events and the theory of sportization. *International Review for the Sociology of Sport, 41,* 259–282.

Walklate, S. (2011). Reframing criminal victimization: Finding a place for vulnerability and resilience. *Theoretical Criminology, 15,* 179–194.

Wrigley, A. (2015). An eliminativist approach to vulnerability. *Bioethics, 29,* 478–487.

Young, I. M. (2005). Throwing like a girl: A phenomenology of feminine body comportment, motility and spatiality. In: I. M. Young (Ed.), *On female body experience: "Throwing Like a girl" and other essays* (pp. 27–45). Oxford: Oxford University Press.

# 9

# ETHNOGRAPHIC VULNERABILITIES

## Power, Politics, and Possibility*

*Devra Waldman, Michael Dao, Hugo Ceron-Anaya, and Michael D. Giardina*

### Proem

This chapter emerged out of shared discussions about ethnography the four of us had beginning at a colloquium hosted by the Department of Sport Management at Florida State University in the Fall of 2021 that one of us (Giardina) organized. Interestingly, the topic of the colloquium was not focused on vulnerability *per se* (whether physical, social, psychological, economic, or otherwise); rather, it was on the broad topic of "Ethnography and Community", and intended to highlight research conducted by three of us (Ceron-Anaya, Dao, and Waldman) in our field-work in Mexico, Vietnam, and India, respectively. Each of us touched on various forms of vulnerability as it had arisen during the conduct of our respective research projects. The invitation from Bryan Clift to contribute to this edited collection came fortuitously later, and we welcomed the opportunity to continue our conversations on the topic. Over the course of many Zoom chats, emails, and text messages, what rose to the fore was not necessarily a focus on a particular kind of explicit topical vulnerability—such as working with individuals experiencing environmental vulnerability (see, e.g., Bunds, 2017)—but rather those unseen, unspoken, unheard, and often unwritten about spaces of vulnerability experienced by the researcher himself or herself. We believe this is an important avenue to explore, for as the sociologist Rosalind Gill (2016) once wrote, there is much to reveal about the unspoken spaces of the research act when we "turn our lens upon our own labor processes, organizational governance, and conditions of production" (p. 40).

Over the course of nine months of conversations, and as we expanded upon and dug into a mix of banal, complex, affective, and in some cases graphic instances in our fieldwork, what came into sharp relief was how *different* our various encounters were with researcher vulnerability:

---

* This is an equally co-authored chapter.

DOI: 10.4324/9781003349266-12

Raced.

Classed.

Gendered.

Powerlessness.

Confusion.

Anxiety.

Importantly, these encounters with vulnerability didn't necessarily make it into our published work or conference presentations when we first recounted our research findings. Rather, we hid them away as unexplored and unwritten forms of vulnerability—encounters written out of existence to protect our research participants, or ourselves, on the printed page, but stories we told amongst friends or colleagues (like William Foote Whyte locating the groundbreaking methodological parts of *Street Corner Society* in Appendix A). But these vulnerabilities were always clearly there, embedded in the "affective labor of human contact and interaction" (Hardt, 1999, p. 95) in our ethnographic research: they informed what we did in the field, and how we did it (and how we thought about what we did after the fact).

For us, then, vulnerability is something that contributes to making and re-making the research act—what we decide to reveal (or not reveal) to participants and the reader, the spaces of our research, and what comes out of our experiences in the field. Put differently, vulnerability is generative—is *productive*; it *tells us something* about our research field, participants, context, and ourselves. This is a point Ruth Behar (1997) makes clear in *The Vulnerable Observer* when she contends regarding the utility of vulnerability in fieldwork:

> Vulnerability doesn't mean that anything personal goes. The exposure of the self who is also a spectator *has to take us somewhere we couldn't otherwise get to*. It has to be essential to the argument, not a decorative flourish, not exposure for its own sake. […] It has to persuade us of the wisdom of not leaving the writing pad blank.
>
> *(emphasis ours)*

Building from Behar, beyond simply a focus *on* vulnerability as a topic of inquiry, we believe there is an epistemological necessity (see Giardina & Donnelly, 2023) *of* vulnerability—for it is unavoidable (and unavoidably present) in the process of engaging with, learning from, and ultimately understanding our ethnographic encounters in the field. And while this vulnerability may be productive in the conduct of research, as we highlight below, it can also be frustrating, frightening, and frequently confusing.

In ethnographic research, vulnerability (with a small v) is often couched in terms of how the researcher makes herself physically vulnerable (as in the case of embodied ethnography; see, e.g., Giardina & Donnelly, 2017; Green, 2016; Mears, 2008) or himself emotionally vulnerable (as in the case of conducting research with trauma survivors; see, e.g., Winfield, 2022). This we can somewhat prepare for, whether in our research design or in our preparation for being in the field. It is present in how we engage with others, and how we present ourselves to them (be they informants, participants, or co-producers of the research act). It is an emotional element that can help gain trust and a sense of belonging in the community (see Parvez, 2018). But vulnerability (with a Capital V) is different and, we would argue, in line with Tine M. Gammeltoft et al.'s (2021) view of existential vulnerability; that is, forms of vulnerability "that arise from concerns that are rooted in an individual's very existence" (p. 2). They go on to explain that existential vulnerability:

> is a *shared* condition of human life, while also taking specific forms within different socio-cultural contexts. [...] The other's freedom is at the heart of existential vulnerability; we are exposed to others, to their actions and assessments of us. This exposure produces vulnerability—as does our awareness of our own power to affect others. *Other people are vulnerable to us, just as we are vulnerable to them.*
>
> *(p. 3, emphasis ours)*

Vulnerability, then, is (at least) a two-way street—though often not equitably so. Our moments of vulnerability in the field *change us*—and our research; they change what comes next in our encounters with certain participants, change the way we interpret situations, and change the way we orient ourselves to future fieldwork.

Rather than try to speak in broad terms or cover in large swathes a discussion of vulnerability (or present an abstract philosophical disquisition about vulnerability), we instead present below a series of narrative collages drawn from our respective ethnographic fieldwork that actively render visible and illustrate our complex and variegated experiences of and with (our own) vulnerability. We do this for several reasons: first, vulnerability is an intensely personal experience, and we would not want to see those experiences collapsed or subsumed into some form of generic accounting, which is why we have each privileged specific—and personal—interactions from our respective fieldwork rather than provide a broad view of ethnographic vulnerability. Second, we are a diverse group of scholars whose perspectives cut across racial, ethnic, and gendered lines; whose individual research has taken place in various parts of the world and thus in very different social, cultural, political, and economic contexts; who are trained in or situated within different academic disciplines (i.e., sociology, geography, physical cultural studies, etc.); and who write from different places in our respective careers (i.e., academic rank, type of institution, political projects, etc.). Put differently, we have each experienced and responded to vulnerability in *different* ways, informed by *different* biographies, and interpreted through *different* theoretical, methodological, and ethico-onto-epistemological lenses. Reading across these perspectives and indeed philosophical orientations to research raises more questions than it answers regarding vulnerability, troubling the ground on which the collective "we" enter the field. We make no apologies for the messiness in doing so, for fieldwork is itself a "messy" enterprise (see Mears, 2008). And third, by reflecting on past fieldwork encounters and re-reading them through the privileging of vulnerability, we can better make sense of (and perhaps even trouble) our findings.

## Narratives from the Field

### *Devra Waldman*

I want to begin by contextualizing two things—my research context and my positionality—in order to situate a vignette from my fieldwork that I will use to discuss *gendered vulnerabilities* in ethnographic research. The majority of my work has taken place in the National Capital Region of India. I came to do research there through learning about how multinational sport organizations have become increasing partners and players in global real estate, often becoming intertwined in developments that center sport identities and brands in "new city" or large-scale gated community projects in urban peripheries looking to court and cater to the new middle classes (see, e.g., Waldman, 2022; Waldman & Weedon, 2019). My PhD fieldwork focused on the spectacular emergence of golf and polo branded large-scaled gated community development in the urbanizing hinterland of Gurgaon—a satellite city of Delhi that has been dubbed India's "Millennial City". In that project, I used ethnographic methodologies grounded in postcolonial theoretical approaches to investigate how these futurist gated communities draw on long-standing colonial logics and global capital networks, how these projects re-shape state/citizen relations, and how the aesthetic role of sport combines with local development practices to produce "cleansed" environments on the basis of class/caste/racialized lines.

My positionality—as a white, North American, cis-gender, female settler-scholar—had a significant impact on shaping who, where, and how I was able to get access to different people and spaces. Because of these specific identity markers, I was seen as inoffensive, unthreatening, and at times naïve and innocent, which I mobilized to facilitate access to elite Indian men who had significant power over real estate development in Gurgaon.

In one encounter, I met one of my informants, an executive at the real estate firm my research was focused on, at a casual outdoor restaurant nestled in a space on the fringes of daunting corporate parks. I first met him early in my fieldwork when I attended a real estate investment conference, after which we had a few meetings and exchanged many emails and phone calls about the company's happenings. Acting somewhat as a gatekeeper for me, he helped get me access inside the community gates, with other company employees, and into various spaces in the corporate offices. We discussed sweeping topics related to the real estate industry, company gossip, ongoing development "successes" and "setbacks" over dinner, but then, as the discussion was winding down, he turned to me and said (direct quote): *"I would like to fuck you tonight"*. Taken aback by his very straightforward declaration, with some part of me hoping he was joking, I tried to diffuse the situation with laughter and redirection. Ignoring what he likely saw as an unconvincing attempt by me to change topics, he said it again, explicitly. This time unable to avoid his pointed comments, I tried to de-escalate by explaining that though I was flattered, this was a professional relationship and I was uncomfortable with that kind of intimacy, and even still, that I was in a monogamous relationship. Finding this unsatisfactory, he pushed back, saying that we were friends, *"friends are allowed to have fun"*, that he was in a relationship too, and that *"women like you from America fuck all the time, so why not me too"*. Frustrated that I did not change my mind, he turned to anger, asking if I found him attractive and if this *"American woman was too snobby to be with him?"*. Eventually, after some negotiation and my attempts to protect his ego (and my safety) by reassuring him of his attractiveness and lying saying that in different circumstances maybe things would play out differently, he backed down. I went home, and I didn't contact him again.

Looking back at my fieldnotes now from that night, there's one phrase that strikes me: *I feel overwhelmed. What should I do? I also feel guilty (but why?), shameful. I feel underprepared.* Though this interaction prompted a range of embodied vulnerabilities, I want to emphasize two in particular—one related to the intersection of race and gender and the other related to thoughts of how my graduate school training left me feeling unprepared.

Postcolonial critiques of ethnographic research have directed important attention to how the formalized study of the "Other" has contributed directly to specific ways of seeing and knowing that perpetuated colonial power, and has highlighted how the very act of invading a specific locality for "research" continues to have colonial implications (Said, 1978; Smith, 1999). There have been essential methodological interventions rightly demanding researchers to critically interrogate their positionality, unpack their complicity and privilege, question the applicability of concepts derived in the Global North to theorize experiences in the Global South, and to address and dismantle hierarchical power dynamics between researchers and those they research. In recounting this interaction, I first want to make clear that my whiteness, gender, and North Americanness afforded me many protections, privileges, and access that would be unavailable to those with different intersecting positionalities than my own (see, e.g., Guiliano, 2011)—all of which are deeply entangled with colonial legacies of India, histories of geoinstitutional imperialism connected to academia, and enduring power dynamics between the Global North and South (see, e.g., McCarthy et al., 2007). I aim to highlight how these protections and privileges are also slippery, contextual, and unstable—instances in which I often found myself in shifting constellations of power (Caretta & Jokinen, 2017). In this case, my experience of embodied vulnerability was partly due to the power he held over me through how he positioned me, and the influence this had on ethnographic research and knowledge production more generally.

As Cupples (2002) notes, our positionality is not just about how and what we feel as researchers, *but also about how we are positioned by those whom we research.* This makes it equally important to situate these experiences, and the reactions of individuals to me, in the broader postcolonial context where this research took place, and to question how my racialized and gendered body influenced encounters I had in the field. Sara Ahmed (2000) argues "encounters between embodied subjects always hesitate between the domain of the particular – the face to face of this encounter – and the general – the framing of the encounter by broader relationships of power and antagonism" (p. 8). Speaking to ongoing relationships within and between Orientalist and Occidentalist stereotypes, by this she means that every interaction between "Self" and "Other" is shaped by not only what is happening in that particular moment, but also broader socio-political histories and "assumed" knowledge of who "the Other" is—"reading the signs on their body, or by reading their body *as* a sign" (Ahmed, 2000, p. 8). Here, my body was read as a sign and a projection of the idea of a "White Woman from the West" which, following Nayak (2006), underscores how intersections of gender and race shape embodied research experiences, especially because the "seemingly knowable object… 'white woman', cannot be understood outside of the specific historical and geographical processes that constitute this subjectivity as intelligible, and the symbolic regimes of language that summon this representation to life" (p. 417). In this way, how my white female body was "knowable" was palatable and emplaced in what could be termed Occidental understandings of representations of North American sexual femininity (Markowitz, 2009).

At the same time, I emphasized in my fieldnotes the vulnerability of feeling unprepared, stemming from failures in methodological training to account for gendered experiences of threat, fear, and sexual violence. As Rebecca Hanson and Patricia Richards (2019) argue, this is a *systemic* problem throughout the halls of academia, where masculinist assumptions surrounding fieldwork still prevail, universities continue to turn a blind eye away from harassment and assault within and beyond its walls, and norms within academia and ethnographic methodological discussions facilitate conspicuous silences around sex(ed) and gender(ed) vulnerabilities. Drawing from Joan Fujimura (2006), gendered experiences of threat and violence in the field become "awkward surplus", scrubbed clean from methodology and reflexivity as they are difficult or risky to fit into narratives about findings and theoretical framings (see also Hanson & Richards, 2019).

Through the recounting of this interaction, I am attempting what Wanda Pillow (2003) terms "uncomfortable reflexivity"—a departure from recounting reflexivity in the more typical and palatable ways. Even as Hanson and Richards (2019) illustrated the silences of these experiences in our "ethnographic tales" despite the all-too-typical encounters of sexual harassment in fieldwork, *it should not be made neat or palatable in its re-telling.* The embodied vulnerability of that particular moment was a result of both gender and race in that context, which resonated in how my body was inscribed with the kind of sexual availability it might signify (Al-Hindi & Kawabata, 2002). What I want to emphasize is that exploring the embodied vulnerability of moments such as this provides the opportunity to interrogate the postcolonial intersectionalities of power in research, and confront and tease out the ongoing workings of Occidentalist and orientalist framings of bodies that continue to operate research encounters (and beyond). Making more visible these uncomfortable, contradictory, and complex moments are important, even crucial, to explore the global hegemonic workings of whiteness, its gendered/

racial malleability, and shifting affects, while also complicating simple binaries of white/other, oppressor/oppressed (Faria & Mollett, 2016). Simultaneously, this too might facilitate a broader move away from *disembodied* methodological discussions about ethnographic fieldwork, and better prepare researchers for fieldwork through a reflection on how our embodied experiences powerfully shape research process, practices, outcomes, and knowledge production.

## Michael Dao

Nhậu, if directly translated from Vietnamese, means to drink. However, drinking is too loose of an idea without providing any context. In the context of social relationships, nhậu is drinking, eating, and socializing with others for either a direct purpose or no purpose at all. It was early in the field, just my first month in Huế, when community members invited me to join them for a night out of nhậu. We were given a private room at a popular "quán nhậu",[1] where we ordered steamed mussels, fried rice, grilled pork ribs, and boxes of Huda Beer.

> I am stranger in the room, barely understanding their Huế dialect. I am the odd one out. But…I don't feel left out. They welcome me by pouring a Huda beer into my glass. One person asks if I want ice. "Yes." I feel accepted. I feel welcomed.

In the middle of this nhậu, a community member sitting to my left touched my left leg, leaned into me, and told me he was happy to meet me, have me in Huế, and hoped he could help with my research. At that moment, nhậu was not about drinking with friends; nhậu was about comradery, community, and culture. I disregarded Western norms of masculinity and heterosexual performance, where I held hands with others, sang national songs, and let the alcohol flow through my veins, being touchier than I am with my own friends. I became vulnerable as I drank toward intoxication, leaving myself open for anyone to challenge my Vietnamese identity and question me about my marital status.[2] I felt I needed to drink to prove my Vietnameseness (to my research participants, but perhaps also to myself?).[3]

> He tells me I'm not really Vietnamese. That I can't be Vietnamese because I was born in America… How can I prove my Vietnameseness? By drinking?

★★★

I returned to my ancestral homeland, Vietnam, in 2016 to conduct a year-long research project exploring how Sport for Development (SfD) activities in Vietnam are contextualized, organized, and implemented through a participatory research approach. To do so, I became a volunteer with *Football for All in Vietnam (FFAV)*, a SfD project located in Thừa Thiên Huế Province.

There I was.
Living in Vietnam.
For a year.

One year was the longest anyone from my family has lived in Vietnam since my parents sought refuge in America. When Vietnamese people say "đi về", the phrase translates to "go home"; so, when we say "đi về Việt Nam" it means to "go home to Vietnam"—as in the homeland of our ancestors. However, I was hit with the harsh reality that it was not for *me* to determine if I was "home"; instead, my acceptance was determined by Vietnamese people and perhaps my ability to nhậu.

To illustrate (my) ethnographic vulnerability, I draw upon the masculine space of drinking alcohol—that is, nhậu—that I regularly embraced to fit in as both a Vietnamese male and a researcher in the field. In Vietnam, nhậu is a way of creating solid relationships; it is not simply drinking beer, socializing, and gossiping after work. In contrast, others do not appreciate the excuses of these gatherings to drink to stumbling drunkenness (see Lincoln, 2016). Nhậu was a *social process* that allowed me to participate in the local culture. Alcohol consumption in Vietnam comes with equivocal emotions, where many people enjoy coming together with family and friends often associated with a sociability underpinned by the communal and familial traditions of the past (Raffin, 2005). Consider the following example:

> "Một hai ba! Dzô!" The cheers came from across the table and the glasses clicked as the touched and vibrated from our hands. Tonight, was another night, like many others nights, consisting of nhàu between FFAV and people from around the province. But the thing is our common link of culture and history brought us together. We may be FFAV staff and they may be provincial authorities, but we are also Vietnamese.

An FFAV staff member told me that to gain access to communities and become collegial with the people of Huế I would have to go for nhậu, *even at moments when I did not want to*. Not participating in this cultural practice could have presented me as a person who did not want to socialize and, in turn, build relationships with people because it exhibited my unwillingness to appreciate a masculine Huế culture. Furthermore, let me say this; I was always invited for nhậu and never declined. Whether at bars, restaurants, and even in homes of community leaders, I sat with people drinking beer or rice whiskey and discussing life. Even if I became inebriated or knew I would be hungover, I felt the need to be present, to prove myself as a Vietnamese researcher (and keep my access) and person (even worse, male).

> The rượu nếp[4] is poured into a teapot to make it easier to pour for consumption. The next thing I knew, the patriarch was pouring the whiskey into small shot glasses and inviting us to try it. It was already 37 degrees Celsius with humidity. I didn't want to drink it…but I knew how rude it would be to decline as he invited us to his home to drink. So… I did.

During nhậu, the research was situated on participants' terms, in their space, and I believe it was when they felt the most comfortable, even if it meant I felt some intoxication. As I illustrate my emotions and experiences with nhậu, I would be remiss not to imagine and appreciate how the people of Huế allowed me to enter their lives and homes. In writing this, I realize while I was challenged and felt this discomfort, the people of Huế must have also felt vulnerable at moments with me. Vulnerability in spaces of Vietnamese drinking allowed for the dismantling of social and historical barriers, and for the forging of true Vietnamese relationships.

> "The War is long over, brother." The district official speaks to me as we become entranced by the copious amounts of rượu nếp and beer flowing through our veins. "There is no division anymore. There is only hope to reconcile and raise Vietnam. Our blood is the same. In my blood is Vietnam and in your blood is Vietnam." I fill his glass with beer. "So, I am more than happy to help you with whatever is needed. What you are doing is something for Vietnam too." I can't speak. There is a knot in my throat. To live across a cultural binary my entire life, then to hear someone say our blood is the same and this research matters was everything. He pours beer into my cup. Dzô!

This district official did not owe me anything. He didn't have to help me with my dissertation research at all. But this reminds me of a Vietnamese myth that describes how Vietnamese people descend from a love affair between Lạc Long Quân, a dragon king, and Âu Cơ, a fairy princess. The story teaches us that all Vietnamese people come from the same origins, and as such, we should care for one another. We share the same ancestors regardless of where we are born.

Drinking alcohol informs physical culture as it becomes a place where ethnicity, class, and gender are produced and reproduced (Joseph, 2012). In this way, I admit, that being a Vietnamese male allowed me the privilege to embrace nhậu. Drinking alcohol is a valued part of Vietnamese identity that has become a norm among Vietnamese males (Lincoln, 2016). This cannot be said for (Vietnamese) women. There is a cultural masculinity I embody that other researchers may not have. Imagine a woman attempting to enter a private room of all Vietnamese men drinking to get drunk—it is not *safe*. But like Joseph (2012) and Donnelly (2014)—both of whom are women—research is fluid in gendered dynamics and drinking alcohol is a cultural space where research becomes vulnerable, dangerous, and unpredictable. Joseph (2012) was warned of the drinking culture among Caribbean cricket players during her research. Similarly, Donnelly (2014) entered the bar to drink with participants during her research on roller derby even when she felt uneasy about it because she found that drinking was part of the process. Drinking makes us vulnerable (physically, emotionally, psychologically)—we lose ourselves, and losing ourselves in the research can be scary, because we are no longer "in control", no longer the distant researcher, and no longer the neutral observer. But, that's the thing, to become vulnerable is to make research real, to fold research into peoples' everyday lives, participants and in many ways to our own. Someone offering you a drink and holding your hand and singing about national identity and history and blood is *real*—it opens you up to emotions and feelings, and in the context of research makes participant and researcher potentially, and productively, vulnerable to the other. Ethnography forces some of us to go beyond the everyday technicism of research (i.e., observing social interactions, writing up fieldnotes, etc.); we are asked to embrace the uncomfortable—like drinking copious amounts of alcohol, and all the physical, emotional, and psychological baggage that follows from there—as a way into the everyday of life of our research participants and the communities and cultural histories they inhabit. Fieldnotes may be incoherent, conversations may not be related to the research, or you may open up your own life to the participants. You may want to avoid going for nhậu but in doing so the people who you wish to talk to and possibly help may never open up. Being physically, emotionally, or ethically vulnerable means knowing that research and people's lives extend beyond the academy—I was vulnerable to them as they were vulnerable to me, though not always at the same time, and not always in the same way. For me, nhậu was a way to embrace Vietnam and the participants, but it was also a way for FFAV and the people of Huế to embrace me in their own ways.

### Hugo Ceron-Anaya

"Hurry up and wait" is the typical formula enlisted personnel use to describe life in the U.S. military. The oxymoronic phrase aims to convey two distinct states. On the one hand, it expresses a condition to be alert and prepared to do something (at the commands of one's superiors). On the other, it communicates a state of stillness, inactivity, and lethargy that emanates from the low-ranked position of the person. The phrase encapsulates how domination takes the form of time control. The "studying up" literature has long pointed out how when the normal class relations favoring researchers over research populations are inverted, the former become vulnerable subjects (Ceron-Anaya, 2019; Donaldson and Poynting, 2013; Gaztambide-Fernández & Howard, 2012; Hoffman, 1980; Hirsch, 1995; Ostrander, 1993; Pierce, 1995; Schneider & Aguiar, 2016).

My research experience doing an ethnography of upper-class golf players in Mexico strongly resemble the case (Ceron-Anaya, 2019). In this nation, golf is a sport played exclusively in private settings, and the average cost of a membership in one of the 13 clubs in Mexico City is around US$37,000 (Ceron-Anaya, 2017). By contrast, the average annual income (after taxes) is only US$15,314 (OECD, 2017). I arrived at golf as a researcher interested in "studying up" class inequalities, not as a fan. The issue of class inequities that brought me to the sport turned out to be a key element in the research process (alongside race and gender, as I detailed in my book *Privilege at Play: Class, Race, Gender, and Golf in Mexico*). At the time of the fieldwork, my class position, as a junior scholar without a permanent job yet, economically situated me near the working class. In some instances, the substantive cultural capital (see Bourdieu, 1977) accumulated in my academic trajectory allowed me to compensate for my limited possession of economic assets. Yet, in most instances, I was the vulnerable subject.

I want to illustrate the argument by using two contrasting examples. First, I want to elaborate on the "interview" with Omar.[5] Through the fieldwork, I interviewed the owner of a company organizing one of the most important amateur golf tournaments in Mexico. The interviewee accepted my request to attend the upcoming leg of the competition, which was going to take place in a prestigious club in the capital city. I joined the event as a guest of the organizing crew, not as a player. Early on the day of the contest, the manager of the organizing team informed me that Omar was the most prominent corporate executive playing that day. He was the regional director of a global technology company. My project used a snowball technique, in which, at the end of the interviews, I asked participants to put me in contact with other golfers. The possibility of contacting a prominent corporate executive and reaching out to his social network was appealing. Before the beginning of the tournament, I approached Omar introducing myself as a researcher. I asked if he was willing to talk about the world of golf in Mexico.

Omar agreed to be interviewed but asked me to look for him at the end of the event, which I knew would be about six hours later. I interviewed the club's manager in the first hours of the day. I also had long conversations about the affluent world of golf with several workers and reporters situated in the tents where golfers stopped for refreshments and looked at all sorts of upscale products (from luxury brands of cars to highly specialized financial services). The interviews with workers were constantly interrupted by the distant appearance of approaching golfers, as workers adopted an attentive attitude toward players' needs and interests. The conversation could only resume when no player was in sight. These interactions followed a "hurry up and wait" flow. Four hours into the event, I had already conducted multiple interviews with workers and filled several pages of my notebook with comments and observations. I was tired but could not leave without talking with Omar; I had to wait.

An hour and a half later, the first players who finished the 18 holes started passing in front of the tents, where all the other workers and I were. I was vigilant, paying careful attention to the large groups of players passing in front of the area. I did not want to miss the opportunity to talk with Omar. I saw him coming while distractedly chatting with another player. I approached him and again asked for an interview. He graciously agreed and sat down with me at the bar. He answered my first question in no more than 30 seconds. I elaborated on the second question, aiming to encourage him to talk more. The answer, however, was even shorter. I kept the strategy, expanding on my question. The third response was similarly brief. As I was trying to rephrase the questions so he would elaborate on the points already asked, he promptly excused himself, saying, "I am sorry, but I need to catch up with someone else." He then moved to the adjacent table and began chatting enthusiastically with other golfers about the tournament they had just played. In no more than three minutes, Omar had finished the interview. As discreetly as possible, I contained my anger and returned to the group of workers packing everything at the center of the course.

The interview with Omar was the most explicit example of my subordination in the field. Notwithstanding, it was not the only instance where time took the form of class domination. For instance, setting up interviews with wealthy golfers was a time-consuming activity. Commonly, after I got someone's contact information, the first step was to contact secretaries who asked for short summaries of the topics I wanted to discuss with their bosses and then questions about my time availability. Regarding the latter, my answer was simple. I could come anytime the person was free to talk. Despite my time flexibility, it was not easy to set up the meetings. I constantly called and emailed secretaries to make their bosses agree on a date and time. On most occasions, the secretary called me back at the last minute to inform me that her boss would not be able to meet with me on that day. Invariably, the call came when I was about to arrive at the interviewee's office or the restaurant where the person had agreed to meet with me. In every one of these cases, I had already driven through heavy traffic for about an hour. Despite my profound frustration, I could not openly complain about the lack of respect for my time with the secretary. As in the case of the short interview with Omar, I graciously thanked the secretary for informing me about the cancelation, sent my regards to the interviewee, and started the process again two or three days later. My fieldwork notebook is full of notes about my irritation with last-minute cancelations, the large amount of time required to set up interviews, and people making me wait for long periods in their offices or restaurants before showing up.

Although the act of waiting may seem like the result of a set of unfortunate external factors—or even just a natural part of ethnographic fieldwork—I argue that this is not a *neutral* situation. Zohre Najafi (2022), in fact, argues that "Marx's critique of class exploitation and commodification of social relations, in the final analysis, consists in the critique of domination of time over man" (p. 1). Making someone wait (for them) is an *ordinary* expression of class domination. By extension, the act of waiting is the manifestation of someone's class vulnerability. The point becomes more evident when the experience of interviewing wealthy golfers is compared with the dynamics of interviewing caddies. The latter are the workers who assist players during the game, carrying the clubs, finding lost balls, and offering advice about the game. In the clubs I visited, caddies were contingent workers who received a salary only when they were called onto the course. Caddies described themselves as members of the working class. Interviewing these workers was considerably more straightforward than the time-consuming process of arranging meetings with club members. For example, a journalist gave me the contact information of a caddy. I called him to arrange an appointment. After I explained why I wanted to talk to him, the worker immediately agreed to be interviewed, telling me that we could meet the following day at the caddies' house at the club where he worked, adding, "I'm always there." Caddies frequently expressed the above idea in a multitude of ways. This was the case of another caddy who explained, "It is common to stay here [at the caddies' house] one or two days waiting for your turn [to work but not being called]. [The] job is unreliable, but we need to stay here taking care of it." I spent several days in different caddie's houses doing ethnographic work, witnessing how the act of waiting is a central feature of a caddie's job.

My research experience doing a "studying up" ethnography frequently implied the act of waiting when I was dealing with golfers, but not in the case of caddies—whom I found I had much in common with relative to our experiences and interactions with those with whom we waited. In line with the first argument presented, time control and the ensuing act of making people wait represent an act of class domination that I could not escape. In my interactions with club members, I was constantly in need to "hurry up and wait" because the class imbalance renders me a vulnerable subject. In this way, it helped me to relate to the caddies and their experiences (and how little the executive golfers considered them), and to understand better how normalized the disregard for their time by those executives was.

### Michael Giardina

*I… don't think I should be here.*

At least, that is what I am thinking to myself as I make my way through the gathered throng of people milling about the Toshiba Plaza in front of the T-Mobile Arena in Las Vegas, Nevada, on a crisp October 2021 evening. Nearly two years into the pandemic, with BioNTech and Moderna vaccines and their respective boosters now more readily accessible in the United States—and more tourist and entertainment destinations "opening up" again—I have traveled here to conduct research on the intersection of sport, promotional culture, and urban development in the city over the last few years.[6]

I make my way through the crowd toward one of the entrances, stopping occasionally to make note of how many people in the plaza are not wearing masks or socially distancing (seems like 50/50). Once at the gate, I use the Ticketmaster app on my smartphone to gain entry; an arena staff member advises fans to "Keep your mask on at all times unless eating or drinking" and waves fans through the gate; mask-clad staffers positioned around the arena hold small signs with similar reminders.

> *But pandemic policies remain inconsistent. The previous night, in order to gain entry to a jazz concert at Dolby Live at Park MGM on the other side of the plaza, attendees not only needed to wear masks but were mandated to use the CLEAR app and complete the requisite Health Pass Entry information request, to which I added a digital vaccine card record.[7]*

I take my seat in the upper bowl next to a late-middle aged couple on one side and a mid-20s group of three friends on the other side; they are all wearing Vegas Golden Knights apparel in some form (i.e., hat, t-shirt, or jersey), and all live within about 30 minutes of the arena. Local residents, in other words. During the litany of usual pregame announcements over the public address system, fans are reminded of the masking requirement and asked to be considerate of their fellow fans. It's early in the season, only the fourth game of the year for the Golden Knights, and with pandemic attendance limits no longer in place the arena is rocking with enthusiastic fans.[8] The couple next to me is celebrating the man's birthday (let's call him Jim); he is a short-haul truck driver, and his partner (Tonya) is an office manager. As the night goes on, and they consume more and more beer, their masks slide farther and farther down their respective faces, their cheering gets louder, and they openly start discussing the mask policy with anyone who will listen to them after they are reminded several times by a weary arena staff member patrolling the stairs to "Please pull those masks up, thank you".

> "This is ridiculous", Jim says with a sigh to no one in particular. "There's like 20,000 people here. What good is a mask going to do?"
> *(I mean, plenty…)*

> "C'mon dear, just put the mask back on", Tonya says, a bit impatiently.
> "It's stupid, though" he says, pulling the mask back up over his nose.
> "If we all get COVID we'll have herd immunity anyway. What's the point now?"
> *This is both epidemiologically and immunologically more complex than that (see, e.g., Randolph & Barreiro, 2020), but I'm not exactly in the mood to engage in this discourse at this point in the evening.*

The Golden Knights score a goal early in the second period to take the lead over the visiting Edmonton Oilers; fans erupt with cheers, high-fives, and fist bumps. Masks come off all around me. Drinks are taken. Masks stay off a bit longer than usual. Arena staffers look exasperated: it's only the third home game of the year; they have 38 more to go.

> *I…I probably shouldn't be here.*

★★★

Trisha Greenhalgh and Ama de-Graft Aikins (2023) assert that the COVID-19 pandemic is not just another aspect of our current context but rather *is* our current context—one that impacts all facets of our everyday lives. Conducting research—especially ethnographic research in which there is by definition a physical presence with and among other bodies and places—naturally carries with it a degree of risk.[9] But from the perspective of researcher vulnerability in a broader sense, conducting ethnography in the new normal context of a pandemic raises some challenging if not disconcerting questions.

First, there are concrete questions and considerations to take from the vignette above vis-à-vis health-related researcher vulnerability. For example, was I asymptomatically COVID-positive as I traversed the various sporting geographies of my field research, potentially passing along aerosolized particulate matter (i.e., airborne transmission of the SARS-CoV-2 virus) as I breathed in and out, despite wearing a KN-95 grade mask while indoors, traveling via airplane, and so forth? In the obverse, were those I came in close contact with COVID-positive and ignoring their symptoms (or refusing to or unable to get tested for diagnostic purposes), thereby exposing me? Would I in extremis bring the potential viral specter of death home to my family and colleagues when I returned from the field? The answer to each of these questions is, troublingly, perhaps. So yes, I was epidemiologically "vulnerable" in the context of carrying out this particular engagement in the field—just as were the other 18,000 or so people in the arena that night who were there to consume a sporting event. On the face of it, these are important technical questions to ask about even being in the field in the first place—and being thanatopolitically vulnerable (see Troyer, 2021) to and within that field.

But that leads me to the second, and perhaps more consequential, consideration for the orientation of this volume—that of the existential vulnerability facing academics in the present context (i.e., pandemic times; see Denzin & Giardina, forthcoming). Much has been written about the turn toward audit culture, bibliometrics, and new managerialism strategies employed within the research university (see, e.g., Cheek, 2018; Spooner, 2018), and the incessant (some might say absurd) lengths academics must often go through to quantify their scholarly impact (see, e.g., Pardo-Guerra, 2022; Shore, 2008). But with some exceptions (see, e.g., Bunds, 2021; Sparkes, 2021), less has been said in the pages of methods-oriented books or in journal articles about the anxiety and internalized pressures and indeed vulnerabilities that are revealed in and through conducting research in this system— and what that does for the practice of research itself.

Put differently, I was able to rationalize the micropolitical factors of being on the ground in Las Vegas to do research in the midst of the pandemic (i.e., I was wearing a high-quality mask, I was both vaccinated and boosted, etc.). As we've learned over the last three years, short of locking ourselves in our homes and cutting off all human contact, there is no failsafe way to avoid exposure to the virus. Thus, taking steps to moderate risk factors (e.g., wearing masks, avoiding crowded indoor spaces with poor ventilation, etc.) has become a banal part of the calculus of conducting research in the field (or traveling on vacation, or going to a restaurant, etc.). Although this is troubling to be sure, what troubles me more is the retrospective accounting of the macropolitical factors governing the research act in the first place.

Specifically, I question why I was in the field at that moment in the first place. Or, put differently, why was I making myself and potential interlocutors (more) vulnerable during a pandemic? Scholarly contribution to the literature? Fair enough. After all, Fine and Abramson (2020) express what many classical field ethnographers had to contend with during this period, writing,

> While physical distancing is necessary, we also must remember why this style of research has been central to sociological inquiry. Many who employ this method contend now, as we once did, that by looking close-up, in real time, we can understand key dynamics of social life in ways that more distant methods cannot.
>
> *(para. 7)*

Or was it to tick another box in the neoliberal accounting metrics for being a "productive" scholar, even during a pandemic? Perhaps. Following Sparkes (2021), maybe I was simply making a spectacle of myself "for purposes of comparison and evaluation by others" in the performance of being an academic. But frankly, I didn't need another publication at that moment—my quantified research self (see Cheek, 2018) is relatively secure in the trappings of tenure and the rank of full professor.

The vulnerability that is revealed and negated in the paragraph above (and throughout my section here) is the crux of the matter. Epidemiologically, I was quite likely vulnerable in the exercise of my research in that moment. But professionally, I wasn't that vulnerable at all. *It was an exercise of privilege to conduct field research during a pandemic; an exercise of privilege to pick how, where, where, and to what extent I conducted that fieldwork; and an exercise in privilege to be retrospectively critical of doing that fieldwork in the first place.* Graduate students, junior scholars, and members of the "academic precariat" (Burton & Bowman, 2022) are not so lucky—they are vulnerable to the very system that renders me not (as) vulnerable (in the sense of not having the luxury to choose to be vulnerable or less vulnerable during the pandemic). As Barr (2020) described our unequal pandemic experiences, "We are *not* all in the same boat. We are just all in the same storm. Some are on super-yachts. Some have just the one oar" (para. 1, emphasis mine). This is true, and also the problem (for many reasons). In the context of this chapter, examining and being honest about our differentiated vulnerabilities—or differently arrayed forms of vulnerabilities—should cause us to take a hard look inward at the kind of work we are doing, who benefits (or does not) from that work, and what we can do to ease or lessen the vulnerabilities to which we may be (un)intentionally contributing.

## Coda

In this chapter, we have endeavored to illustrate the different ways researchers become vulnerable subjects in the fieldwork. Even though their large amount of cultural capital materialized in academic credentials, the vignettes presented in this chapter show moments in which ethnographers feel pushed to participate in hazardous activities, engage in dangerous situations, feel belittled, and question their actions in the field. In specific contexts, the power dynamics that commonly favor the researcher over the research subjects can get inverted. It is in these instances that we become vulnerable. Although the latter is a condition generally associated with a set of negative connotations, we would like to reverse the common understanding about it. This does not mean that we aim to minimize the vulnerable situations we encountered in our respective projects. On the contrary, we want to use these adverse events as regenerative experiences.

We argue that the unpleasant, dangerous, or risky situations described in this chapter offer new angles to rethink ethnographic fieldwork. First, we illustrated in our vignettes how cultural norms, structural forces, social demands, and personal identities are not only part of our analytical toolkits. In multiple degrees, we are part of the same social worlds we aim to explain, and hence we are also subject to its forces. The situations described here represent cautionary tales for other ethnographers. These stories do not seek to scare scholars from pursuing similar projects. Instead, the episodes want to make researchers attentive to a set of unpleasant and threatening situations that they may find in their research. As social scientists, we know about structural forces and their effect on people. Yet, we were not fully prepared to see the impact of those structural conditions in our research endeavors. By highlighting these situations, we aim to emphasize the need to be mindful of our unavoidable structural and personal vulnerabilities during the fieldwork.

Second, it is relevant to recognize that vulnerability never takes a single form. The stories presented seek to reiterate the myriad ways ethnographers could experience vulnerable situations. In some cases, researchers' social, psychological, and physical fragility emanates from cultural norms that turn scholars into outsiders. In others, our marginalized position is based on social assumptions about how our gendered and sexed bodies should act. An ethnographer's positioned weakness could also come from the broader set of power relations that organize a field, which inevitably acts on all subjects in the social space, including the researcher. In the same vein, an ethnographer could also experience a vulnerable situation based on the social pressure that expects academics to produce, even at the cost of their well-being. The vignettes also illustrate a series of accounts not frequently presented in methodological discussions about how to conduct ethnographic fieldwork.

Finally, we also want to highlight the analytical dimension these ethnographic encounters possess. In the four stories, we each became vulnerable because our identities and assets were viewed as unimportant, questionable, or submissive. For Devra, it was her embodied and gendered vulnerability; for Michael Dao it was the intersection of nationality and masculinity; for Hugo, it was a vulnerability brought on by class domination; and for Michael Giardina it was both the epidemiological vulnerability alongside the political vulnerability negated in the academy. The vulnerable positions we either opted into or were forced to take (even for a brief period) represent the opposite location of where powerful individuals reside. The vignettes are reversed descriptions of how a dominant subject would be perceived and treated. Being vulnerable is a condition that illustrates the characteristics of those living within the borders of the social field. Therefore, it is possible to infer how power looks and acts by reversing these stories. Analytically, these commonly untold stories offer a crucial opportunity for ethnographers to capture the human experience relationally, to trouble both their experiences in the field and the findings generated therefrom, and to reconsider the productive possibility and potentiality of vulnerability within the research act.

## Notes

1 Quán nhậu is a nhậu restaurant that are often frequented by groups of men and the hostesses are women serving men.
2 In relation to gender and masculinity, I was often asked if I was single and if I was interested in marrying a Vietnamese woman.

3 As a Vietnamese person born in the United States, I am often questioned of how truly Vietnamese I am.
4 Rice Whiskey.
5 All names are pseudonyms.
6 During that time (c. 2018–2021), three new major professional sports franchises came into being in the city, and roughly $5 billion worth of new sport and/or entertainment-focused venues were completed or began construction (e.g., Allegiant Stadium, T-Mobile Arena, MSG Sphere, Dolby Live at Park MGM, Stadium Swim Sportsbook at Circa Resort & Casino, etc.).
7 Much has been made (see, e.g., Esmonde, 2019; Lupton, 2019) about fitness trackers and the associated biometric data surveillance issues, but concert-goers happily (or at least grudgingly) acceded to the demands of the document verification system that has become increasingly popular at major U.S. airports and sporting events during the pandemic.
8 T-Mobile Arena is generally considered to be one of the loudest arenas in the league; this particular game drew an announced crowd of 17,978, which is actually above the stated capacity of the arena (17,367) for hockey.
9 Goodall (in Stewart, Hess, Tracy, & Goodall, 2009) has previously discussed questions of risk in ethnography as something to be considered in the conduct of one's research (i.e., the kinds of groups we might study, the locations of those studies, or the risk we might cause to our participants or to our personal or professional self).

## References

Ahmed, S. (2000). *Strange Encounters: Embodied Others in Post-Coloniality*. London: Routledge.

Al-Hindi, K. F., & Kawabata, H. (2002). Toward a more fully reflexive feminist geography. In P. J. Moss (Ed.), *Feminist Geography in Practice: Research and Methods* (pp. 103–115). London: Blackwell.

Atkinson, P., Delamont, S., & Housely, W. (2008). *Contours of Culture: Complex Ethnography and the Ethnography of Complexity*. Lanham, MD: AltaMira.

Barr, D. (2020). We are not all in the same boat. DamionBarr.com. https://www.damianbarr.com/latest/tag/We+are+not+all+in+the+same+boat.+We+are+all+in+the+same+storm

Behar, R. (1997). *The Vulnerable Observer: Anthropology That Breaks Your Heart*. Boston, MA: Beacon Press.

Bourdieu, P. (1977). Cultural reproduction and social reproduction. In J. Karabel & A. H. Halsey (Eds.), *Power and Ideology in Education* (pp. 487–511). Oxford University Press.

Bunds, K. S. (2017). *Sport, Politics, and the Charity Industry: Running for Water*. London: Routledge.

Bunds, K. S. (2021). "Please let it stop": Fear, anxiety, and uncertainty on the neoliberal tenure track. *Qualitative Inquiry, 27*, 1040–1047.

Burton, S., & Bowman, B. (2022). The academic precariat: Understanding life and labour in the neoliberal academy. *British Journal of Sociology of Education, 43*, 497–512.

Caretta, M. A., & Jokinen, J. C. (2017). Conflating privilege and vulnerability: A reflexive analysis of emotions and positionality in postgraduate fieldwork. *The Professional Geographer, 69*(2), 275–283. https://doi.org/10.1080/00330124.2016.1252268

Ceron-Anaya, H. (2017). Not everybody is a golfer: Bourdieu and affluent bodies in Mexico. *Journal of Contemporary Ethnography, 46*(3), 285–309.

Ceron-Anaya, H. (2019). *Privilege at Play: Class, Race, Gender, and Golf in Mexico*. New York: Oxford University Press.

Cheek, J. (2018). The marketization of research: Implications for qualitative inquiry. In N. K. Denzin, & Y. S. Lincoln (Eds.), *The SAGE Handbook of Qualitative Research* (5th ed., pp. 322–340). Thousand Oaks, CA: Sage.

Coffey, A. (1999). *The Ethnographic Self.* Thousand Oaks, CA: Sage.

Cupples, J. (2002). The field as a landscape of desire: Sex and sexuality in geographical fieldwork. *Area, 34*(4), 382–390.

Donaldson, M., & Poynting, S. (2013). Peering upwards: Researching ruling-class men. In *Men, Masculinities and Methodologies* (pp. 157–169). New York: Springer.

Donnelly, M. K. (2014). Drinking with the derby girls: Exploring the hidden ethnography in research of women's flat track roller derby. *International Review for the Sociology of Sport, 49*, 346–366.

Esmonde, K. (2019). Training, tracking, and traversing: Digital materiality and the production of bodies and/in space in runners' fitness tracking apps. *Leisure Studies, 38*, 908–917.

Faria, C., & Mollett, S. (2016). Critical feminist reflexivity and the politics of whiteness in the 'field'. *Gender, Place & Culture, 23*(1), 79–93. https://doi.org/10.1080/09663 69X.2014.958065

Fine, G. A., & Abramson, C. M. (2020). Ethnography in the time of COVID-19. *Footnotes: A Magazine of the American Sociological Association,* May/June, p. 9.

Fujimura, J. H. (2006). Sex genes: A critical sociomaterial approach to the politics and molecular genetics of sex determination. *Signs: Journal of Women in Culture and Society, 32*(1), 49–82. https://doi.org/10.1086/505612

Gammeltoft, T. M., Huyền Diệu, B. T., Kim Dung, V. T., Đức Anh, V., Minh Hiếu, L., & Thị Ái, N. (2021). Existential vulnerability: An ethnographic study of everyday lives with diabetes in Vietnam. *Anthropology & Medicine.* https://doi.org/10.1080/13648470.2021. 1994334. Online ahead of print.

Gaztambide-Fernández, R. A., & Howard, A. (2012). Access, status, and representation: Some reflections from two ethnographic studies of elite schools. *Anthropology & Education Quarterly, 43*(3), 289–305.

Giardina, M. D., & Donnelly, M. K. (Eds.) (2017). *Physical Culture and Embodied Ethnography: Theory, Method, and Praxis.* London: Routledge.

Giardina, M. D., & Donnelly, M. K. (2023). Ethnographic futures: Embodied, diffractive, and decolonizing approaches. In N. K. Denzin, Y. S. Lincoln, M. D. Giardina, & G. S. Cannella (Eds.), *The SAGE Handbook of Qualitative Research* (6th ed.) (pp. 351–368). Thousand Oaks, CA: Sage.

Giardina, M. D., & Newman, J. I. (2011). What is this 'physical' in physical cultural studies. *Sociology of Sport Journal, 28*, 36–63.

Gill, R. (2016). Breaking the silence: The hidden injuries of the neo-liberal academy. *Feministicsche Studien, 34*, 39–55.

Green, K. (2016). Tales from the mat: Narrating men and meaning making in the mixed martial arts gym. *Journal of Contemporary Ethnography, 45*, 419–450.

Greenhalgh, T., & de-Graft Aikins, A. (2023). Qualitative research and public health science: Case studies from the COVID-19 pandemic. In N. K. Denzin, Y. S. Lincoln, M. D. Giardina, & G. S. Cannella (Eds.), *The SAGE Handbook of Qualitative Research* (6th ed.) (pp. 501–518). Thousand Oaks, CA: Sage.

Guiliano, J. (2011). Chasing objectivity? Critical reflections on history, identity, and the public performance of Indian mascots. *Cultural Studies ↔ Critical Methodologies, 11*(6), 535–543. https://doi.org/10.1177/1532708611426108.

Hanson, R., & Richards, P. (2019). *Harassed: Gender, Bodies, and Ethnographic Research.* Berkeley, CA: University of California Press.

Hardt, M. (1999). Affective labor. *Boundary, 2*(26), 89–100.

Hirsch, P. M. (1995). Tales from the field: Learning from researchers' accounts. In R. Hertz, & J. B. Imber (Eds.), *Studying Elites Using Qualitative Methods* (pp. 74–79). Thousand Oaks, CA: Sage.

Hoffman, J. E. (1980). Problems of access in the study of social elites and boards of directors. In W. Shaffir, & R. A. Stebbins (Eds.), *Field Work Experience: Qualitative Approaches to Social Research* (pp. 45–56. New York: St. Martins.

Joseph, J. (2012). Around the boundary: Alcohol and older Caribbean-Canadian men. *Leisure Studies, 31,* 147–163.

Lincoln, M. (2016). Alcohol and drinking cultures in Vietnam: A review. *Drug and Alcohol Dependence, 159,* 1–8.

Lupton, D. (2019). "It's made me a lot more aware": A new materialist analysis of health self-tracking. *Media International Australia, 171,* 66–79.

Markowitz, D. (2009). Occidental dreams: Orientalism and history in The Second Sex. *Signs, 34,* 271–294.

McCarthy, C., Durham, A. S., Engel, L. C., Filmer, A. L., Giardina, M. D., & Malagrecra, M. A. (Eds.) (2007). *Globalizing Cultural Studies: Ethnographic Interventions in Theory, Method, and Policy.* New York, NY: Peter Lang.

Mears, A. (2008). Discipline of the catwalk: Gender, power, and uncertainty in fashion modeling. *Ethnography, 9,* 429–456.

Najafi, Z. (2022). Dialectical relation of temporal domination and class exploitation in Marx's value theory. *Capital & Class,* online first https://doi.org/10.1177/0309816822111437

Nayak, A. (2006). After race: Ethnography, race and post-race theory. *Ethnic and Racial Studies, 29*(3), 411–430. https://doi.org/10.1080/01419870600597818

OECD. 2017. Average annual wages. OECD Employment and Labour Market Statistics (database). Accessed July 10, 2018. https://doi.org/10.1787/f5dc582e-en

Ostrander, S. A. (1993). "Surely you're not in this just to be helpful" Access, rapport, and interviews in three studies of elites. *Journal of Contemporary Ethnography, 22*(1), 7–27.

Pardo-Guerra, J. P. (2022). *The Quantified Scholar: How Research Evaluations Transformed the British Social Sciences.* New York: Columbia University Press.

Parvez, Z. F. (2018). The sorrow of parting: Ethnographic depth and the role of emotions. *Journal of Contemporary Ethnography, 47,* 454–483.

Pierce, J. (1995). Reflections of fieldwork in a complex organization: Lawyers, ethnographic authority, and lethal weapons. In R. Hertz, & J. B. Imber (Eds.), *Studying Elites Using Qualitative Methods* (pp. 94–110). Thousand Oaks, CA, Sage.

Pillow, W. (2003). Confession, catharsis, or cure? Rethinking the uses of reflexivity as methodological power in qualitative research. *International Journal of Qualitative Studies in Education, 16*(2), 175–196. https://doi.org/10.1080/0951839032000060635

Randolph, H. E., & Barreiro, L. B. (2020). Herd immunity: Understanding COVID-19. *Immunity, 52,* 373–741.

Said, E. (1978). *Orientalism.* New York: Random House.

Shore, C. (2008). Audit culture and illiberal governance: Universities and the politics of accountability. *Anthropological Theory, 8,* 278–298.

Smith, L. T. (1999). *Decolonizing Methodologies: Research and Indigenous Peoples.* London: Zed Books.

Stewart, K. A., Hess, A., Tracy, S. J., & Goodall, H. L., Jr. (2009). Risky research: Investigating the 'perils' of ethnography. In N. K. Denzin & M. D. Giardina (Eds.), *Qualitative Inquiry and Social Justice* (pp. 198–216). London: Routledge.

Raffin, A. (2005). *Youth Mobilization in Vichy Indochina and Its Legacies, 1940 to 1970*. Lanham, MD: Lexington Books.

Schneider, C. J., & L. L. Aguiar (2016). *Researching amongst Elites: Challenges and Opportunities in Studying Up*. London: Routledge.

Sparkes, A. C. (2021). Making a spectacle of oneself in the academy using the H-index: From becoming an artificial person to laughing at absurdities. *Qualitative Inquiry, 37*, 1027–1039.

Spooner, M. (2018). Qualitative research and global audit culture: The politics of productivity, accountability, and possibility. In N. K. Denzin, & Y. S. Lincoln (Eds.), *The SAGE Handbook of Qualitative Research* (5th ed.) (pp. 894–914). Thousand Oaks, CA: Sage.

Troyer, J. (2021). On the politics of death. *The MIT Press Reader*. https://thereader.mitpress.mit.edu/thanatopolitics-on-the-politics-of-death/

Wacquant, L. (2004). *Body & Soul: Notebooks of an Apprentice Boxer*. New York: Oxford University Press.

Waldman, D. (2022). Aiming for the 'green': (Post)colonial and aesthetic politics in the design of a purified gated environment. https://onlinelibrary.wiley.com/doi/full/10.1111/1468-2427.13077

Waldman, D., & Weedon, G. (2019). Postcolonialism, pristine natures, and producing the village green: Pastoral Englishness in Indian cricket-themed gated communities. In *Sport, Development and Environmental Sustainability* (pp. 64–78). London: Routledge.

Winfield, T. P. (2022). Vulnerable research: Competencies for trauma and justice-informed ethnography. *Journal of Contemporary Ethnography, 51*, 135–170.

# SECTION III

# Embracing Researcher Vulnerability

# 10

# FEMME PRAXIS

## Using femme theory to foster vulnerability within research design and institutions

*Rhea Ashley Hoskin and Lilith A. Whiley*

### Introduction

Have you ever crafted an email and then revised it to remove exclamation points, fearing that you may come across as overly emotional, infantile, unprofessional, too "people pleasing" or – worse – ditzy (Waseleski, 2006)? Or, maybe, you picked a suit over a dress for an important presentation, because it looked more professional, and people are more apt to take you seriously in a suit (Hoskin, 2019). Regardless of a person's gender identity or gender expression, many academics find themselves in a position where they need to strategically perform in a less feminine or more masculine way (Banchefsky et al., 2016; Hoskin, 2019, 2020). This gendered code-switching can be performed in terms of aesthetics, whereby someone feels they are taken less seriously in a dress than when they are in a suit, but this gendered power shift can also inform affective behaviour, professional relationships, institutional power, and research. Indeed, one could argue that the latter subtly cues the former: too often, academia and research do not welcome "the feminine", thus reifying a culture of stoicism, claimed "objectivity", invulnerability, and moreover, *anti*-vulnerability.

Throughout this chapter, we do not use the term femininity and womanly synonymously. Rather, we use femininity to refer to the set of characteristics, behaviours, and traits historically associated with women but equally available across bodies and identities (see Taylor & Hoskin, 2023 for a full operationalization). By examining femininity as a set of characteristics available to "all" and, yet, discouraged when expressed by most to different degrees, we seek to illuminate the co-constituted nature of femmephobia (i.e., the systematic devaluation and regulation of femininity [Hoskin, 2017a, 2020]) and anti-vulnerability that proliferate within masculine domains like academia. Here, we offer femme theory as a means of challenging both the gender and power structures that perpetuate anti-vulnerability. Of course,

DOI: 10.4324/9781003349266-14

we are not the first scholars to ponder the gendered power structures within academia. Indeed, others before us have spotlighted the harsh inequalities faced by feminine and feminised people under the toxic masculinism of science and knowledge production (e.g., Bell et al., 2019; Biggs et al., 2018; Bleijenbergh et al., 2013; Bourabain, 2021; Boustani & Taylor, 2020; Fotaki, 2011, 2013; Huopalainen & Satama, 2019; Jackson, 2017, 2021; Karami et al., 2020; Lund & Tienari, 2019; Mähldck, 2021; Mandalaki & Pérezts, 2021; Meriläinen, Salmela, & Valtonen, 2022; Savigny, 2017; Sobande & Wells, 2023).

Traditionally, norms of masculinist science (e.g., Lather, 1988) require that researchers frame their work as superseding or supplanting their predecessors – exposing a gap wherein the contribution ameliorates. Rather than perpetuating validation via domination, this chapter is written in the spirit of collaboration and humble co-creation. It is in this spirit that we seek to contribute to the existing bodies of literature cited above by offering femme theory and our framework of femme-torship (Hoskin & Whiley, 2023) as helpful resources in materializing the value of vulnerability and femininity in academia.

In an analysis of one million doctoral dissertations between 1980 and 2010, Kim et al. (2022) found a widespread bias against feminine research that was distinct from bias towards woman-focused research. Arguably, this bias is a product of how femininity is constructed and, more specifically, how knowledge is gendered. Femininity is often associated with emotionality and sentimentality (Cvetkovich, 1992) – base emotions that are purportedly anathema to more masculine traits like cerebral reason, high-minded rationality, and scholarly science (Bagilhole, 2002; Savigny, 2017). And, importantly, these masculinist norms are fostered, normalized, and reproduced through interpersonal relationships (including mentorship styles), and approaches to research that delegitimate feminine-coded ways of being and knowing. For instance, mentors may advise mentees to avoid feminine dresses, pink clothing, and other aesthetic markers of western femininity such as painted nails and coloured hair in order to be taken more seriously. They may also advise against appearing overly emotional, sensitive, or nurturing towards others; for doing so renders them incompetent in the eyes of their peers (see Bonnes, 2022). These are examples of "lean in" advice that is based on em**power**ment discourses, which "mentor" women and other minorities to emulate masculine characteristics, rather than challenge the imperative and valuing of masculinity itself (Jackson, 2017).

Such approaches uphold the current gender-value system that prioritizes masculinity and existing power structures. As a result, rather than changing existing power structures to fit minority populations, these approaches encourage those who have been historically excluded from power to "pretend" to fit into a mould built to keep them oppressed, reifying the status quo while instilling feelings of imposter syndrome and outsiderness (Beard, 2017). Change, however, requires transforming systems and structures. As we will argue, systems, structures, and approaches that reify masculine ontologies and epistemologies may also foster a culture of anti-femininity – and all that is coded feminine – through affective, embodied, and communicative norms, as well as gendered power structures. In response, a growing body of scholarship has reconsidered the academic imperative of anti-femininity, arguing instead for the valuation of traits deemed feminine in academia and research; for instance, vulnerability.

## Vulnerability and femininity

Vulnerability and femininity are co-constructed, as are the underlying structures that maintain their devaluation. In the western world, vulnerability has been coded as feminine (Ziarek, 2013) and perceived as synonymous with submissiveness and feebleness (Schwartz, 2022). As femme theorists would argue, it is vulnerability's very association with femininity that makes it especially damning. Gilson (2016) points out that, "the vexing nature of vulnerability can be attributed to the way it is associated with both femininity and with weakness and dependency" (p. 71). Like femininity, vulnerability is seen as "weakness, softness, permeability, a sense of being affected, imprinted upon, or entered and shattered" (Dahl, 2017, p. 35). Within masculinist epistemologies, to be vulnerable is to be susceptible "to harmful wrongs, exploitation, or threats" (Mackenzie et al., 2014, p. 6). Invulnerability thus becomes a means of maintaining a privileged position in a neoliberal socio-economic system – a "marker of achievement and status" (Gilson, 2016, p. 76). It is true that invulnerability can afford a cloak of protection, especially given that minoritized bodies (e.g., feminine bodies and bodies of sexual and ethnic minority women) have historically been "subject to systemic violation, exploitation, objectification, and commodification" (Gilson, 2016, p. 75), making invulnerability desirable, protective, and often reserved for those in power. Indeed, (vulnerable) women are marginalized in academia, excluded from promotions, and sexually harassed (Mansfield et al., 2019). Feminine topics are less likely to be published in, so-called, high impact journals and are less likely to be awarded prized research funding that "make" careers (Cislak et al., 2018; Kim et al., 2022); feminine bodies, epistemologies, and lived experiences are thus vulnerable against masculinist notions of academic success. Yet, invulnerability is a double-edged sword and can also be used to justify the perpetuation of gendered racism. For instance, perceptions of Black women as being strong, tough, and domineering (in other words, invulnerable) limit the recourses that are available to prevent injustice and, on the contrary, rationalize victim blaming (Donovan, 2011). It seems that in this case, as in many others, femininities of colour simply cannot win as both vulnerability and invulnerability are used to justify and reproduce inequalities.

The myth that toughness and sensitivity are mutually exclusive is perpetuated under neoliberalism, which provides fuel for incendiary toxic masculinisms (Schwartz, 2020). Fierce competition, exceptionalism, and exclusionary individuality are embedded in neoliberal logics (Goerisch et al., 2019). Success is positioned as hyperproduction (read exploitation), the pursuit of (masculine) mastery and dominion, and control under the guise of talent management. These are manifest in the competitive pursuit of what are deemed to be high-ranking journals (Bell et al., 2019), the constant impetus for the discovery of novel and ground-breaking information at the expense of authentic research (Jane, 2015), the misuse of peer review to stall and block competitors (Cawley, 2011), and exclusivity of who is regarded as worthy to be "mentored" (Goerisch et al., 2019). While neoliberalism and toxic masculinism complement and validate each other in these ways, the

> exploitable feminine subject emerges in contrast to men [...] Her objectification is counterposed to his capacity to operate as an active subject, her passivity to his action on his own behalf, the essential triviality of both her productive and household contribution to the centrality of his.
>
> *(Salzinger, 2016, p. 9)*

Agency is positioned as incompatible with (feminine) vulnerability for vulnerable bodies are lacking in the prized power and are unable to mobilize change or transform their weak position (Gilson, 2016). Like Schwartz (2020), we too challenge this masculinist misconstruction of vulnerability as without agency and refute that vulnerability is automatically weak and anathema to autonomy by queering such simplistic dichotomous notions of agency and vulnerability. We do so by applying a femme theory lens and pointing out that femme lesbians partnered with stone butches have long embodied both the active and the passive in simultaneously being receptive and pursuing (Harris & Crocker, 1997). Femme theory thus enables a more nuanced understanding of vulnerability, one that is compatible with agency and is neither devalued nor necessarily subjugated. Indeed, the negative connotations associated with vulnerability emerge from patriarchal social constructions that associate femininity with weakness. Instead, we propose that feminine values and characteristics that have been scorned and derogated by masculinist society, such as vulnerability, sensitivity, and emotionality, can and should be truly valuable (Schwartz, 2020).

## The value of vulnerability

Despite reigning toxic masculinist discourses in the academy, there is much value in both vulnerability and femininity. Indeed, despite the numerous ways in which both have been disparaged within the academy and beyond, there is great value in centring both, particularly within academia. Vulnerability offers up the possibility of "inspiring people and connecting on a deeper level" (Lopez, 2018, p. 11). This is especially important to the research process as vulnerability is key in developing trust and a foundation for forming a rapport with research participants. The trust that is developed between researcher and participant (or co-creator) balances the traditional hierarchical power between those who are researching and those who are being researched (for instance, the difference between numbering participants and respecting them via pseudonyms). Moreover, participants entrust researchers with personal, sensitive, and at times, traumatic or incriminating lived experiences, placing them in a position of hyper-vulnerability. Confidentiality and anonymity are thus rightly recognized paramount to participant safety – so too are they to researcher safety. Trust is imperative throughout the research process, including during data interpretation and analysis. There is indeed much value to participative methodologies that tap into participants' ways of knowing such as Action Research, storytelling, life histories, and narratives, but also methodologies that co-produce knowledge and position participants as co-researchers and co-constructors of knowledge. Trust can nurture and foster genuine collaboration over tickbox "advisory groups". Moreover, trust and vulnerability can strive to equalize, for example, in our aims to decolonize research methodologies, the cultivation of trust and vulnerability facilitates working "with" communities and groups by breaking down the toxic masculinist researcher/research power dynamics normatively accepted in science.

Within the academy, the relationship between mentor/mentee and senior researcher/early career researcher can also benefit from expressing vulnerability instead of fostering a masculinist culture of false bravado and dominance. Our institutions are inundated with anecdotal evidence of mentors advising masculine comportment and warning against the feminine, ranging from advice on what to wear to career strategizing. Simultaneously, research institutions are facing a crisis of PhD and early career mental health concerns; perhaps a product of the culture in which supervisors have been found to steal the work of early career researchers, abuse their power and authority, block promotions, sexually harass, and demand free labour (Herbenick et al., 2019; Woolston, 2019). Certainly, among those who hold power in the current masculinist academy, there is a lot to gain by reproducing these abhorrent logics to further instrumental goals, and position vulnerability as the "antithesis" of success (Fletcher, 1994). As academics, we work in a highly competitive system where being "right" is highly prized at the expense of intellectual humility. But is this approach or environment conducive to rigorous knowledge production?

In conjunction with positivistic paradigms, neoliberal masculinist competitive environments enable publication bias for scholars who are expected to produce and narrate "perfect" research instead of authentic and transparent communication of failures, no doubt contributing to the current replication crisis. Alluring results lead researchers to "make choices about data collection and analysis which increase the chance of false-positives [...] and novel effects [which] are more likely to be published than studies showing no effect" (Brembs, Button, & Munafo, 2015, p. 2). Indeed, some have gone as far as fabricating data to boast of publications in "top" journals (Wiggins & Christopherson, 2019). Yet, failure, mistakes, and imperfections enable learning (Meyer et al., 2017). This is one of the reasons why there is growing support for publishing quantitative papers that show no statistically significant effects or reproduce prior research (and are therefore unoriginal). There is scientific merit indeed in valuing this work too, not as failed experiments or unoriginality relegated to, so-called, low-impact journals, but as rightfully contributing to knowledge and epistemological corpus. Moreover, cultivating vulnerability in qualitative studies, via reflexivity can make for more authentic research. For instance, Bjørkeng et al. (2014) advocate for, "researchers being rendered questionable by recognizing their processual, relational, and ethical engagement with those whom they research" (p. 329). By embracing vulnerability as researchers, we may aspire towards an ontology and epistemology that is "formed between the others and ourselves through exploring, co-creating, and dwelling together" (ibid).

Acknowledging imperfections, self-awareness, and humility are linked (Mane, 2019). These values, as well as openness and generosity, become paramount to ethical and reflexive research (Rhodes & Carlsen, 2018); yet, these cannot be reached without the unseating of masculinist ego and superiority, and the risking of vulnerability. Rather than a detriment to success, vulnerability is paramount; it is "essential to education and to learning"; it is about "openness to being wrong and venturing one's ideas, beliefs, and feelings nonetheless … the ability to put oneself in and learn from situations in which one is the unknowing, foreign, and perhaps uncomfortable party" (Gilson, 2014, p. 309). Vulnerability enables curiosity and a learning orientation (Church & Samuelson, 2017). Although humility has not been valued much in the west, and boldness has been favoured in its stead (Jackson, 2021), this has not been the case in eastern traditions wherein introversion, quietness, and listening hold higher esteem than being loud, self-promotion, and being forceful. The gendered assumptions playing out in the reproduction of these qualities are evident. Take, for example, how women's ostensible "meekness, shyness, and modesty" are perceived as limiting characteristics that need to be shed in order to achieve, to *lean in*: "What I view as a strength, willingness to learn from others and the capacity to model that trait from a position of power, looks like weakness and softness to others with more macho and charismatic orientations" (Jackson, 2021, p. 27). Yet, the embodiment and manifestation of this type of femme praxis requires "hard emotional labour" (Jackson, 2019; Jackson & Sundaram, 2020) to challenge the status quo, hierarchical norms, and masculine ascendency. Doing so involves epistemic humility and vulnerability: shedding the (false) security that we know best, certainty, and the comfort of arrogance to embrace the unknown – and this discomfort goes against what many in the academy perform, reproduce, and demand.

### Gender economies of invulnerability

While there is an accumulating body of scholarship articulating the importance of vulnerability, given the ways in which femininity and vulnerability are co-constituted, how can we foster vulnerability while existing in an institution that values masculine over feminine epistemologies and ways of being? Thus, nurturing vulnerability in academia and research requires larger systemic and structural changes – and methodological frameworks capable of making such challenges. Moreover, while there is push back against existing structures that demand invulnerability, there exist few methodological tools or theoretical frameworks adept at centring and making use of vulnerability while also challenging masculine ascendency that maintains the current value system. To do so, we connect anti-vulnerability to gendered economic systems whereby masculinity is perpetually valued over femininity.

This gendered economic system is evident in the distribution of incentives and rewards and the determination of what is "worthy" labour. Femme theory offers a framework and methodological tool to dismantle these toxic masculinist neoliberal structures that value, among other things, invulnerability (Hoskin & Blair, 2022).

## Femme theory

The term femme originates from 1940s/1950s lesbian communities wherein feminine lesbians (or femmes) were partnered with more masculine lesbians (or butches) (Nestle, 1992). The term has expanded as an identity category to encompass a wide range of people who have a certain relationship to femininity – who have either been denied femininity historically, who experience marginalized femininity, or who challenge the norms of femininity as dictated by patriarchal gender structures (Blair & Hoskin, 2015, 2016). Alongside this growth of femme identities, femme theory has emerged as a framework through which to make visible and de-centre the otherwise taken-for-granted masculine epistemologies, focusing instead on feminine epistemologies as valuable overlooked contributions (Hoskin, 2021; Hoskin & Blair, 2022). Femme theorists argue that the tendency to overlook and devalue the many contributions of feminine epistemologies is a product of femme-phobia; or, the ways in which society systematically denigrates and regulates femininity (Hoskin, 2017a, 2019, 2020). Importantly, while femininity and woman or female share longstanding historical connections, particularly those enforced under patriarchal rule, femme theory sees gender expression (i.e., femininity) as a separate construct with overlapping histories of gender and sex (i.e., woman or female) deserving of deliberate scholarly attention. The importance of considering gender expression as a separate construct can be connected to the 1940s lesbian communities, where women embodied masculine/butch, feminine/femme, or androgynous; and, each of which contributes to unique experiences based on gender expression. And, of course, femme lesbian communities teach us that there is so much more to femininity than the desire to appease the male gaze.

### Femme theory as method and research tool

By theorizing femmes' various relationships to femininity, feminine ontologies beyond serving a male gaze, and the ways in which femininity is filtered through power and marginalization, femme theory offers a means of understanding and making visible femininity's relation to power within an intersectional framework (Carbado et al., 2013; Crenshaw, 1989). Moreover, femme theory offers an additional dimension to the near-ubiquitous theorizations of femininity as solely a tool of the patriarchy used to oppress women (e.g., Brownmiller, 1984; Friedan, 1963; see Hoskin, 2017b for an overview). While the use of femininity to oppress women has deep historical roots that continue to grow well into the 21st century, femme theory argues that this is just one perspective – and a partial perspective, at that (Haraway, 1988). Importantly, the additional perspective garnered through femme theory is achieved via the centring of marginalized community voices – both historic and contemporary.

By bringing the "margins to the centre" (hooks, 2000), femme theory makes visible what is otherwise taken for granted as the naturalized masculine norm; a naturalization process that functions to calcify existing power structures, particularly those relating to masculine ascendency and feminine subordination. Like feminism, femme theory is a "flexible framework" that "offers a simultaneous way to express an epistemology (knowledge), a methodology (the production of knowledge), an ontology (one's subjective way of being in the world), and a praxis (the translation of knowledge into actions that produce beneficial social change)" (Allen, 2022, p. 1). Across each of these domains, femme theory offers tools to identify and challenge masculinism and femmephobia. Femme theory asks scholars to "bring feminine multiplicities and feminine devaluation into focus within interdisciplinary and intersectional research" and to "recognize feminine intersections as central to understanding the ebbs and flows of power" (for a full overview see Hoskin, 2021, p. 13). Through femme theory, research and institutional practices can be examined and revised to make femininity salient, challenge masculine centrality, and revalue femininity. Such tools are particularly useful for those interested in promoting practices of vulnerability.

### Femme-toring as femme praxis

In addition to being a tool integral in the challenging of masculinist epistemologies central to the norms and values of academia, femme theory also generates the concept of femme-torship and, thus, offers a means of systemically challenging these norms as they continue to be produced interpersonally (Hoskin & Whiley, 2023). Like femininity and vulnerability, the importance of relationality is also overlooked within research, the academy, and institutions more broadly. Indeed, vulnerability is itself an important aspect of relationality and relational knowledge (Meriläinen, Salmela, & Valtonen, 2022). Thus, if we are to incorporate vulnerability within research design and practice, this begs the question: How can such a task be achieved without first changing the way we treat and interact with each other, and the norms governing these interactions? Catalysing change via interpersonal relations could offer an effective means through which to enact femme-inine praxis and, in turn, foster vulnerability, but to do so without causing harm, a broader systemic change of values is necessary – otherwise, it would be simply ushering already marginalized groups into an even more disparaged position.

Think for a moment about the cultural archetype of the superstar professor, researcher, colleague, or mentor: how does this archetype treat their colleagues and mentees, and interact within the institution at large? Think further about the qualities, traits, and approaches that are characteristic of this archetype. Typically, we argue, the interpersonal relationships and traits of this academic archetype are infused with masculinist epistemologies; and, more specifically *men*-toring. For example, perhaps this exercise conjured up an image of an academic who is domineering, rigid, controlling, egotistical, apathetic, over-authoritarian, invested in hierarchy, micromanaging of their students, competitive among colleagues, and so forth. As femme theorists, we see these traits as being masculine-coded, and as contrasting the more feminine-coded qualities observable within the academy (see Figure 10.1). Importantly, these qualities are naturalized, unnamed, and rarely contextualized as masculine (vs. feminine) coded – they are especially insidious in their implicitness. Mentoring style of interpersonal relations is frequently cited as a supervisory style, but can be found among colleagues as well. It is a gendered practice that legitimizes masculine ascendency and supports the devaluing of the feminine – or femmephobia – to ensure the institutional patriarchal status quo (e.g., domination, hierarchy, publish or perish culture, high-ranking publications, "prestigious" editorships, angry reviews that tear down aspiring researchers instead of supporting development etc.). As scholars invested in fostering socially just practices of vulnerability, we need to start thinking about cultivating new ways of "mentoring" and engaging with one another – peer to peer, student to professor, or researcher to community – so that we do not simply reproduce old hierarchies. And, we must also consider how gender-coded relational norms of academia that prize invulnerability act as an impediment to social justice pursuits.

On the other side of the binary lies a generative approach to not only instigate the relationships we aspire to build and prioritize interconnectivity over hierarchy, but also foster practices of vulnerability within and outside of the research process. Thus, instead of men-toring, we offer femme-toring as a form of relational femme praxis that recognizes the value of feminine-coded qualities. The femme praxis of femme-toring reflects the transformation from "theory into action in order to change the world" (Allen, 2022, p. 12). Moreover, we argue that femme-toring can function as a catalyst to achieve broader systemic change within research, academic institutions more widely, and, importantly, nurture an environment wherein qualities coded feminine (such as vulnerability) may flourish. Illustrating the world-making potential of femme praxis, consider the institutional norms against which femme-torship may be considered a type of "failure". Like many queer theorists, femme theorists argue that failure offers a productive means of challenging the status quo (Hoskin & Taylor, 2019). By failing to approximate the masculinist norms in the academy premised on individualism, invulnerability, and stoicism, femme-torship challenges the existing power structures that denigrate femininity and, by extension, limit researchers' ability to adopt practices of vulnerability. Femme theory and the femme praxis of femme-toring, we argue, function as methods for fostering vulnerability within the institution, infusing it within research design, effectively training mentees to explore their own vulnerability, and reshaping institutions. This is achieved through the application of femme theory and also the femme-torship principles of softness, collaboration, and yielding (Hoskin and Whiley, 2023).

## Softness

Femme theorists look at "soft" feminine qualities as a means of rethinking power structures and value systems. Schwartz (2020) illustrates how softness entails

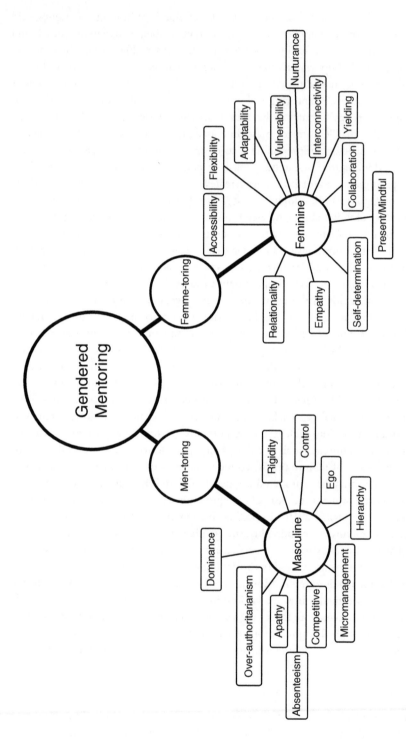

**FIGURE 10.1** Gendered Mentoring.

emotionality, tenderness, interdependence, vulnerability, and relationality, and positions it as a form of "healing" (p. 5). Indeed, early psychoanalytical theorists associated the feminine with kindness (e.g., Jung). And, although these qualities are typically denigrated within masculinist power structures like academia and research, femmes and femme scholarship have a long history of nuancing vulnerability, demonstrating new power relations not premised on dominance and hierarchy. By acknowledging our softness, we can reframe and challenge toxic masculinisms of egoism, dominance, and rigid hierarchy. These characteristics, although traditionally associated with gains, contribute neither to socially just communities nor ethically sound research practices. On the contrary, femme-torship values softness, suppleness, and permeance, enabling us to listen and to learn and helping us to acknowledge the limits of our knowledge. This epistemic humility is key; acknowledging the boundaries of our knowledge is an integral part of learning, and one that can be fostered by softness and permeance to others (and their views).

## Collaboration

Feminist action rejects the "zero-sum game" (i.e., if you win, then I lose) way of thinking that is based on toxic status quo norms, gender-coded ontologies of dominance and hierarchy, and that reify racism, sexism, heteronormativity, and ableism. In her compelling analysis of how racism (and other forms of oppression) hurt everyone, McGee (2002) argues for the "solidarity dividend", that dismantles the zero-sum game of "you win/I lose", moving instead towards focusing on the public good, and acknowledging how "we truly need each other" (p. 271). Indeed, solidarity with others and collaboration through community "are critical, intersectional, antiracist feminist goals that are needed to transform society" (Allen, 2022, p. 27). Collaboration can also be demonstrated within research teams where papers may be the outcome of shared labour, for example, by genuine co-authorship in resulting publications and authentic acknowledgement of support, especially by research assistants and early career faculty. Collaboration is inherently non-hierarchical in structure; it de-centres invulnerability, independence, and individualism by forging connections and relationality. Moreover, collegiality across research teams can facilitate a more interconnected science, one in which scholars build upon the work of others, feel inspired, and inspire in turn instead of positioning others as rivals and needing to prove originality at the expense of collaboration. In these ways, collaboration stands in opposition to masculinist norms of competitiveness, over-authoritarianism, hierarchy, rigidity, and control that limit researcher and institutional vulnerability.

## Yielding

While masculine-coded power structures position power as power *over* and domination, feminine forms of power can and do look different. Yielding, for instance, is considered a feminine form of power by femme theorists (Barton & Huebner,

2022). Indeed, yielding requires flexibility, adaptability, relationality, and malleability while simultaneously maintaining one's own integral form (Barton & Huebner, 2022). Yielding necessitates humbleness in the face of learning, for instance, by listening carefully to participants and giving voice to their lived experiences and by being open to co-constructions of knowledge. Yielding stands in direct opposition to masculine norms of unyielding, toughness, rigidity, refusal to admit wrong-doing, insistence on "alpha" status, and aggressive responses to perceived slights. Like collaboration, these masculinist norms within research and academia limit scholarly efforts to cultivate vulnerability within these domains; one cannot be vulnerable within a culture that demands unyielding dominance. Through femme-torship and femme theory, however, we can foster both theory and praxis to cultivate vulnerability and shift masculinist economies of worth.

## Epistemological and methodological tools for vulnerability

We argue that femme theory and praxis, as methods of cultivating vulnerability, hold the capacity to radically shift sexist, racist, homophobic, transphobic, and femmephobic practices and align with egalitarian aims such as moving towards decolonizing research methods. Indeed, by shaping how research (and research institutions) are organised, femme theory and femme-toring offer effective epistemological and ontological tools, grounded in femme principles, to facilitate radically feminine ways of being/knowing. Through femme theory, we aim to detangle and make visible how power itself is coded as masculine; and, operating within a binary model of gender vulnerability is coded as feminine. Within this dichotomy, feminine power is inconceivable and, thus, vulnerability worthless. Implicit power hierarchies and structures are embedded into all relations, whether we name them or not. Some may be more egalitarian than others, but oftentimes the existing power structures go unnamed and thus are left to replicate existing hierarchies through various vectors of the institution (e.g., mentees, colleagues, peers, within research). Conversely, recent years have witnessed the impact of naming the unnamed. Take, for instance, the global impact of #MeToo and naming that which has been swept under the rug or naturalized for centuries. Giving language to social phenomena can catalyse systemic change. Through femme theory and praxis, we hope to name masculine ascendency and femmephobia within the academy, thereby fostering practices of vulnerability throughout the institution.

Femme praxis helps to name the qualities and behaviours that calcify existing power structures and provides a compass to keep our relational behaviour aligned with our political agenda; to continuously recalibrate our actions with our values. Moreover, femme theory opens cognitive space for agentic vulnerability via femme-toring practices and interpersonal relationality, softness, collaboration, and yielding. Our aim is not to argue that femininity is supreme and reigns over masculinity. Everyone of all genders has within them the capacity to *feel* – pain, loss, joy, love – and vulnerability is the "ontological condition of humanity" (Rogers et al., 2012, p. 19). We do, however, point out that "vulnerability is predominantly understood as feminising and subsequently as negative, scary, shameful and, above all, something to be avoided and protected against" (Dahl, 2017, p. 41).

At the same time, academia functions in an individualistic neoliberal world that aims to redirect political pressure onto the individual to avoid changes to the status quo. This system claims meritocracy and favours individualized competition over benefits to the collective; under this guise, individual failures are to blame, and discriminatory institutional structures are absolved of responsibility even as efforts towards inclusivity are claimed, commodified, and converted into "something considered valuable by the university management" (Lund & Tienari, 2019, p. 108). Indeed, within this culture, we contend that academia would commodify vulnerability if it could extract monetary value. For example, neoliberalism could "reclaim [vulnerability] as a new virtue to be cultivated" (Ziarek, 2013, p. 67) via self-help and self-management books, organizational training workshops, and in doing so, feed into the very system that we aim to critique. This would also not be the first time that neoliberalism has benefited from performing feminism, for example, Tzanakou and Pearce (2019, p. 1191) argue that the Athena Swan equality charter is a "product of neoliberalization" in that it enables universities to do just enough equality work to be seen in a favourable light, yet leads to limited genuine institutional change, especially for women of colour and LGBT folx. Yes, we see the irony of our argumentation and do not want to position vulnerability as the opposite end of the spectrum of "lean in" approaches. We are not advocating for step-by-step guides on "how to" perform vulnerability nor do we support organizations corporatizing vulnerability via human resource management practices such as training and coaching. We do, however, advocate for workshops on femmephobia in which participants learn to unpack their own femmephobic attitudes and identify those that permeate their surrounding world. We are not providing a different tool with which to play the academic game and win; instead, we are proposing to change the very system and the values upon which it rests.

## Conclusion

Just as anti-vulnerability and invulnerability are perpetuated and solidified at interpersonal, internalized, institutional, and structural levels, so too must our approach to catalysing the change required to cultivate practices of vulnerability reflect each of these domains. Through femme theory and praxis, gender economies that denigrate vulnerability are challenged across domains through reflexivity and reflection, naming practices, femme-toring, and the promotion of open dialogue about the gendered coding of power and worth.

The relationship between power, marginality, and resistance is such that power remains in constant dialogue – or renegotiation – with resistance from the margins (i.e., counter-discourses; Foucault, 1978). These counter-discourses provide the minute shifts in power necessary to spark broader change; and, thus through this relationship, change emerges gradually. Given the co-constituted norms of anti-femininity and anti-vulnerability that proliferate within the academy, if change surrounding vulnerability is our goal then in considering vulnerability so too must we consider issues of gendered power. Operating within a masculinist institution, we see femme praxis and vulnerability as counter-discourses, emerging from the institutional margins and providing the minute shifts in power necessary to challenge the status quo.

## References

Allen, K. R. (2022). Feminist theory, method, and praxis: Toward a critical consciousness for family and close relationship scholars. *Journal of Social and Personal Relationships, 40*(3), 899–936.

Bagilhole, B. (2002). *Women in Non-Traditional Occupations: Challenging Men.* New York, NY: Springer.

Banchefsky, S., Westfall, J., Park, B., & Judd, C. M. (2016). But you don't look like a scientist!: Women scientists with feminine appearance are deemed less likely to be scientists. *Sex Roles, 75*(3), 95–109.

Barton, B., & Huebner, L. (2022). Feminine power: A new articulation. *Psychology & Sexuality, 13*(1), 23–32.

Beard, M. (2017). *Women & Power: A Manifesto.* Glasgow: Profile Books.

Bell, E., Meriläinen, S., Taylor, S., & Tienari, J. (2019). Time's up! Feminist theory and activism meets organization studies. *Human Relations, 72*(1), 4–22.

Bjørkeng, K., Carlsen, A., Rhodes, C., Cooren, F., Vaara, E., Langley, A., & Tsoukas, H. (2014). From self-reflexivity to other-vulnerability in the research process1. *Language and Communication at Work: Discourse, Narrativity, and Organizing, 4,* 325.

Biggs, J., Hawley, P. H., & Biernat, M. (2018). The academic conference as a chilly climate for women: Effects of gender representation on experiences of sexism, coping responses, and career intentions. *Sex Roles, 78,* 394–408.

Blair, K. L., & Hoskin, R. A. (2015). Experiences of femme identity: Coming out, invisibility and femmephobia. *Psychology & Sexuality, 6*(3), 229–244.

Blair, K. L., & Hoskin, R. A. (2016). Contemporary understandings of femme identities and related experiences of discrimination. *Psychology & Sexuality, 7*(2), 101–115.

Bleijenbergh, I. L., van Engen, M. L., & Vinkenburg, C. J. (2013). Othering women: Fluid images of the ideal academic. *Equality, Diversity and Inclusion: An International Journal, 32*(1), 22–35.

Bonnes, S. (2022). Femininity anchors: Heterosexual relationships and pregnancy as sites of harassment for US servicewomen. *American Sociological Review, 87*(4), 618–643.

Boustani, K., & Taylor, K. A. (2020). Navigating LGBTQ+ discrimination in academia: Where do we go from here? *The Biochemist, 42*(3), 16–20.

Bourabain, D. (2021). Everyday sexism and racism in the ivory tower: The experiences of early career researchers on the intersection of gender and ethnicity in the academic workplace. *Gender, Work & Organization, 28*(1), 248–267.

Brembs, B., Button, K., & Munafo, M. (2015). Deep impact: Unintended consequences of journal rank. *Frontiers in Human Neuroscience, 7*(291), 1–12.

Brownmiller, S. (1984). *Femininity.* New York: Fawcett Columbine.

Carbado, D. W., Crenshaw, K. W., Mays, V. M., & Tomlinson, B. (2013). Intersectionality: Mapping the movements of a theory. *Du Bois Review: Social Science Research on Race, 10*(2), 303–312.

Cawley (2011) An analysis of the ethics of peer review and other traditional academic publishing practices. *International Journal of Social Science and Humanity*, *1*(3), 205–213.

Cislak, A., Formanowicz, M., & Saguy, T. (2018). Bias against research on gender bias. *Scientometrics*, *115*(1), 189–200.

Church, I. M., & Samuelson, P. L. (2017). *Intellectual Humility: An Introduction to the Philosophy and Science*. London: Bloomsbury Publishing.

Crenshaw, K. (1989). Demarginalizing the intersection of race and sex: A Black feminist critique of antidiscrimination doctrine, feminist theory, and antiracist politics. *University of Chicago Legal Forum*, *53*(1), 139–167.

Cvetkovich, A. (1992). *Mixed Feelings*. New Brunswick, NJ: Rutgers University Press.

Dahl, U. (2017). Femmebodiment: Notes on queer feminine shapes of vulnerability. *Feminist Theory*, *18*(1), 35–53.

Donovan, R. A. (2011). Tough or tender: (Dis) Similarities in white college students' perceptions of black and white women. *Psychology of Women Quarterly*, *35*(3), 458–468.

Fletcher, J. K. (1994). Castrating the female advantage: Feminist standpoint research and management science. *Journal of Management Inquiry*, *3*(1), 74–82.

Fotaki, M. (2011). The sublime object of desire (for knowledge): Sexuality at work in business and management schools in England. *British Journal of Management*, *22*(1), 42–53.

Fotaki, M. (2013). No woman is like a man (in academia): The masculine symbolic order and the unwanted female body. *Organization Studies*, *34*(9), 1251–1275.

Foucault, M. (1978). *The History of Sexuality: An Introduction*. New York: Random House, Inc.

Friedan, B. (1963). *The Feminine Mystique*. New York, NY: W.W. Norton & Company.

Gilson, E. (2014). *The Ethics of Vulnerability: A Feminist Analysis of Social Life and Practice*. New York: Routledge.

Gilson, E. (2016). Vulnerability and victimization: Rethinking key concepts in feminist discourses on sexual violence. *Signs: Journal of Women in Culture and Society*, *42*(1), 71–98.

Goerisch, D., Basilier, J., Rosener, A., McKee, K., Hunt, J., & Parker, T. (2019). Mentoring with: Reimaging mentoring across the university. *Gender, Place and Culture*, *26*(12), 1740–1758.

Haraway, D. (1988). Situated knowledges: The science question in feminism and the privilege of partial perspective. *Feminist Studies*, *14*(3), 575–599.

Harris, L., & Crocker, E. (1997). *Femme: Feminists Lesbians and Bad Girls*. New York: Routledge.

Herbenick, D., van Anders, S. M., Brotto, L. A., Chivers, M. L., Jawed-Wessel, S., & Galarza, J. (2019). Sexual harassment in the field of sexuality research. *Archives of Sexual Behaviour*, *48*(4), 997–1006.

hooks, b. (2000). *Feminist Theory: From Margin to Center* (2nd ed.). Cambridge, MA: South End Press.

Hoskin, R. A. (2017a). Femme theory: Refocusing the intersectional lens. *Atlantis: Critical Studies in Gender, Culture & Social Justice*, *38*(1), 95–109.

Hoskin, R. A. (2017b). Femme interventions and the proper feminist subject: Critical approaches to decolonizing western feminist pedagogies. *Cogent Social Sciences*, *3*(1), 1–16.

Hoskin, R. A. (2019). Femmephobia: The role of anti-femininity and gender policing in LGBTQ+ people's experiences of discrimination. *Sex Roles*, *81*(11), 686–703.

Hoskin, R. A. (2020). "Femininity' it's the aesthetic of subordination": Examining femmephobia, the gender binary, and experiences of oppression among sexual and gender minorities. *Archives of Sexual Behaviour*, *49*(7), 2319–2339.

Hoskin, R. A. (2021). Can femme be theory? Exploring the epistemological and methodological possibilities of femme. *Journal of Lesbian Studies*, *25*(1), 1–17.

Hoskin, R. A., & Blair, K. L. (2022). Critical femininities: A 'new' approach to gender theory. *Psychology & Sexuality, 12*(1), 1–8.

Hoskin, R. A., & Taylor, A. (2019). Femme resistance: The fem (me) inine art of failure. *Psychology & Sexuality, 10*(4), 281–300.

Hoskin, R. A., & Whiley, L. (2023). Femme-toring: Leveraging critical femininities and femme theory to cultivate alternative approaches to mentoring. *Gender, Work & Organization.*

Huopalainen, A. S., & Satama, S. T. (2019). Mothers and researchers in the making: Negotiating 'new' motherhood within the 'new' academia. *Human Relations, 72*(1), 98–121.

Jackson, L. (2017). Leaning out in higher education: A structural, postcolonial perspective. *Policy Futures in Education, 15*(3), 295–308.

Jackson, L. (2019). The smiling philosopher: Emotional labour, gender, and harassment in conference spaces. *Educational Philosophy and Theory, 51*(7), 693–701.

Jackson, L. (2021). Humility and vulnerability, or leaning in? Personal reflections on leadership and difference in global universities. *Universities & Intellectuals, 1*(1), 24–29.

Jackson, C. & Sundaram, V. (2020). *Lad Culture in Higher Education: Sexism, Sexual Harassment and Violence.* New York, NY: Routledge.

Jane, E. (2015). Flaming? What flaming? The pitfalls and potentials of researching online hostility. *Ethics and Information Technology, 17*(1), 65–87.

Karami, A., White, C. N., Ford, K., Swan, S., & Spinel, M. Y. (2020). Unwanted advances in higher education: Uncovering sexual harassment experiences in academia with text mining. *Information Processing & Management, 57*(2), 102167.

Kim, L., Smith, D. S., Hofstra, B., & McFarland, D. A. (2022). Gendered knowledge in fields and academic careers. *Research Policy, 51*(1), 104411.

Lather, P. (1988). Feminist perspectives on empowering research methodologies. *Women's Studies International Forum, 11*(6), 569–581.

Lopez, S. O. (2018). Vulnerability in leadership: The power of the courage to descend. Retrieved from: https://www.proquest.com/openview/b95faa6263a8fc8f5ae8c23ff2aee0a4/1?pq-origsite=gscholar&cbl=18750

Lund, R., & Tienari, J. (2019). Passion, care, and eros in the gendered neoliberal university. *Organization, 26*(1), 98–121.

Mackenzie, C., Rogers, W., & Dodds, S. (Eds.). (2014). *Vulnerability: New Essays in Ethics and Feminist Philosophy.* Oxford: Oxford University Press.

Mandalaki, E., & Pérezts, M. (2021). Abjection overruled! Time to dismantle sexist cyberbullying in academia. *Organization, 30*(1), 1–13.

Mählck, P. (2021). Equality, diversity and inclusion: How can diversity practice challenge racism, sexism and white privilege in the globalised academy? In M. Carlson, B. E. Halldórsdóttir, B. Baranović, A.-S. Holm, S. Lappalainen, & A. Spehar (Eds.), *Gender and Education in Politics, Policy and Practice* (pp. 55–69). Cham: Springer.

Mane, A. S. D. (2019). Establishing psychological safety in teams and the role of vulnerability and inclusive leadership. Retrieved from: https://studenttheses.uu.nl/handle/20.500.12932/33564

Mansfield, B., Lave, R., McSweeney, K., Bonds, A., Cockburn, J., Domosh, M., & Radel, C. (2019). It's time to recognize how men's careers benefit from sexually harassing women in academia. *Human Geography, 12*(1), 82–87.

Meriläinen, S., Salmela, T., & Valtonen, A. (2022). Vulnerable relational knowing that matters. *Gender, Work & Organization, 29*(1), 79–91.

McGee, M. (2002). Hooked on higher education and other tales from adjunct faculty organizing. *Social Text, 20*(1), 61–80.

Meyer, F., Le Fevre, D. M., & Robinson, V. M. (2017). How leaders communicate their vulnerability: Implications for trust building. *International Journal of Educational Management, 31*(2). 221–235.

Nestle, J. (Ed.). (1992). *The Persistent Desire: A Femme-Butch Reader.* New York: Alyson Books.

Rhodes, C., & Carlsen, A. (2018). The teaching of the other: Ethical vulnerability and generous reciprocity in the research process. *Human Relations, 71*(10), 1295–1318.

Rogers, W., Mackenzie, C., & Dodds, S. (2012). Why bioethics needs a concept of vulnerability. *IJFAB: International Journal of Feminist Approaches to Bioethics, 5*(2), 11–38.

Salzinger, L. (2016). Re-marking men: Masculinity as a terrain of the neoliberal economy. *Critical Historical Studies, 3*(1). Retrieved from: https://escholarship.org/content/qt6n144139/qt6n144139.pdf

Savigny, H. (2017). Cultural sexism is ordinary: Writing and re-writing women in academia. *Gender, Work & Organization, 24*(6), 643–655.

Sobande, F., & Wells, J. R. (2023). The poetic identity work and sisterhood of Black women becoming academics. *Gender, Work & Organization, 30*(2), 469–484.

Schwartz, A. (2020). Soft femme theory: Femme internet aesthetics and the politics of "softness". *Social Media + Society, 6*(4), 2056305120978366.

Schwartz, A. (2022). Radical vulnerability: Selfies as a femme-inine mode of resistance. *Psychology & Sexuality, 13*(1), 43–56.

Taylor, A., & Hoskin, R. A. (2023). Fat femininities: On the convergence of fat studies and critical femininities. *Fat Studies, 12*(1), 72–85.

Tzanakou, C., & Pearce, R. (2019). Moderate feminism within or against the neoliberal university? The example of Athena SWAN. *Gender, Work & Organization, 26*(8), 1191–1211.

Waseleski, C. (2006). Gender and the use of exclamation points in computer-mediated communication: An analysis of exclamations posted to two electronic discussion lists. *Journal of Computer-Mediated Communication, 11*(4), 1012–1024.

Wiggins, B. J., & Christopherson, C. D. (2019). The replication crisis in psychology: An overview for theoretical and philosophical psychology. *Journal of Theoretical and Philosophical Psychology, 39*(4), 202.

Woolston, C. (2019). PhDs: The tortuous truth. *Nature, 575*(7782), 403–407.

Ziarek, E. P. (2013). From parody to the event; from affect to freedom: Observations on the feminine sublime in modernism. In Jean-Michel Rabate (Ed.), *A Handbook of Modernism Studies* (pp. 399–413). Chichester: Wiley Blackwell.

# 11

# FRAMING TRANSDISCIPLINARY RESEARCH AS AN ASSEMBLAGE

## A case study from a mental health setting

*Mark Batterham and Aled Singleton*

## Introduction

In this chapter, two authors, Mark, a practising mental health nurse, and Aled, an early career human geography researcher, report and reflect on the issues of vulnerability as they collaborate on bringing the practice of walking therapy to support mental health recovery. Due to factors such as lack of resources and the risk-averse nature of clinical practice, the research journey is often in flux and its boundaries are stretched and squeezed. To reflect how these slippery characteristics were encountered, we have framed this account as what we call a *transdisciplinary assemblage*. This conceptual model, which we define in the first section of this chapter, allows us to explore four cases of vulnerability at key moments. Point A relates how bringing walking therapy into clinical practice challenges the risk culture of the organisation and reveals the weak position of nurses as leaders in research. Point B shows how the influence of geographical thinkers causes the work to accelerate too quickly and nearly brings the whole process to a premature end. Point C is principally a period of strength as the process of interviewing service users and practitioners is underway. However, this latter moment is also a chance for us as researchers to stop, reflect, and better understand ourselves as subjects in the process. In this stage, Aled appreciates how precarious academic contracts restrict his work and Mark wrestles with the realities of incorporating meaningful service user involvement. Arriving at Point D, there is a particular weakness realising that there may be no resources to take the approach further.

We firstly explain why we have combined the terms *transdisciplinary* and *assemblage* and outline why it is useful.

DOI: 10.4324/9781003349266-15

## How we understand and define the transdisciplinary assemblage

The background of this writing is the research experience of developing, documenting, analysing, and making the case to further embed walking therapy within clinical practice. The walking therapy in this case was formalised and expanded by mental health practitioners with the aim of taking practice outside the physical confines of the institution and to help service users (re)gain confidence in public space. As the practice developed it became attracted to – and to some degree enveloped within – forces beyond the day-to-day relationships between service users and practitioners. For example, nurse Mark was apprehended by an abortive attempt to gain research funding in Stage B. In Stage C, there was a need to bring in the expertise of social researcher Aled to lead the interviews for a formal service evaluation. His precarious employment in academia made this task harder. The burden that this put upon the individual is not uncommon. We argue that our case of pursuing walking therapy, and therapy whilst walking, in a mental health setting became a subject in its own right. Trying to advance the practice means that it is now an entity which exists beyond the people or the institutions concerned.

We reason that the research process starts to have some of the characters of an *assemblage*, as originally developed by Gilles Delueuze and Félix Guattari in *Capitalism and Schizophrenia* (1977). Writers such as Bruno Latour (2007) have developed assemblage thinking into further theories, but it is human geographers who seem particularly interested in the latter concept. For example, Woodward, Dixon, and Jones (2009, p. 401) explain how:

> Deleuze presents a world encountered from the perspectives of movement and force relations: rather than structured, whole objects (the human, the subject, what have you), there are continuously interconnecting multitudes of partial objects affecting and being affected by other partial objects, constituting – if only for a moment –assemblages that appear to cohere by working together or initiating processes that are specific to that relation.

The attention to movement and forces is important to the case presented in this writing. For example, institutional processes both threaten and give opportunities to develop the practice of walking therapy. Outside the institution, the unexpected COVID-19 pandemic opens up new possibilities at Point C. Therefore, the aim of using Deleuze and Guattari's assemblage theory in our work is to reflect on the vulnerabilities we have faced and perhaps relax a little. By accepting that entities are never fixed, pre-determined, or that they have a completely stable ontological form, we can see our research journey perhaps as an adventure movie. The protagonist has a chance meeting, they squeeze through a door as it is about to close, they are chased down a street, and eventually they emerge into sunlight at the conclusion.

The term *transdisciplinary* is important to our study of researcher vulnerability because it goes beyond the mixing together of disciplines that is generally considered to be *interdisciplinary*. Lawrence (2004, p. 489) puts transdisciplinary practice into terms that researchers studying vulnerability will understand: 'This implies the giving up of sovereignty over knowledge, the generation of new insight and knowledge by collaboration, and the capacity to consider the know-how of professionals and lay-people.' We will start with Point A, which reveals the potential for a mental health service to encourage and accommodate walking therapies. In this case, we specifically focus on how the mental health nurse becomes vulnerable when they move closer to the discipline of human geography. Stylistically this is written in the present tense and the third person to show how the events unfold. As such this approach is designed to invite the reader to imagine how they would act in such a situation.

## Point A: The opportunity to develop new practices in mental health

There is potential to innovate in the mental health system in England as it has undergone fundamental and far-reaching changes over recent decades, for example, the significant shift to community care in the early 1990s and 'National Service Frameworks' introduced by the New Labour government (Department of Health, 1999). These policy drives established new specialist community services, as well as directing clinical provision. Not all of these services have survived, but the modern landscape of mental health care is barely recognisable from those not-so-distant days when service users were housed and treated together in large asylums. Indeed, McGrath and Reavey (2015) note that few individuals with severe mental health difficulties are now cared for within specialist institutions; the majority occupy geographical spaces alongside persons who do not share similar experiences. Although specialist services may *reach in* to mental health wards and other institutional environments, the community is their main operational territory. This spatial level, namely around the city and nearby areas, is the focus of our research. This general shift towards community care has obvious benefits, but concerns have been raised regarding the isolating reality of service users' day-to-day existence (Sayce, 1999; Parr, 2011). The walls of the 19th- and early 20th-century asylum have been replaced by the spatial consequences of the enduring image of the psychiatric patient and the indifferent politics of neoliberalism. Many mental health service users continue to experience discrimination and alienation and the patchwork of community services and resources developed over many years to support recovery has been unpicked, and in places completely dismantled. Under austerity and its contemporary manifestation, adequate provision for one of society's most vulnerable groups is, like many other social matters, deemed a luxury we can no longer afford. This hollowing out of state and voluntary sector support has been re-packaged as an emancipatory opportunity for service user self-management (Deering, 2016).

The new spatial arrangements of mental health care throw up new problems for research. Through exercises such as audits and service evaluations, organisations acknowledge their own vulnerability and are open to changes in the conceptualisation and planning of interventions. Although convincing arguments to look beyond conventional knowledge limits exist – for example, see Abrahamyan Empson et al. (2020) – three related factors operate to slow or thwart innovative practice within contemporary mental health care in England. First, much of the mental health system retains a focus on the monitoring and management of risk, shaping relationships and day-to-day service delivery in a way that reflects this priority (Deering et al., 2019). The routine use, and design of the psychiatric clinic itself, embodies this preoccupation with risk (McGrath & Reavey, 2013) and undermines efforts to forge a therapeutic alliance. Second, mental health services are chronically under-staffed. As of writing this, the current (Q3, 2021/22) registered nurse vacancy rates in mental health services are 21.7% in the South East of England and 16% in the South West (NHS Digital, 2022). Third, as innovators in this case study, mental health nurses are criticised from within their own ranks for lacking a clear purpose and sense of identity, instead acting as mere handmaidens to a more powerful medical establishment (Barker & Buchanan-Barker, 2011). Even where nurses have involved themselves in radical movements challenging oppressive practice, such as the closure of the Italian asylums in the 1960s and 1970s (see Foot, 2014), they have tended to follow the lead of their superiors. This vocational self-doubt combines with a defensive risk culture, and what are at times overwhelming job demands, to create a climate where nurses feel vulnerable and consequently hesitant to innovate through practice development or research. Indeed, even where nurses are enthusiastic to involve themselves in research, the pivotal nature of their clinical roles can mean that opportunities are withheld or even withdrawn. This long-standing problem is critical to this discussion of the authors' vulnerability as researchers as it is a nurse (co-author Mark Batterham) who has collaborated with other frontline staff to initiate the changes discussed below.

Notwithstanding the operational pressures and constraints, there is scope and motivation amongst mental health workers operating in community services to develop and broaden the interventions offered. Clinical guidelines promote a more holistic approach to care that opens the way for treatments that extend beyond medical orthodoxy. Within and beyond the case study area, 'wellbeing groups' have been set up to reduce social isolation and improve physical health. In our locality, long-standing social activities include a weekly badminton group and a Saturday morning coffee group. There is an occasional bouldering group and an annual bodyboarding trip. These groups represent a progressive shift from conventional practice and prioritise the relational dimension of recovery, yet they are spatially bounded.

Mark and his colleagues spotted an opportunity to meet the presenting clinical needs of mental health service users in the early stages of recovery by expanding on the activities already offered to include a walking group. Their reasons were threefold. First, understanding that walking with others provides individuals who may be experiencing difficulties with social contact with a choice to opt in or out of conversation. Second, the organisers hypothesised that the shared and companionable experience of walking together would allow for different and perhaps deeper conversations to take place. As Rebecca Solnit (2001) notes, walking is as much a social and conversational activity as it is a means of individual fulfilment. Finally, they felt that group walks may help defuse the threat of the city. Urban living is a known risk factor for the development of particular mental health problems, for example see Vassos et al. (2012), and there is growing evidence that it may also impact recovery. By way of illustration, busy city streets have been found to increase negative beliefs about the self and others for service users struggling with persecutory delusions (Freeman et al., 2015) and highly stimulating urban spaces can leave individuals feeling overwhelmed (Söderström et al., 2016).

The first outing took place in the spring of 2019 and the group has continued to operate, with breaks over the colder winter months and briefly during the first national lockdown in 2020 to halt the spread of coronavirus. The initial walks were not explicitly staged as opportunities for gathering data; nobody takes field notes, makes surveys or conducts interviews, and brief records are only made after the event. Whether explicitly done for research or not, walking practices change the power dynamics and thus relative vulnerability of both the service user and staff member. This is explained in the Evans and Jones (2011, p. 850) participatory scale of walking interventions, with the practitioner-led 'guided walks' at the bottom and interviewee-led 'natural go-along' walks at the top. As a result, there is a tension between a walk that can help one service user gain confidence through leading, but which may make it harder for the member of staff to manage timings or step in if things go wrong. On the other hand, the practitioner being overly concerned with practicalities and managing risk means that they are less able to spend time focused on service users. In this case, most group walks are planned and led by mental health staff, with a handful of routes organised by service users. In Point D, we reflect on the benefits derived from embracing these potential pitfalls and furthering our approach, with a former service user who previously led a walk becoming part of the team selected to present a conference paper. First, we will explain how the practice is developed through Point B. In this phase, Mark is inspired by the work of Aled, a social researcher promoting walking techniques outside of clinical practice. By trying to encourage democratic involvement in the research process, but eventually failing, Mark's efforts are put in jeopardy.

## Point B: Weakness revealed by accelerating too early

In September 2019, Mark takes a day of study leave from his job in the health service and meets Aled, who is slightly out of his comfort zone, presenting to a group mostly researching the psychological aspects of climate change initiatives. Having met over a hot drink, the two sit next to each other. Aled presents initial findings from his research into place attachment and the lifecourse, where he encourages participation through walking interviews and walking tours (Evans & Jones, 2011). The two stop for a deeper chat over lunch, and swap email addresses. Aled writes later that day and attaches a paper by Tina Richardson (2017) which presents 'schizocartography' as an urban walking technique, and which relies heavily on assemblage theory. Important terminology is introduced, and efforts seem underway to find a space between disciplines. Mark's immediate response is to recognise the therapeutic potential of Aled's walking method, noting that he will talk to his colleagues. Aled invites Mark to a public event using participatory walking that he has organised for the Economic and Social Research Council Festival of Science in November 2019.

Early in 2020, Mark approaches Aled asking to meet, explaining that he is applying for some funding and needs some guidance on participatory methods. He writes: 'I need to propose ways in which I will address the gaps in my knowledge and skillset… I think the methods you have been using in your study are very relevant to my proposal.' The assemblage starts to resemble how Richardson (2017, p. 6) describes the practitioner-analyst(s) being '…not distanced from the space under examination: they choose the tools and at the same time recognize their own subjectivity in the moment that becomes the assemblage.' This assemblage pursuing walking interventions now includes Mark, the service users he works with, his colleagues, the location in southern England and is bridging into concepts from human geography and a potential new working relationship with Aled. The meeting does not happen due to the start of the pandemic. The lines of communication between the two run cold, until Aled emails Mark at the end of August 2020.

Mark writes back to Aled on 3 September 2020 to say that:

> Unfortunately my [funding] application was rejected: mainly, it seems, because it was too sociological and not clinical enough. So I am in the process of speaking to various contacts to see if I can re-orientate my proposal in a way that will be more fundable yet remain innovative, relevant & interesting.

It transpires that Mark had applied for a research fellowship which would have paid for half of his time, over two years, to lay the ground for a geographical research project alongside his clinical practice. Had it been successful Mark would have been given the time, space, and training to develop a study proposal focussing on the everyday practices of young people living in neighbourhoods that hold a greater risk to the development of serious mental health problems. Not getting the funding meant that the walking groups would continue as before, supported by the goodwill of staff members with busy schedules, and with little scope to design a research approach or gather data.

The assemblage has been thwarted in its moves to interrogate what Mark calls 'sociological' and therefore the doors to the social sciences, including human geography, are impeded. However, Mark shows a degree of resilience and explains that he wants to get some further understanding of human geography and relationships between stress and urban life and asks Aled for some guidance. Aled writes back:

> My work is towards the experimental end of things and – given my supervisors and funders [Economic and Social Research Council] – more about understanding sociological factors rather than the individual. That said, I would be very interested to know more about the clinical.

In the subsequent emails, Mark and Aled agree to meet. The pandemic rules out a face-to-face meeting, and so they connect online. Mark shares some work on restorative environments, citing the work of Weber and Trojan (2018), and explains that he is embarking on an internal service evaluation to evaluate the group and one-to-one walks between service users and mental health staff. As indicated in Point A, such service reviews are the gateway to practice being accepted. Completing such an exercise would enable the nurse to strengthen their position as a producer of knowledge. Moreover, Mark acknowledges that he cannot lead this project on his own. For example, he cannot simultaneously play the role of the champion for walking therapy, the researcher and also the person providing a degree of quality assurance.

A meeting in January 2021 starts to form a service evaluation working group, which includes a junior psychiatrist working with Mark and a clinical academic psychologist. The latter two professionals extend the range of disciplines within the research assemblage. In many ways there would be a trade-off: the service evaluation would have greater credibility, but the social science component risked being compromised. Nevertheless, Aled would bring a geographical approach to potentially interview staff and service users. Beyond the members of the working group, there is an internal approval procedure to follow before the service evaluation can work. Fortunately, there is scope for the service evaluation to focus more on the experience of collaboration and co-production, rather than systematically reviewing impact. Two recent articles published by *Advances in Mental Health* provide useful precedents for service evaluations completed with the limited time and resources available to Mark and team, namely focused on one-to-one semi-structured interviews with a small number of staff and service users. Specifically, Kearney et al. (2021) report on an arts-based family initiative and Patel et al. (2021) focus on cognitive behavioural therapy groups for postnatal women.

Framing the evaluation more around service user involvement and innovation, and less as an account of clinical outcomes, would play to the strengths of the research team. As a human geographer, Aled would consider the spatial qualities of where the walking therapy had taken place. The *public realm* is important to American sociologist Richard Sennett, who states that: 'in public, people can access unfamiliar knowledge, expanding the horizons of their information' (2010, p. 261). The opportunity to use public space was taken up more widely as the coronavirus pandemic washed in from spring 2020. For example, some clinical appointments that would ordinarily be held in an institutional setting moved outside. Individuals diagnosed with severe mental health problems are not always comfortable with telephone or video conferencing interactions, for example because of the nature of their ongoing symptoms. Consequently, many medical reviews, less formal contacts, and even structured therapeutic sessions started to take place on the streets and in the parks. By necessity, walking became a method for delivering broader mental health care. This scenario created an excellent opportunity for our walking therapy research project to gather evidence.

In Point C, we will find out how the research team responds to this opening. There is a chance for Mark to step back and Aled to arrive to conduct in-depth conversations for the service evaluation. In the following writing, there is an analysis of the interviews themselves and a chance for Mark and Aled to speak in the first person and give their own more personal reflections. Though this moment is largely positive, inherent fragilities are revealed due to the nature of Aled's employment and the limited time available. From this position we approach Point D, where the future of this ongoing work is open to a new set of possibilities.

## Point C: An illusion of strength

Across three visits in the spring of 2021 Aled interviews a psychiatrist, two mental health workers, an employment support worker and two service users. Two of the staff interviews are conducted outside, as the weather is good and also because mask-wearing is still enforced within the building but not outside. Service user participants are required to be interviewed within the walls of the institution and a mental health worker sits in as Aled conducts the discussions. This arrangement is at odds with the matters being discussed, namely the repositioning of social relations. When viewed through the lens of power, we are left wondering whether institutional research processes unintentionally return service users to a position of passivity and vulnerability. Psychiatric environments have been found to stigmatise and devalue service users, as well as reinforcing safety and risk management rather than therapeutic interaction as the primary service concern (McGrath & Reavey, 2013). In this case, service user autonomy is traded in to appease the institution's own sense of vulnerability.

Early analysis from the data gathered during these interviews reveals a conscious rescripting of the therapeutic relationship through co-operation and a creative shift towards the spatial in the delivery of mental health care. For example, the walking group passes through busy urban neighbourhoods, historic centres, and quiet woodlands. Gentle conversations take place and new associations are formed as the small group makes its way over peripheral hills and along repurposed former industrial routes. Seeds of hope are sown as service users in the early stages of their recovery walk alongside their peers approaching discharge.

An interview with a psychiatrist reveals that individual appointments and medical reviews, for so long routinely conducted within institutional settings or private homes, are increasingly taking place outside. Staff speak about abandoning the familiarity, security, and authority of the clinic for the more textured and less formal spaces of the urban street or park.

> I just think [walking] really helps with engagement for us. Instead of coming into my clinic and 'come and have a seat'. It just feels so sterile.
>
> *Psychiatrist*

The psychiatric environment of control signalled by locked doors, alarms, and strengthened glass is exchanged for a stroll together down a rural lane or a cup of coffee on a bench overlooking a canal. This unorthodox practice, already existent by the onset of the coronavirus pandemic in March 2020, is propelled and legitimised by its restrictions. It stands in quiet determined defiance of the conventional norms and inglorious history of the mental health system. At points, the dominant culture sought to reassert its traditional ways of doing through peer pressure thinly disguised as banter.

> They laugh at me and say, you know, 'Off for another walk? Off for a game of badminton?' Yeah, I want [service users] to see me make a fool of myself and teach me how to play.
>
> *Psychiatrist*

The psychiatrist has an important role to play in advancing walking therapy being adopted within the service. As such, latter comments give an idea of how such innovative practice could be apprehended because practitioners lose confidence to try new approaches.

The group activities and individual practices can both be understood as a conscious embrace of vulnerability on the part of frontline mental health staff. Indeed, taking the research out of the institution is a deliberate move away from environments of monitoring and control. Grbin (2015) acknowledges the influence of architectural arrangements on social relations. For example, it allows mental health workers to pursue a more humanistic approach to care that offers hope, promotes dignity, and foregrounds relationality (Kogstad et al., 2011). The following quote gives an introduction to taking practice outside:

> It was kind of a nice opportunity for them to feel some autonomy because they chose the route because they know the area.
>
> *Employment support worker*

This latter practice is consistent with the participatory typology described by Evans and Jones (2011). For many individuals working in mental health, it accords with their personal values and allows them to reconnect with their original vocational motivations. A change in practice can however have a personal cost in terms of time and the demands of work. Staff appear to consider this a price they must pay if they are to deliver care in the manner they consider best. It enables the relationship between the service user and the mental health system to be redrawn in a more democratic and less imposing direction.

> Being side by side and going in a direction when the surroundings are changing, I think there's something a little bit less kind of putting someone on the spot or under pressure than a sit-down face to face meeting.
>
> *Employment support worker*

Indeed, an example of service user resistance to clinical settings is provided by the psychiatrist interviewed. They describe a young woman who would often shut down in a clinic room, clearly troubled by her exacerbated symptoms. Walking together in the service user's local park, the conversation was easier, broader, and crucially more productive.

In contrast to scrutinising the presenting mental state of the individual service user within a sterile clinical setting, a focus on the activity of walking is identified as helping to foster a welcoming and safe therapeutic space. As well as being a shared experience, both of the service users interviewed describe attending group walks as a personal achievement, literally *stepping out* towards recovery. On the practitioner side, the psychiatrist and other frontline workers are much less able to shape the outdoor session than when an appointment is held in their own clinic. Perhaps they will remain vulnerable until new procedures are developed in due course.

Thus far we have explained how this research project has developed and changed over time. Framing this journey as a transdisciplinary assemblage has allowed us to engage with the complexity of the relations between the different actors and the constraints put upon the individuals. Sometimes it felt like the goal of developing walking therapy had become engulfed in something else completely. Having completed the individual interview stage for the service evaluation, there are some positive developments in terms of Mark gaining support to promote involvement from service users. The assemblage takes a different form as there is another discipline which demands attention.

## Emerging from the assemblage allows a chance to reflect

As Aled conducts these interviews in the spring of 2021, the assemblage is boosted and reformed as Mark gains an internal grant to develop a research proposal. The focus is the spatial dimension of recovery described in Point A, and whose wings were clipped in Point B. Moreover, the health service specifically encourages service user and carer involvement, a sharply progressive aspiration. A recently discharged service user who had led walks for their peers becomes an 'involvee' researcher and helps facilitate group discussions with those still in treatment. Mark finds himself working alongside someone he used to care for, and with whom he walked alongside during the course of treatment. This demands a degree of magnanimity from Mark and may make it more difficult for him to appear as the producer of knowledge for some service users. Resources and power shift towards the service user dimension of the assemblage, impacting on both subjectivities and processes. Most significantly, a former recipient of care is recast as a specialist research assistant, presenting their newly acquired knowledge to the very same clinical staff who used to treat them. The assemblage seems to have achieved the main characteristics which Polk (2015, p. 111) demands of the transdisciplinary approach: 'the inclusion of both multiple disciplines and practice-based knowledge and expertise in the knowledge production process.' As this moment arrives, we step forward and reflect on our positions.

## Mark's reflection

Reflecting on our transdisciplinary assemblage, our experience has at times felt like turning up to a fashionable dinner party in the wrong clothes and with an imposter (Aled) as my plus one. The hosts seem well-disposed to our demeanour, yet eye us cautiously as we enthuse excitedly about unfamiliar and seemingly alien writers and concepts. As we offer our coats in the entrance lobby, we try to catch the eye of some of the regular guests gathered inside. They themselves debate the past, discuss the matters of the day, and dispute the way ahead. The third figurative member of our group (the service user) paces nervously outside, hoping to be admitted at an opportune moment through the rear door. It is this opportunity, this space, this potential to connect that defines our assemblage.

My role as a practitioner-researcher has simultaneously been one of *education* (disseminating information relating to the spatial dimension of mental health), *persuasion* (stating and modelling the case for new, more lateral forms of clinical and research practice), and *organisation* (mobilising resources within and beyond the health service). Granted, it is a position of individual vulnerability but through the development of collaborations and networks, it has forged collective strength. A direction made now to terminate walking practices or exclude service users from the research process would appear reactionary.

*Within* our assemblage, Aled's position as an outsider seems to impact on the research process in a number of ways. As a human geographer independent of the health service, he is untainted by the omnipresent undercurrent of monitoring. This enables his interviews with service users to be more curious and less complicated. Indeed, Aled's comparative ignorance of matters pertaining to psychiatric illnesses places service user participants in a position of relative power. Although Aled drafted the interview schedule with me, the service users hold superior knowledge about the clinical context and chose what and how much to reveal. This relational dimension was magnified in the interviews with clinicians and support workers. Health staff can appear defensive when quizzed on their practice by their peers (Råheim et al., 2016), and so Aled's neutrality may allow for more open, reflective discussions. In both sets of interviews, Aled places himself in a position of vulnerability as he sets about 'studying up' (Nader, 1972; Rose, 1997). He risks being dismissed as a green and ignorant outsider, yet utilises this vulnerability to establish rapport in discussing topics of potential sensitivity.

## Aled's reflection

As planning for Stage C started, I was in possession of a doctorate, but my monthly PhD stipend had ended and I was holding an honorary (unpaid) position at my own institution. I was now part of the significant academic workforce chasing precarious employment through short-term funding (Morgan & Wood, 2017). To undertake the interviews with Mark, I would effectively be on loan to the health service. Being in a situation which is familiar to many recently qualified doctors of philosophy (Herschberg et al., 2018) meant that I was in the habit of keeping positive by projecting my forward programme of work. For example, I wrote about these yet-to-commence interviews in an abstract to a significant geographical conference. A quick acceptance for the latter paper gave our little team confidence, but there is an irony that we could have had nothing of substance to present. In this sense, I was bringing a degree of susceptibility to the work, and to my own reputation, before research had even begun.

The interviews were carried out over three separate sessions. Some of the health service staff meetings were staged in the playing grounds attached to the institution, where a voice recorder was placed on the bench between us. This setting both helped to comply with COVID-19 restrictions at the time and furthered the theme of being outside the clinic. Before launching into the prescribed questions on the topic guide, I wanted to come across as somebody who had been through the process of walking therapy myself. I followed what feminist geographer Kim England wrote in her much-cited paper on reflexivity and positionality: 'We need to locate ourselves in our work and to reflect on how our location influences the questions we ask, how we conduct our research, and how we write our research' (1994, p. 87). I shared how walking with friends and counsellors had helped me during a period when my father had terminal cancer, and subsequently through a period of grief after his death. Although I risked not coming across as an expert, appropriate self-disclosure can help move the relationship between researcher and researched to a more equal footing. Moreover, the discussion of sensitive topics in particular appears to provide space for sharing personal accounts (Dickson-Swift et al., 2007). The transcripts show that this approach helped both service users and mental health practitioners to open up. As I listened through the interviews again, I gained knowledge about the specialist community mental health service, its terminology, and the staff perspective.

The final stage of the interviews was with service users. For procedural reasons, these were staged inside a 1920s building accessed through stone steps. I was shown through various doors and taken down a corridor to a little room with windows that barely opened. As standard health service practice, I was advised that I could activate a mobile alarm if the situation became dangerous. Having a support worker to accompany me meant that there was not an obvious physical threat, such as described by Liamputtong (2007). However, the atmosphere was initially unsteadying and affected my ability to do the interview. I had certainly felt more confident and potentially more able to quickly develop a rapport with the other person when the interviews had been delivered outside. The experience helped to sense that such austere and bounded spaces impact on the research dynamic. Indeed, McGrath and Reavey (2015, p. 213) argue that confined spaces offer 'little capacity for movement, action or engagement with others.' Moreover, I fear what may have happened if the recollection of a walk could have triggered the memory of an episode of acute distress.

The practice of delivering mental health care in the public realm has opened all parties – Aled, Mark, service users, and colleagues – to uncertainties and unknown opportunities. Stage D of the assemblage is the period when our research project renders in plain view what is often invisible, namely conference presentations, preparing papers for academic journals, and applying for research funding. We now theorise what it means to plan this next stage.

## Point D: Does this use of assemblage theory allow us to draw conclusions?

So far, our research journey has shadowed Anderson and McFarlane's (2011) three main characteristics of assemblages: the transdisciplinary nature of our collaboration relates to the *heterogeneous elements*; the opportunities that have arisen through points A, B, and C resemble *processes of emergence*; and our current position is *open to transformation*. At the time of writing, we find ourselves at a point of being exposed. We have been through a process where we have responded to challenges and have gathered first-hand experiences. There is a growing momentum for service users to shape the next stage of the work. The assemblage resembles more of an 'actant-rhizomatic' entity which geographer Nigel Thrift (2000, p. 1) describes as being valued, if it is ever accepted, within structures and institutions only after a series of performative actions. The performative notion seems apt as we expose ourselves to the judgement of our peers and crucially those who can propel or condemn the research assemblage that we have created. Readily available resources to take the work forward are scarce. Mark awaits the outcome of his study proposal whilst the recently mobilised service users watch on. Aled's attention may be taken up by something else. The clock ticks steadily louder with each passing day. Will it end with a chime or an explosion, and would the latter spell the end?

We have cleared a path to a more democratic and inclusive research space by embracing what being vulnerable means for our practice (Lambert & Carr, 2018). The service users that are now joining us in deliberative discussions for further research (including presenting to a conference in the summer of 2022) are generally those we have accompanied on group walks. This exemplifies the shifting positions and *lines of flight* of our assemblage as we move from conventional practice, through innovation, to transdisciplinary research (Lawrence, 2004; Polk, 2015). Our final thought is to underline the conceptual value of this assemblage approach. By tracing the four points of a transformative process, namely: entry (A); accelerating too early (B); an illusion of strength (C); and now realising that the practice has reached a point of danger (D), we can write in the first person (plural and individual) and see our research journey. We can either push harder or accept that the assemblage may have run its course for reasons of not being able to resolve our own disciplinary constraints, resource shortage, or an unsupportive policy environment.

Ours is not a tale of yearning, nor one of resentment. However, we should pay heed to what queer and feminist human geographer Eden Kinkaid (2020, p. 469) warns us about the assemblage: 'The danger is that, in disavowing social categories, assemblage thinking may further obscure the operations of power and inequality.' We have presented a celebration of the possible, the messy, the uncertain, the disruptive, the mobile and the unpredictable. As a case study it offers other researchers a different framework to conceptualise how to respond to vulnerabilities. Ultimately some actors are more powerful than us and many constraints are beyond ourselves and our own efforts.

## Disclaimer

The views expressed in this chapter are those of the individual authors and do not necessarily represent those of the organisations by whom they are employed.

## Acknowledgements

Mark thanks colleagues and service users who have joined us at various points in this journey. Aled is grateful for financial support from Swansea University and the Economic and Social Research Council Fellowship Grant ES/W007568/1.

## References

Abrahamyan Empson, L., Baumann, P. S., Söderström, O., Codeluppi, Z., Söderström, D., & Conus, P. (2020). Urbanicity: The need for new avenues to explore the link between urban living and psychosis. *Early Intervention in Psychiatry, 14*(4), 398–409. https://doi.org/10.1111/eip.12861

Anderson, B., & McFarlane, C. (2011). Assemblage and geography. *Area, 43*(2): 124–127. https://doi.org/10.1111/j.1475-4762.2011.01004.x

Barker, P., & Buchanan-Barker, P. (2011). Myth of mental health nursing and the challenge of recovery. *International Journal of Mental Health Nursing, 20*(5), 337–344. https://doi.org/10.1111/j.1447-0349.2010.00734.x

Deering, K. (2016). Neoliberalism and self-management: The case for social justice. *Mental Health Nursing Journal, 36*(4), 10–12.

Deering, K., Pawson, C., Summers, N., & Williams, J. (2019). Patient perspectives of helpful risk management practices within mental health services. A mixed studies systematic review of primary research. *Journal of Psychiatric and Mental Health Nursing, 26*(5–6), 185–197. https://doi.org/10.1111/jpm.12521

Deleuze, G., & Guattari, F.(1977). *Capitalism and schizophrenia* (Vol. 1). New York: Viking Press.

Department of Health (1999). *National service framework: Mental health.* https://www.gov.uk/government/publications/quality-standards-for-mental-health-services [Accessed 16 March 2022]

Dickson-Swift, V., James, E. L., Kippen, S., & Liamputtong, P. (2007). Doing sensitive research: What challenges do qualitative researchers face? *Qualitative Research, 7*(3), 327–353. https://doi.org/10.1177/1468794107078515

England, K. V. L. (1994). Getting personal: Reflexivity, positionality, and feminist research. *The Professional Geographer, 46*(1), 80–89. https://doi.org/10.1111/j.0033-0124.1994.00080.x

Evans, J., & Jones, P. (2011). The walking interview: Methodology, mobility and place. *Applied Geography, 31*(2), 849–858. https://doi.org/10.1016/j.apgeog.2010.09.005

Foot, J. (2014). Franco Basaglia and the radical psychiatry movement in Italy, 1961–78. *Critical and Radical Social Work, 2*(2), 235. https://doi.org/10.1332/204986014X14002292074708

Freeman, D., Emsley, R., Dunn, G., Fowler, D., Bebbington, P., Kuipers, E., ... Garety, P. (2015). The stress of the street for patients with persecutory delusions: a test of the symptomatic and psychological effects of going outside into a busy urban area. *Schizophrenia Bulletin*, *41*(4), 971–979. https://doi.org/10.1093/schbul/sbu173

Grbin, M. (2015). Foucault and space. *Sociološki pregled*, *49*(3), 305–312. https://doi.org/10.5937/socpreg1503305G

Herschberg, C., Benschop, Y., & van den Brink, M. (2018). Precarious postdocs: A comparative study on recruitment and selection of early-career researchers. *Scandinavian Journal of Management*, *34*(4), 303–310. https://doi.org/10.1016/j.scaman.2018.10.001

Kearney, L., McCree, C., & Brazener, L. (2021). Making it together: A service evaluation of creative families: An arts and mental health partnership, *Advances in Mental Health*, *19*(2), 139–151. https://doi.org/10.1080/18387357.2019.1684828

Kinkaid, E. (2020). Can assemblage think difference? A feminist critique of assemblage geographies. *Progress in Human Geography*, *44*(3), 457–472. https://doi.org/10.1177/0309132519836162

Kogstad, R. E., Ekeland, T. J., & Hummelvoll, J. K. (2011). In defence of a humanistic approach to mental health care: Recovery processes investigated with the help of clients' narratives on turning points and processes of gradual change. *Journal of Psychiatric and Mental Health Nursing*, *18*(6), 479–486. https://doi.org/10.1111/j.1365-2850.2011.01695.x

Lambert, N., & Carr, S. (2018). 'Outside the original remit': Co-production in UK mental health research, lessons from the field. *International Journal of Mental Health Nursing*, *27*(4), 1273–1281. https://doi.org/10.1111/inm.12499

Latour, B. (2007). *Reassembling the social: An introduction to actor-network-theory*. Oxford: Oxford University Press.

Lawrence, R. J. (2004). Housing and health: From interdisciplinary principles to transdisciplinary research and practice. *Futures*, *36*(4), 487–502. https://doi.org/10.1016/j.futures.2003.10.001

Liamputtong, P. (2007). *Researching the vulnerable*. London: SAGE Publications, Ltd. https://doi.org/10.4135/9781849209861

McGrath, L., & Reavey, P. (2013). Heterotopias of control: Placing the material in experiences of mental health service use and community living. *Health & Place*, *22*, 123–131. https://doi.org/10.1016/j.healthplace.2013.03.010

McGrath, L., & Reavey, P. (2015). Seeking fluid possibility and solid ground: Space and movement in mental health service users' experiences of 'crisis'. *Social Science & Medicine*, *128*, 115–125. https://doi.org/10.1016/j.healthplace.2013.03.010

Morgan, G., & Wood, J. (2017). The 'academic career' in the era of flexploitation. In E. Armano, A. Bove, & A. Murgia (Eds.), *Mapping precariousness, labour insecurity and uncertain livelihoods: Subjectivities and resistance* (pp. 82–97). Abingdon: Routledge.

Nader, L. (1972). Up the anthropologist: Perspectives gained from studying up. In D. Hymes (Ed.), *Reinventing anthropology* (pp. 284–311). New York: Pantheon Books.

NHS Digital (2022). NHS vacancy statistics England April 2015 – December 2021 experimental statistics. *NHS*. https://digital.nhs.uk/data-and-information/publications/statistical/nhs-vacancies-survey/ [Accessed 16 March 2022]

Parr, H. (2011). *Mental health and social space: Towards inclusionary geographies?*. Hoboken, NJ: John Wiley & Sons.

Patel, R., Ezzamel, S., & Horley, N. (2021). Improving access to cognitive behavioural therapy groups for postnatal women following partnership work: A service evaluation. *Advances in Mental Health*, *19*(2), 127–138. https://doi.org/10.1080/18387357.2020.1761263

Polk, M. (2015). Transdisciplinary co-production: Designing and testing a transdisciplinary research framework for societal problem solving. *Futures, 65*, 110–122. https://doi.org/10.1016/j.futures.2014.11.001

Råheim, M., Magnussen, L. H., Sekse, R. J. T., Lunde, Å., Jacobsen, T., & Blystad, A. (2016). Researcher–researched relationship in qualitative research: Shifts in positions and researcher vulnerability. *International Journal of Qualitative Studies on Health and Well-Being, 11*(1), 30996. https://doi.org/10.3402/qhw.v11.30996

Richardson, T. (2017). Assembling the assemblage: Developing schizocartography in support of an urban semiology. *Humanities, 6*, 47. https://doi.org/10.3390/h6030047

Rose, G. (1997). Situating knowledges: Positionality, reflexivities and other tactics. *Progress in Human Geography, 21*(3), 305–320. https://doi.org/10.1191/030913297673302122

Sayce, L. (1999). *From psychiatric patient to citizen: Overcoming discrimination and social exclusion.* New York: Macmillan International Higher Education. https://psycnet.apa.org/doi/10.1007/978-1-349-27833-6

Sennett, R. (2010). The public realm. In Bridge, G., & Watson, S. (Eds.), *The Blackwell city reader* (pp. 261–271). Hoboken, NJ: Wiley.

Söderström, O., Empson, L. A., Codeluppi, Z., Söderström, D., Baumann, P. S., & Conus, P. (2016). Unpacking 'the City': An experience-based approach to the role of urban living in psychosis. *Health & Place, 42*, 104–110. https://doi.org/10.1016/j.healthplace.2016.09.002

Solnit, R. (2001). *Wanderlust: A history of walking.* London: Penguin.

Thrift, N. (2000). Afterwords. *Environment and Planning D: Society and Space, 18*(2), 213–255. https://doi.org/10.1068/d214t

Vassos, E., Pedersen, C. B., Murray, R. M., Collier, D. A., & Lewis, C. M. (2012). Meta-analysis of the association of urbanicity with schizophrenia. *Schizophrenia Bulletin, 38*(6), 1118–1123. https://doi.org/10.1093/schbul/sbs096

Weber, A. M., & Trojan, J. (2018). The restorative value of the urban environment: A systematic review of the existing literature. *Environmental Health Insights, 12*. https://doi.org/10.1177%2F1178630218812805

Woodward, K., Dixon, D. P., & Jones III, J. P. (2009). Poststructuralism/poststructuralist geographies. In Kitchin, R. & Thrift, N. (Eds.), *International encyclopedia of human geography* (Vol. 8, pp. 396–407). Amsterdam: Elsevier.

# 12

# 'PLEASE EXPLAIN TO ME HOW I'M VULNERABLE'

## Learning How to Rework Experiences of Researcher Vulnerability by Listening Carefully to Care-Experienced Young People

*Dawn Mannay*

### The Label of Vulnerability

This section begins by defining and examining the term vulnerable in preparation for the following section, which explores how vulnerability has been attributed to and rejected by the children and young people that I have worked with in research studies and related activities. This leads to a contemplation of how vulnerability operates bidirectionally in fieldwork and a consideration of its impacts on researchers, which can be both debilitating and productive. The final section positions vulnerability as a property of academic structures, policies, and conventions. It challenges individualised conceptions of personal vulnerability and failure, which can obscure unrealistic institutional expectations for productivity, performance, and perfection. The chapter was written as a reflection of my experiences working in Higher Educational Institutions in the geographical context of Wales, UK.

So, the starting point is to understand what is meant by vulnerability. The word 'vulnerable', like all other words has a definition, and the quality of being vulnerable is described as being 'able to be easily hurt, influenced, or attacked' (Cambridge Dictionary, 2022). Derived from the Latin 'vulnerare', meaning 'to wound', the term is used across academic fields to denote people at risk and factors that reduce the ability to respond to threats (Ford et al., 2018, p. 189). The application of this term can be problematic as being able to 'be easily hurt' can be attributed to a paucity of resilience, or some form of individual lack, rather than the wider social and economic inequalities that mean that some people negotiate more difficulties in their everyday lives than others. As Priestley (2020, p. 521) contends, the neoliberal narrative of agency situates the successful subject as an empowered decision-maker, who is responsible for their good fortune, meaning that the vulnerable are 'held accountable for their own demise'.

DOI: 10.4324/9781003349266-16

This idea of individual lack is inherent in the neoliberal justice narrative (Littler, 2018), where 'vulnerable' families are positioned in an individualising and pathologising discourse, which 'emphasises social mobility as the problem of people experiencing poverty' (Folkes, 2019, p. 15). Similarly, in the field of disability studies the labelling of individuals as 'vulnerable', 'resilient', or 'non-resilient' has also been explored. For example, Hutcheon and Lashewicz (2014) propose that being labelled as 'at risk' presumes different-ness, which leads to the positioning of individuals as vulnerable, with expectations around who is reliant enough to overcome different-ness and negotiate risk, and who lacks the personal resilience to 'overcome' and fit in with prescribed notions of sameness. Vulnerability research raises critical questions about 'why people and places are vulnerable (or not)' (Ford et al., 2018, p. 201), and the following section focuses on the positioning of care-experienced young people as at risk and vulnerable.

## 'Lack' Labelling

Care-experienced children and young people are well aware of the identities ascribed to them and the abbreviated form of 'Looked After Children' – LAC, which marks out those who have had contact with the care system.[1] Care-experienced young people have rejected this label, explaining that they do not like being 'referred to as "LAC" as they are not "lacking" in anything' (Children's Commissioner for Wales, 2016, p. 11). Research evidence confirms that care-experienced young people face inequalities in relation to education, employment, and housing (Allnatt, 2019; Artamonovaa et al., 2020; Brady & Gilligan, 2019; Girling, 2019; Harrison, 2020; Mannay et al., 2017), which can have a negative impact on mental health and well-being (Baker et al., 2019; Mannay et al., 2022). However, although research data, patterns, and probabilities position care-experienced young people at an increased risk of disadvantage (Long et al., 2017; O'Higgins et al., 2015), it is important to separate ideas of vulnerability in terms of individual young people themselves and the wider social structures that impact on their everyday lives.

I have been involved in a series of research studies and associated activities with care-experienced children and young people, which were carried out over an extended period of time and contributed to a Research Excellence Framework (REF) Impact Case Study[2] (Boffey et al., 2021; Mannay et al., 2015; Mannay et al., 2018a; Mannay et al., 2022; Mobedji & Mannay, 2018; Roberts et al., 2020). These activities provided an opportunity to gain insights about the impact of being seen as 'at risk' and the unintended consequences of well-intended actions to support children and young people positioned as vulnerable.

A number of studies have documented the ways in which children and young people encounter unsupportive professional practices that inscribe indices of difference by stigmatising their care status and undermining their expectations for achievement (Harker et al., 2003; McLeod, 2010). This inscription of difference was documented by the care-experienced children and young people in and leaving care that we worked with in a study interested in their educational experiences in

Wales (Mannay et al., 2017). One of the young people in this study discussed how their move into the care system impacted on how they were perceived in the space of the school.

> As soon as I went into care, then went back to school and my teachers, majority of them, treated me completely different, because I was in care they moved me down sets, they put me in special help, they gave me – put me in support groups. And I was just like I don't need all this shit, I've only moved house, that's it I was like yeah I might be in care but the only difference to me is I've moved house, that's it... they looked at all my papers and where I was in my levels and that and they was like you're more than capable of being in top set but we don't think you're going to be able to cope.

In this account, the young person illustrated a recognition of the ways in which their care status was interpreted by teachers as a 'vulnerability', the shift to a new housing arrangement bringing the assumption that they would not 'be able to cope'. Benjamin et al. (2003) maintains that in educational discourses for the successful subject position to flourish, the failing subject is necessary, and this young person had been shifted away from the signifier of the 'capable... top set' to a position where 'special help' was required. In relation to earlier vulnerability studies, this suggests that the school felt that the young person did not have the 'personal resilience' to 'overcome' (Hutcheon & Lashewicz, 2014). Teachers' expectations can lead to a 'self-fulfilling prophecy' (Rosenthal & Jacobson, 1968), and the expectation that care-experienced children and young people are vulnerable, failing subjects, can contribute to negative educational experiences and to disrupted educational trajectories as noted in the following account from a care-experienced young person.

> I'd always wanted to go. Just when college and school messed up like the first time, I kind of just thought that I'd wait until I was a mature student and figure out what I actually wanted to do. Like mainly because everyone always told me that I couldn't. So, it was just a kind of thing of I wanted to go just because I could.

In this account again, the young person had received the message that they 'couldn't' in spaces of education and social care. As with other care-experienced young people (Brady & Gilligan, 2020), transition to higher education was delayed and the pathway to university was taken later, shifting from the 'couldn't' to the 'could'. However, returning to education at a later point may not be an option for all young people and the structural inequalities associated with being in care can continue alongside a continuance of labelling with the status of 'vulnerable'.

Conceptions of vulnerability also featured in a study that I was involved with that explored the experiences of young people in and leaving care during the COVID-19 pandemic in Wales (Roberts et al., 2021a, 2021b). Emerging adulthood is considered a risky and vulnerable period for care leavers and the COVID-19 pandemic, and its restrictions had differential outcomes for already marginalised communities (Patel et al., 2007; Withers, 2020). For this young parent in the study financial issues arose due to the restrictions of the COVID-19 pandemic and associated delays with economic resources.

> I might as well have no fucking support off them... d'you know what I mean? The most support I need is money, that's what I need, people say 'what's money, you don't need money', that's the only support I need, for someone to help me. Then they start telling me that I can't cope... So, I'm thinking well the one minute you're saying you can't help me and the next minute you're saying I can't cope with anything.

During the COVID-19 pandemic, care-experienced young people reported isolation, digital exclusion, financial precarity, and precarious access to support and services (Leicestershire Cares, 2021; O'Higgins et al., 2020). For this young person, this meant that they did not have resources for essential commodities such as food and heating. However, in reaching out to services, there was a disjuncture between what the participant was requesting help with and how she was positioned because of her care biography.

> I'm vulnerable, I'm a vulnerable person because I'm a kid in care. So, what you saying, all kids in care are vulnerable. If I'm vulnerable right I wouldn't be in the situation that I'm in, and if I'm vulnerable I wouldn't have a clue what I'm doing. If I was vulnerable, I'd be going out doing whatever with whoever and seeing whoever. I am doing that, no, I'm sat at in the van, I'm in a relationship, I been with him two and a half year. D'you know what I mean, I'm settled down with a child, sorted my life out. But no, I'm vulnerable.

In previous studies, it has been noted that self-reliance was described as a resource by the care leavers but not by their caseworkers (Sulimani-Aidana & Melkmanb, 2018), and here the participant felt that her self-reliance was overlooked. The positioning of the 'vulnerable person' was actively rejected as a blanket attribute that is assigned to all care leavers, rather than one based on her as an individual and as a mother. Young people who become parents are often impacted by discourses of stigma and risk, and surveillance of their parenting practices (Brady & Brown, 2013; Mannay et al., 2018b). For care-experienced parents, these forms of judgement and surveillance are even more significant (Roberts, 2017, 2019), and notions of vulnerability are embedded in social work practice and decision-making.

This section has explored the ways in which the care status of young people can engender an ascription of vulnerability in educational and social care discourses. It has also illustrated how young people, whilst recognising changes in their lives, structural barriers and social inequalities, actively reject the assumption that they are themselves vulnerable, lacking, or failing subjects. While ideas of vulnerability are attached to care leavers and other groups positioned as at risk or risky, and to some extent practitioners, for example, in relation to vicarious trauma (Middleton & Potter, 2015), there is far less attention given to the vulnerability of academic researchers who work alongside care-experienced children and young people. The following sections focus on the relational aspects of researcher vulnerability, considering why researchers may be of risk of harm, and what can be learnt from the accounts of care-experienced young people to reframe vulnerability as a structural challenge, rather than an individual failure.

## Researcher Vulnerability

Resonances of the ideal of scientific objectivity mean that research outputs often conceal the presence of the researcher (Ryan-Flood & Gill, 2010), creating the impression that the researcher is 'an unfortunate necessity for the production of research, rather than its beating heart' (Loughran & Mannay, 2018, p. 2). As Folkes (2022, n.p.) contends, 'it is crucial that positionality is engaged with not only in relation to methodology, but within wider theoretical and analytical writing'. There is a recognition in qualitative research of how the researcher relates to the communities that they work within as transient insiders and outsiders (Coffey, 1999; Roberts, 2018). There is also a growing acknowledgement of how emotion is intertwined into the spatial and temporal elements of qualitative research as well as academic research careers (Carroll, 2018; Fink, 2018). However, despite an engagement with positionality and the emotional lifeworld of research, less attention is given to researcher vulnerability.

There are arguments that vulnerable populations are exposed to research epistemologies, methodologies, and practices that can 'exacerbate their vulnerability' (Wilson & Stephen Neville, 2009, p. 69). In working with care-experienced children and young people, then, the issue of participant vulnerability is centralised in applications to the ethics board and a duty of care informed the research design of these studies (Shaw & Holland, 2014), working with partner organisations to ensure both the appropriateness of participants to take part in the project and continued access to support. However, as Braun and Clarke (2021, p. 26) contend, for all participants, the impacts of being involved in research can be 'minimal, or significant, or even transformative… in good and bad ways'. This process of transformation is of course bidirectional because the 'researcher never entirely leaves the field' and 'the field never entirely leaves the researcher' (Pole & Hillyard, 2017, p. 109).

With these impacts in mind, for me researcher vulnerability emerged when I was exposed to the emotional worlds of care-experienced participants. As discussed in the previous section, participants shared the ways in which their care status framed them as vulnerable, lacking, and less capable, and this had often unintended, yet potentially adverse effects on their everyday lives and trajectories. Similar accounts were found in the literature reviews for these studies, with many research studies reporting comparable patterns, suggesting that things were not improving across time (Jackson & Sachdev, 2001; Jackson et al., 2005). This inability for research to impact on policy and practice made me begin to question my role as yet another researcher, whose research may make no difference to care-experienced communities. This left me vulnerable and exposed to the criticism that academia often fails to make any positive changes in the lives of participants, as the research process accrues more benefits for the researcher than the researched.

This vulnerability came from comparing the studies I was involved with and those that went before, considering whether this research could contribute to informed policy or practice changes, or whether things would stay the same. It also came from young people in the studies who understood and articulated that previous research they had contributed to had not changed or benefitted their everyday lives, as one young person commented, '*you come and ask questions and go, nothing ever changes*'. This uncomfortableness of the 'researcher as a vampire' positioning has been reported in other studies (Ward, 2015, p. 170), and it left me vulnerable, easily hurt, because I could not make any guarantees that this time something would change.

There was an associated guilt in claiming 'vulnerability' because I recognised that the vulnerabilities of the researcher are not comparable to the inequalities faced and negotiated by the care-experienced communities that I worked alongside. A feeling that any sense of personal vulnerability should not be experienced, felt, or recognised. However, rather than slipping into inertia, this vulnerability and defencelessness was useful as it pushed me to explore different ways to advocate for the rights and interests of participants (Hugman et al., 2011).

In my earlier doctoral research that explored the structural equalities of class (Mannay, 2012), like the young person above I agreed 'nothing ever changes' and felt paralysed by the enormity of the history of the structural inequalities that I encountered. However, the direct challenge in my first project with care-experienced young people that 'nothing ever changes' engendered a sense of responsibility to channel my energies into negotiating change. I was also inspired and motivated by young people in the same study, who, as discussed in the previous section, had been told that they 'couldn't' but moved from a position of 'couldn't' to one of 'could'.

In listening carefully to care-experienced young people, and then working alongside young people, partner organisations and like-minded colleagues, we were able to create a range of multimodal impact activities and resources.[3] These were designed to inform policy and practice, and films, magazines, and music videos were used to communicate messages from care-experienced children and young people. Training sessions were also provided across the UK with practicing and trainee teachers, youth workers, social workers, foster and kinship carers, local authorities, and third-sector organisations. The study and its initial outputs were followed by additional research projects. Some of these studies were instigated by calls from care-experienced young people and third-sector organisations (see Roberts et al., 2020, 2021a, 2021b). The later studies also built in this requirement to make a change, beyond the standard reports or journal articles, and were again followed by multimodal outputs and an emphasis on informing policy and practice.

Accordingly, in considering what it means to be vulnerable, the researcher can attempt to move beyond helplessness and reconsider how to negotiate new forms of ethical practice in the generation and sharing of qualitative research and its key messages. This cognitive reframing involves shifting a conceptual viewpoint in relation to how a situation is experienced, placing the situation in a different frame that fits the concrete circumstances equally well but changes its meaning (Robson & Troutman-Jordan, 2014). However, as considered in the following section, despite the opportunities of this cognitive reframing and the move from inertia to action, there are further vulnerabilities in this engagement work because of the risk factors and threats that accompany impact agendas.

## Impact Vulnerability

This section challenges individualised conceptions of personal vulnerability by examining the complex layers of pressure that researchers negotiate. It begins by considering issues of performativity in the academy. The section reflects on how the motivation to create impact and change can be threatened by the administrative demands of documenting impact and a lack of institutional appreciation of the time-intensive work required to build trustful relationships and the emotional labour that this entails. The weight of structural expectations is further emphasised in relation to COVID-19, which has seen researchers exhausted by the demands of radically different working practices and heightened expectations around delivering pastoral care to students. An additional reference to my personal journey is offered to illustrate how even when under immense pressure, academics continue to juggle unmanageable workloads because they do not want to identify or be identified as unable to cope, as faulty, or as vulnerable. At this point, the section returns to the lessons learnt from care-experienced young people who rejected the label of the vulnerable subject. An argument is put forward that institutions need to ensure that individual researchers are adequately supported by addressing the structural vulnerabilities inherent to organisations that place individual academics at risk.

The move towards impact from working with care-experienced children and young people was a grassroots response to the issues they raised and what they thought should change. However, there is a wider impact agenda that sits within and beyond academic institutions and acts as a mechanism to assess and categorise impact performance. This imperative for impact can be seen as another pressure for researchers, and 'we are increasingly subject to a range of administrative processes that demand that we can demonstrate that the research that we carry out, and the outputs that result from it, possess some utility to non-academics and that they possess causal powers to influence the world in some way or another' (Knowles & Burrows, 2014, p. 242). Consequently, there is an argument that demands for impact can put pressure on academic staff, contributing to an audit culture where researchers are already continually measured and evaluated. These forms of pressure have also been considered more recently by Leigh (2021, p. 72) who outlines the 'time pressured work of the qualitative researcher in the neoliberal academy [which] emphasises outputs, excellence in research, teaching and impact'.

In the hierarchy of academic work activities, those that are quantifiable and directly increase university rankings are positioned as valuable. These values can become unconsciously internalised by researchers who have reported feeling as if they are squandering their time when there is no immediate tangible outcome, even when their activities, such as building trust with communities, are an essential aspect of qualitative research (Costas Batlle & Carr, 2021). Similarly, reflecting on their work in a long-term collaborative project with care-experienced young people, as Research Assistants, with other work commitments, Staples et al. (2019, p. 207) noted:

> Displaying and managing patience, compassion, warmth and calmness are all part of facilitating CASCADE Voices.[4] This emotion-work has been argued to be expected of and practised by women to a greater extent than men in academic research but not valued in the same way as other aspects of research (Reay, 2004). The gendered division and misrecognition of emotional labour is not the domain of this chapter, but it is noted because we are seeking to provide a reflexive account of the group and its functioning.

Staples et al.'s (2019) work with CASCADE Voices centralises the building of trust highlighted by Costas Batlle and Carr (2021), which also involves training young people in research methods, so they are not only experts by experience in relation to their care histories, but also have expertise in conducting research, evaluating findings, and suggesting new directions for future studies. CASCADE Voices have been central to the studies that I have reflected on in this chapter and relationships between young people and researchers can be sustained over a long period of time. For example, Louise Roberts' post-doctoral research was a direct response to a suggestion from care-experienced parents that more research was needed in this area, this later led to presentations to key stakeholders and the Welsh Government, and a book which included a chapter by a care-experienced parent (Roberts, 2021).

As such, this work has been embedded in wider networks and relationships that are built on fostering change and sustained engagement. There is then an aim to see impacts, in policy and practice, on a large scale or incrementally in small but significant steps at the level of the individual. However, the impact agenda is interested in quantifiable impacts that are measurable and this necessitates forms of recording, and different strategies to ensure that impact can be measured against the REF. This brings a new layer of administrative work, where activities need to consider how impact can be measured, what this data will look like, and how it should be recorded. If there is no sufficient institutional support, then this can leave researchers vulnerable to overwork and fatigue.

Impact work begins with a study and a report, but to be considered as an Impact Case Study the original research needs to generate academic journal articles, chapters, or books that would be considered of high enough quality in relation to the

REF. This is only the first step. In this example, there was a seven-year gap between the initial study and the announcement of the results of the Impact Case Study in relation to the REF. In the initial study, there were a team of committed researchers, they had work hours dedicated to the project, and went over and above their roles in terms of time, energy, and contribution to deliver the project. However, they did not have an assigned workload to continue on the journey to impact.

There was associated funding that was drawn on to facilitate the generation of multimodal outputs and to enable travel across the UK to deliver workshops and training to key stakeholders. There were also limited opportunities to apply for some days of staff time to help with some activities and administration. However, the team that began the project is only tied to the project and contractual research- ers must move onto different studies and projects. As such, requesting help to travel 200 miles to deliver a workshop and then type 200 feedback cards into a spread- sheet is too much to ask from colleagues who are already trying to negotiate com- peting demands and deadlines. There has been support from individuals, which was always appreciated, but again there is a burden of guilt that they are fitting in additional work. In this way, despite the collaborative nature and the interactions that characterise impact work, it can at times seem a lonely journey to the Impact Case Study with the weight of continuing to share recommendations from young people and the vulnerability that if you do not then avenues to change will remain untravelled.

The ways in which the journey to the Impact Case Study relies on an individual researcher is illustrative of vulnerabilities in the wider mechanisms of academic prac- tice and the organisations that fund research. Ideally, impact needs to be part of the initial funding proposal. In advocating for this resourcing, I am not simply referring to the production of a few follow-up outputs that are more engaging and accessible than the report. Instead, impact requires a sufficient period of paid staff time so that there is capacity to engender change from research. Many social researchers are motivated to inform policy and practice, and to contribute to positive changes, but time is the facilitator and barrier to achieving impact. Additionally, even where time can be found to develop incremental changes in the lives of individuals, these are not necessarily the measurable outcomes favoured by the impact agenda. This planning, delivery, and recording of measurable impact is an additional layer of labour contributing to the 'time pressured work of the qualitative researcher in the neoliberal academy' (Leigh, 2021, p. 72).

It is also useful here to reflect on the impacts of the COVID-19 pandemic which engendered a series of unexpected impacts and vulnerabilities. Carruthers Thomas (2022) has documented UK women academics' experiences of working practices and academic identity during and beyond the COVID-19 pandemic in the #DearDiaryProject. These poignant accounts illustrate negative impacts of the emotional labour involved in supporting students alongside unmanageable aca- demic labour for research projects, publications, and impact activities. These effects and their legacies were also observed by Morrish (2021, n.p.):

The post-pandemic academy will be staffed and managed by people who are exhausted and emotionally drained. If we don't want universities to be full of victims and victimisers, it is time for an audit of emotional labour and to ensure this is reciprocal and focussed on the needs, feelings and intentions of all involved in the very human chains of relations that are inherent to higher education contexts.

In writing and recounting my experiences of this work, there is again a vulnerability. Academic researchers do not want to appear as a fault in the system, as someone who cannot keep up with the work, as someone at risk and has some individual failing that works to 'reduce the ability to respond to threats' (Ford et al., 2018, p. 189). As a non-traditional student who returned to education as a mother of two children, living in an area categorised as lacking, there was a misalignment with statistical probabilities and my position in the academy. My educational journey was characterised with barriers that have been experienced by others who return to academic study and markers of difference endure (Mannay & Ward, 2020; Morgan, 2016). Moving to an academic career has not removed these markers of difference. This can be positive when students that I teach say it was good to see someone 'like them' in a recognition of my accent. My same way of speaking can also align with Loughran's (2018, p. 256) reflections on her glottal stop[5] and the ways in which academics 'hear my voice and seem to mentally write me off'. In academia, the age of my children, and later grandchildren, has also instigated comments of 'teen mom' and my holiday destinations have been categorised as somewhere that 'common people go', as such I have needed to guard against any risk of appearing vulnerable.

Aligning with the account from the young person introduced earlier in this chapter, this return to education and an academic career meant the 'couldn't' changed to 'could'. The essence of the 'could' amidst barriers necessitated a commitment of time and effort in gaining qualifications, and this continues in teaching, research, and other activities – sustaining the 'could'. My work is also motivated, as noted in the previous section, by the communities I work with and the need to move beyond research outcomes where 'nothing ever changes'. As Mason (2021) contends, engaged scholarship can necessitate personal and professional sacrifice, but there are limits to capacity that also need to be recognised.

In thinking through these limits to capacity, and the tensions in my own practice in relation to the 'could', the 'should' and the realities of work that may make me vulnerable or seen as vulnerable, there is a question of the individual versus the structural. This was poignantly communicated in the quote from the care-experienced young person interviewed in the pandemic presented earlier in this chapter in its full form:

> I'm vulnerable, I'm a vulnerable person... If I'm vulnerable right I wouldn't be in the situation that I'm in, and if I'm vulnerable I wouldn't have a clue what I'm doing. [I] sorted my life out. But no, I'm vulnerable.

This is very much a rejection of and challenge to individualised conceptions of personal vulnerability and a call to recognise the external, structural issues that would be difficult for anyone to negotiate. Listening to and considering this position can help academic researchers to stop and consider vulnerabilities as a property of the structure of work rather than the failings of the individual. This is not to say that I do not make mistakes or have doubts, academic research is always emerging and developing, continually bringing opportunities for new learning. However, it is useful to look beyond the window to the self and consider structures, policies, and conventions within academia itself. There is an emphasis on productivity in academia, but also efficiency, so when researchers feel overwhelmed this may not reflect that they are too easily harmed because they are vulnerable individuals. Rather, changes need to be made more widely to ensure that risk to harm is minimised, recognising that systems themselves have vulnerabilities.

## Concluding Thoughts

This chapter began by exploring how vulnerability is framed, considering who is positioned as vulnerable and the ways in which individual lack is inherent in the neoliberal narratives, and the label of lacking is attributed unevenly to particular communities. Drawing across projects involving care-experienced children and young people, the chapter documented examples of the unintended consequences of self-fulfilling prophecies that position those with care histories as not being 'able to cope'. This had costs for young people's educational trajectories and even when they moved from being 'in care' and were categorised as a care leaver, faulty attributions meant that they were still viewed through the lens of vulnerability. The accounts of these young people raised questions about interpretations of vulnerability in individuals and communities, challenging vulnerability as a reflection of people and collectives, and reconceptualising vulnerability as responses to wider structural inequalities and stigmas that attempt to infantilise care-experienced communities by locating vulnerability within the person.

The chapter then considered the ways in which the accounts of young people can provide an opportunity to recognise and rework researcher vulnerability. The chapter suggested that it is important for researchers to recognise emotion and feelings of vulnerability because these forms of fragility can be drawn on as a motivation to engender change. In my own work, thinking through previous studies that were unable to effect change, and listening to young people confirm that 'nothing ever changes' offered an opportunity to think through my own vulnerabilities. This reflection on the role of the researcher and the resilience of young people acted as a motivational resource to move beyond barriers of helplessness and inertia and explore ways to foster change and sustain engagement with sharing messages from young people.

However, there are expectations to research, publish, teach, and demonstrate measurable impact that can again position researchers as vulnerable if they are unable to keep up with these competing pressures and demonstrate excellence. In listening to the accounts of young people, there is an opportunity to reject this individualised notion of lack and to question whether issues of vulnerability are an artefact of the structure of academia. Researchers can be made to feel vulnerable when they do not have adequate resources and generating impact from research is resource and time intensive. As such, this chapter has argued that funders need to consider the investment necessary to enable genuine forms of impact that can make a difference, and that academic institutions that benefit from measurements of impact need to ensure that individual researchers are adequately supported. In the same way that researchers need to recognise their vulnerabilities so do wider organisations. They can ask the question 'please explain to me how I'm vulnerable' and in the same way that researchers listen to participants, they could engage with academics to explore ways to ensure that the current risks to harm are tackled.

## Acknowledgements

I would like to thank all the children and young people that I have worked with and learnt from as well as all the colleagues, partners, and funding bodies that have been involved in research, projects, and impact activities.

## Notes

1 The care system is an umbrella term that incorporates services for children and young people who are living under the care of the state. Care-experienced children are those who are either looked after by the state under Wales national legislation or were previously looked after by the state. Care arrangements can include foster, kinship, and residential care placements.
2 The REF is a system for assessing the quality of research in UK higher education institutions and impact is defined as an effect on, change or benefit to the economy, society, culture, public policy or services, health, the environment or quality of life, beyond academia – see https://impact.ref.ac.uk/casestudies/About.aspx.
3 Examples of some of these resources can be found at https://www.exchangewales.org/lace/.
4 CASCADE Voices is a research advisory group that was developed through collaboration between the Children's Social Care Research and Development Centre (CASCADE) and Voices from Care Cymru. They advise on the design of research projects, suggest new research directions, act as peer researchers, and respond to the findings of studies.
5 The glottal stop is a voiceless stop sound made in the throat, often replacing a 't' in spoken English (for example, for 'letter', 'le'er'). It is a usual feature of working-class London accents.

## References

Allnatt, G. (2019). Transitions from care to higher education: A case study of a young person's journey. In D. Mannay, A. Rees & Roberts, L. (Eds.), *Children and young people 'looked after'? Education, intervention and the everyday culture of care in Wales* (pp. 69–82). Cardiff: University of Wales Press.
Artamonovaa, A., das Dores Guerreirob, M. & Höjer, I. (2020). Time and context shaping the transition from out-of-home care to adulthood in Portugal. *Children and Youth Services Review*, 115, 105–115.

Baker, C., Briheim-Crookall, L., Magnus, L. & Selwyn, J. (2019). *Our lives beyond care: Care leavers' views on their well-being in 2018.* London: Coram Voice.

Benjamin, S., Nind, M., Hall, K., Collins, J. & Sheeby, K. (2003). Moments of inclusion and exclusion: Children negotiating classroom contexts. *British Journal of Sociology of Education,* 24(5), 547–558.

Boffey, M., Mannay, D., Vaughan, R. & Wooders, C. (2021). *The Fostering Communities programme - Walking tall: Stage two evaluation.* Project Report. Cardiff: The Fostering Network in Wales.

Brady, G. & Brown, G. (2013). Rewarding but let's talk about the challenges: Using arts-based methods in research with young mothers. *Methodological Innovations Online,* 8(1), 99–112.

Brady, E. & Gilligan, R. (2019). Exploring diversity in the educational pathways of care-experienced adults: Findings from a life course study of education and care. *Children and Youth Services Review,* 104, 104379.

Brady, E. & Gilligan, R. (2020). The role of agency in shaping the educational journeys of care-experienced adults: Insights from a life course study of education and care. *Children and Society,* 34(2), 121–135.

Braun, V. & Clarke, V. (2021). The ebbs and flows of qualitative research. Time, change, and the slow wheel of interpretation. In B. Clift, J. Gore, S. Gustafsson, S. Bekker, I. Costas Batlle & J. Hatchard (Eds.), *Temporality in qualitative inquiry: Theories, methods and practices* (pp. 22–38). Abingdon: Routledge.

Cambridge Dictionary (2022). Cambridge University Press. Available at https://dictionary. cambridge.org/dictionary/english/vulnerability

Carroll, K. (2018). Approaching bereavement research with heartfelt positivity. In T. Loughran & D. Mannay (Eds.), *Emotion and the researcher: Sites, subjectivities, and relationships, Vol. 16. Studies in qualitative methodology* (pp. 1–18). Bingley: Emerald.

Carruthers Thomas, K. (2022). *Dear Diary: Equality implications for female academics of changes to working practices in lockdown and beyond.* Available at www.deardiaryresearch.co.uk

Children's Commissioner for Wales (2016). *The right care: Children's rights in residential care.* Swansea: Children's Commissioner for Wales.

Coffey, A. (1999). *The ethnographic self: Fieldwork and the representation of identity.* London: Sage.

Costas Batlle, I. & Carr, S. (2021). Trust and relationships in qualitative research. In B. Clift, J. Gore, S. Gustafsson, S. Bekker, I. Costas Batlle & J. Hatchard (Eds.), *Temporality in qualitative inquiry: Theories, methods and practices* (pp. 158–171). Abingdon: Routledge.

Fink, J. (2018). Foreword. In T. Loughran & D. Mannay (Eds.), *Emotion and the researcher: Sites, subjectivities, and relationships, Vol. 16. Studies in qualitative methodology* (pp. xvii–xix). Bingley: Emerald.

Folkes, L. (2019). Collective (re)imaginings of social mobility: Insights from place-based, classed and gendered (im)mobility narratives. PhD Thesis, Cardiff University.

Folkes, L. (2022). Moving beyond 'shopping list' positionality: Using kitchen table reflexivity and in/visible tools to develop reflexive qualitative research. *Qualitative Research.* https:// doi.org/10.1177/14687941221098922

Ford, J. D., Pearce, T., McDowell, G., Berrang-Ford, L., Sayles, J. S. & Belfer, A. (2018). Vulnerability and its discontents: The past, present, and future of climate change vulnerability research. *Climatic Change,* 151, 189–203.

Girling, R. (2019). Yet another change: The experience of movement for children and young people looked after. In D. Mannay, A. Rees & Roberts, L. (Eds.), *Children and young people 'looked after'? Education, intervention and the everyday culture of care in Wales* (pp. 127–139). Cardiff: University of Wales Press.

Harker, R. M., Dobel-Ober, D., Lawrence, J., Berridge, D. & Sinclair, R. (2003). Who takes care of education? Looked after children's perceptions of support for educational progress, *Child and Family Social Work*, 8, 89–100.

Harrison, N. (2020). Patterns of participation in higher education for care-experienced students in England: Why has there not been more progress? *Studies in Higher Education*, 45(9), 1986–2000.

Hugman, R., Pittaway, E. & Bartolomei, L. (2011). When 'do no harm' is not enough: The ethics of research with refugees and other vulnerable groups. *British Journal of Social Work*, 41(7), 1271–1287.

Hutcheon, E. & Lashewicz, B. (2014). Theorizing resilience: Critiquing and unbounding a marginalizing concept. *Disability & Society*, 29(9), 1383–1397.

Jackson, S., Ajayi, S. & Quigley, M. (2005). *Going to university from care*. London: Institute of Education, University of London.

Jackson, S. & Sachdev, D. (2001). *Better education, better futures. Research, practice and the views of young people in public care*. Barkingside: Barnardo's. Available at http://www.barnardos.org.uk/bettered.pdf

Knowles, C. & Burrows, R. (2014). The impact of impact. *Etnográfica*, 18(2), 237–254.

Leicestershire Cares (2021). *Life under lockdown: A rapid assessment of the impact of the lockdown on young people in Leicester*. Leicestershire and Rutland. Leicestershire: Leicestershire Cares.

Leigh, J. (2021). What would a rhythmanalysis of qualitative researcher's life look like? In B. Clift, J. Gore, S. Gustafsson, S. Bekker, I. Costas Batlle & J. Hatchard (Eds.), *Temporality in qualitative inquiry: Theories, methods and practices* (pp. 72–92). Abingdon: Routledge.

Littler, J. (2018). *Against meritocracy- culture, power and myths of mobility*. Abingdon: Routledge.

Long, S. J., Evans, R. E., Fletcher, A., Hewitt, G., Murphy, S., Young, H. & Moore, G. F. (2017). Comparison of substance use, subjective well-being and interpersonal relationships among young people in foster care and private households: A cross sectional analysis of the school health research network survey in Wales. *BMJ Open*. Available at https://bmjopen.bmj.com/content/7/2/e014198.info

Loughran, T. (2018). Blind spots and moments of estrangement: Subjectivity, class and education in British autobiographical histories. In T. Loughran & D. Mannay (Eds.), *Emotion and the researcher: Sites, subjectivities, and relationships., Vol. 16. Studies in qualitative methodology* (pp. 245–259). Bingley: Emerald.

Loughran, T. & Mannay, D. (2018). Introduction: Why emotion matters. In T. Loughran & D. Mannay (Eds.), *Emotion and the researcher: Sites, subjectivities, and relationships, Vol. 16. Studies in qualitative methodology* (pp. 1–18). Bingley: Emerald.

Mannay, D. (2012). Mothers and daughters on the margins: gender, generation and education. PhD Thesis, Cardiff University.

Mannay, D., Boffey, M., Cummings, A., Cunningham, E., Davies, B., Stabler, L., Vaughan, R., Wooders, C. & Evans, R. (2022). *The strengths and challenges of online services and interventions to support the mental health and wellbeing of care-experienced children and young people: A study exploring the views of young people, carers, and social care professionals in Wales during the Coronavirus pandemic*. Project Report. Cardiff: The Fostering Network in Wales.

Mannay, D., Creaghan, J., Gallagher, D., Mason, S., Morgan, M. & Grant, A. (2018b). 'Watching what I'm doing, watching how I'm doing it': Exploring the everyday experiences of surveillance and silenced voices among marginalised mothers in Welsh low-income locales. In T. Taylor & K. Bloch (Eds.), *Marginalized mothers, mothering from the margins. Advances in gender research* (Vol. 25, pp. 25–40). Bingley: Emerald.

Mannay, D., Evans, R., Staples, E., Hallett, S., Roberts, L., Rees, A. & Andrews, D. (2017). The consequences of being labelled 'looked-after': Exploring the educational experiences of looked-after children and young people in Wales. *British Educational Research Journal*, 43(4), 683–699.

Mannay, D., Smith, P., Turney, C., Jennings, S. & Davies, P. (2018a). *The value of cultural and creative engagement: Understanding the experiences and opinions of care-experienced young people and foster carers in Wales*. Project Report. Cardiff: Wales Millennium Centre.

Mannay, D., Staples, E., Hallett, S., Roberts, L., Rees, A., Evans, R. & Andrews, D. (2015). *Understanding the educational experiences and opinions, attainment, achievement and aspirations of looked after children in Wales*. Cardiff: Welsh Government.

Mannay, D. & Ward, M. R. M. (2020). The Coffee Club: An initiative to support mature and non-traditional higher education students in Wales. In G. Crimmins (Ed.), *Strategies for supporting inclusion and diversity in the academy: Higher Education, aspiration and inequality* (pp. 169–184). London: Palgrave Macmillan.

Mason, W. (2021). Radically slow? Reflections on time, temporality and pace, in engaged scholarship. In B. Clift, J. Gore, S. Gustafsson, S. Bekker, I. Costas Batlle & J. Hatchard (Eds.), *Temporality in qualitative inquiry: Theories, methods and practices* (pp. 142–157). Abingdon: Routledge.

McLeod, A. (2010). 'A friend and an equal': Do young people in care seek the impossible from their social workers? *British Journal of Social Work*, 40, 772–788.

Middleton, J. S. & Potter, C. C. (2015). Relationship between vicarious traumatization and turnover among child welfare professionals. *Journal of Public Child Welfare*, 9(2), 195–216.

Mobedji, S. & Mannay, D. (2018). *'Just listen': Care-experienced young people's views of the child protection system in Wales*. Project Report. Cardiff: The Fostering Network.

Morgan, M. (2016). Re-educating Rhian: experiences of working-class mature student mothers. In D. Mannay (Ed.), *Our changing land: Revisiting gender, class and identity in contemporary Wales. Gender studies in Wales*(pp. 112–129). Cardiff: University of Wales Press.

Morrish, L. (2021). Emotional labour in the post-pandemic university. Blog, 31 October. [online]. Available at https://postpandemicuniversity.net/2021/10/31/emotional-labour-in-the-post-pandemic-academy/

O'Higgins, A., Canning, R. & Taylor, J. (2020). Care in the time of Covid: summary. Available at https://careinthetimeofcovid.org/

O'Higgins, A., Sebba, J. & Luke, N. (2015). *What is the relationship between being in care and the educational outcomes of children? An international systematic review*. Oxford: Rees Centre.

Patel, V., Flisher, A. J., Hetrick, S. & McGorry, P. (2007). Mental health of young people: A global public-health challenge. *Lancet*, 369(9569), 1302–1313.

Pole, C. & Hillyard, S. (2017). When it's time to go. In C. Pole & S. Hillyard (Eds.), *Doing fieldwork* (pp. 107–122). London: Sage.

Priestley, A. (2020). Care experienced young people: Agency and empowerment. *Children & Society*, 34, 521–536.

Reay, D. (2004). Cultural capitalists and academic habitus: Classed and gendered labour in UK higher education. *Women's Studies International Forum*, 27(1), 31–39.

Roberts, E. (2018). The transient insider. Identity and intimacy in home and community research. In T. Loughran & D. Mannay (Eds.), *Emotion and the researcher: Sites, subjectivities, and relationships, Vol. 16. Studies in qualitative methodology* (pp. 113–126). Bingley: Emerald.

Roberts, L. (2017). A small-scale qualitative scoping study into the experiences of looked after children and care leavers Who are parents in Wales. *Child & Family Social Work*, 22(3), 1274–1282.

Roberts, L. (2019). 'A family of my own': When young people in and leaving state care become parents in Wales. In D. Mannay, A. Rees & L. Roberts (Eds.), *Children and young people 'looked after'? Education, intervention and the everyday culture of care in Wales* (pp. 140–152). Cardiff: University of Wales Press.

Roberts, L. (2021). *The children of looked after children: Outcomes, experiences and ensuring meaningful support to young parents in and leaving care*. Bristol: Policy Press.

Roberts, L., Mannay, D., Rees, A., Bayfield, H., Corliss, C., Diaz, C. & Vaughan, R. (2021a). 'It's been a massive struggle': Exploring the experiences of young people leaving care during COVID-19. *Young*, 29(4), 81–99.

Roberts, L., Rees, A., Bayfield, H., Corliss, C., Diaz, C, Mannay, D. & Vaughan, R. (2020). *Young people leaving care, practitioners and the coronavirus (COVID 19) pandemic: Experiences, support, and lessons for the future*. Project Report. Cardiff: CASCADE/Cardiff University.

Roberts, L., Rees, A., Mannay, D., Bayfield, H., Corliss, C., Diaz, C. & Vaughan, R. (2021b). Corporate parenting in a pandemic: Considering the delivery and receipt of support to care leavers in Wales during Covid-19. *Children and Youth Services Review*, 128, 106155.

Robson, J. P., Jr. & Troutman-Jordan, M. (2014). A concept analysis of cognitive reframing. *Journal of Theory Construction & Testing*, 18(2), 55–59.

Rosenthal, R. & Jacobson, L. (1968). *Pygmalion in the classroom*. New York: Holt, Rinehart & Winston.

Ryan-Flood, R. & Gill, R. (Eds.) (2010). *Secrecy and silence in the research process*. Abingdon: Routledge.

Shaw, I. & Holland, S. (2014). *Doing qualitative research in social work*. London: Sage.

Staples, E., Roberts, L., Lyttleton-Smith, J., Hallett, S. & CASCADE Voices. (2019). Enabling care experienced young people's participation in research: CASCADE voices. In D. Mannay, A. Rees & L. Roberts (Eds.), *Children and young people 'looked after'? Education, intervention and the everyday culture of care in Wales* (pp. 196–209). Cardiff: University of Wales Press.

Sulimani-Aidana, Y. & Melkmanb, E. (2018). Risk and resilience in the transition to adulthood from the point of view of care leavers and caseworkers. *Children and Youth Services Review*, 88, 135–140.

Ward, M. R. M. (2015). *From labouring to learning, working-class masculinities, education and de-industrialization*. Basingstoke: Palgrave Macmillan.

Wilson, D. & Neville, S. (2009). Culturally safe research with vulnerable populations. *Contemporary Nurse*, 33(1), 69–79.

Withers, A. (2020). Not in this together. *Social Work 2020-21 under Covid-19 Magazine*. Available at https://sw2020covid19.group.shef.ac.uk/2020/07/14/not-in-it-together/

# INDEX

Note: Locators in *italic* refer to figure, **bold** refer to table and those followed by "n" refer to end notes.